SOME TIMES
IN AMERICA

SOME TIMES
IN AMERICA

And a Life in a Year at the *New Yorker*

ALEXANDER CHANCELLOR

CARROLL & GRAF PUBLISHERS, INC.
NEW YORK

Illustrations by Benoît Jacques

Copyright © 1999 by Alexander Chancellor

First Carroll & Graf edition 2000

Carroll & Graf Publishers, Inc.
19 West 21st Street
New York, NY 10010-6805

Library of Congress Cataloging-in-Publication Data is available.

ISBN: 0-7867-0710-0

Manufactured in the United States of America

CONTENTS

1) Introductory Music   1

2) The Gentleman Hack   23

3) The Smell of Beeswax   41

4) Cigarettes and Whisky   65

5) Eat Here Now!   81

6) The Talk of the Town   101

7) Down in the Street   123

8) The Quest for Truth   131

9) He is an Englishman   145

10) The Principle of Lunch   163

11) The Democratic Dawn   181

12) The Merry Widows   199

13) Passing the Time   219

14) The Fourth Estate   241

15) Out in the Country   269

16) Goodbye to It All   289

FOR SUSIE

CHAPTER 1

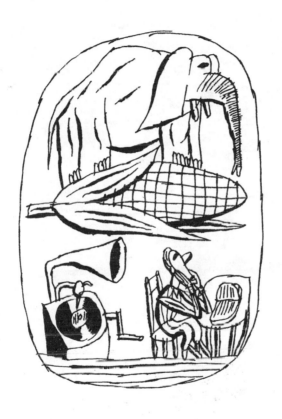

Introductory Music

This is an account of one Englishman's relationship with the United States. It has not been an intense relationship—I have, for instance, spent less than three years in the country during my sixty years of life—but it has been, for me, an important one that reached a curious apogee in the 1990s when I became for a year the editor of 'The Talk of the Town' section of the *New Yorker* magazine. I owe this improbable experience to Tina Brown, whom I have known since she left Oxford University in England in 1975 and applied to me unsuccessfully for her first job in journalism. My time at the *New Yorker* is the core of this book, but I am going to begin at the beginning.

I was born at the beginning of the Second World War when my parents were living in a country house in Hertfordshire, thirty miles north of London, and also had a flat overlooking the front of St Paul's Cathedral in the heart of the City. The flat could not have been more dangerously located, being in the principal target area for Hitler's bombs, and it was a miracle that it survived the blitz. I have always thought it odd that my parents kept me there as a baby when most London children were evacuated for safety to the countryside, but they seem to have been oblivious to the risk. The flat suited my father not only because it was very cheap but also because it was only a few minutes' walk from his office in Fleet Street where he presided as general manager over the international news agency Reuters. Although my parents were not especially rich and my father had to work for a living, they both came from old landed families and felt themselves part of the English upper class. So from childhood I absorbed the prejudices of that class towards America.

The upper class was generally more anti-American than the working class, because it felt more directly affronted by America's assumption of Britain's former role as a world power; and it expressed its hostility in bizarre ways. The comforts that America alone in the world could afford were derided as vulgar and effeminate. Air-conditioning was seen as unhealthy and debilitating. Central heating was regarded as perhaps necessary in America where the weather was terrible, but superfluous in the British Isles which enjoyed the perfect climate. Britain, we were taught at school, had the great good fortune to be washed by the warm water of the Gulf Stream which came all the way from Mexico to pamper us.

Iced water was another thing we were taught to despise. The Americans put ice in their water because it came warm out of the tap. Our water, on the other hand, was always exquisitely cold if we would only be patient and run it for long enough. Putting ice in water was typical of the exaggerations of Americans, such as their swanky cars, their enormous refrigerators, and their inhumanly tall buildings. Americans might sometimes be well-intentioned, but they were too vulgar to be the world's top nation, a role which had been tailor-made for small but sophisticated Britain.

Actually, I knew from a very early age that there was rather more to the Americans than we were told. My father's job often took him across the Atlantic, even during the war, and he would bring us back presents from New York. In 1944, he returned with a heavy set of 78 rpm records of *Oklahoma!*, the new hit Rodgers and Hammerstein musical, which, aged four, I would listen to on a wind-up gramophone in my mother's bedroom. Before long I knew the words of all the songs by heart and would sing them lustily, even though I didn't understand them.

' "The corn is as high as an elephant's eye," ' I would

chirp, ' "and it looks like it's climbing clean up to the sky." '
Corn to me meant wheat, not maize, and how could wheat
grow to the height of an elephant's eye? What too was 'a
little brown maverick' and why did it wink its eye? And
what was a 'surrey with a fringe on the top'? These were
impenetrable mysteries, but still the songs from *Oklahoma!*
conjured up an exciting image of America. I could picture
a vast land of waving corn and big-hearted farmers and
cowmen shouting 'Yeow' as they buried their rivalries in
the struggle to forge a new state.

When *Oklahoma!* eventually came to the Drury Lane
Theatre in London in 1947, I was taken to see it and was
overwhelmed by its glamour and exuberance, even though
I was rather frightened by the psychopathic farmhand Judd.
By that time I was seven years old and enjoying, with my
brother and two sisters, a comfortable and sheltered life in
the country. We had a large white porticoed house supported by a small staff of domestic servants. But the post-
war pall of gloom that hung over Britain touched
everybody, including us. Food rationing affected the well-
off as well as the poor; and we had rabbit, shot on our
land, for almost every meal. Even now I can hardly bring
myself to eat rabbit, however imaginatively cooked.

Already by then I had had direct experience of American
munificence. Wishing to support the British war effort in
some way, a very rich businessman in California called
Philip Chancellor had sought out a British family bearing
his name upon whom to bestow largess. I don't know how
he found us—it might have been through the telephone directory, for my parents had certainly never heard of him
before—but he sent us regular food parcels from the United
States which we consumed with rapture. I think it was
through Philip Chancellor that I got to know what ham
tasted like. Some time after the war he came to visit us in
England with a woman we were told was his eighth wife.
We had thought till then that Henry VIII, with six wives,
held the world record for serial matrimony, so we were

much impressed and not a little shocked. Nor did Mr Chancellor's generosity end when prosperity returned. When my brother John got married in 1959, he lent him his house in Acapulco, Mexico, for the honeymoon.

The arrival of *Oklahoma!* in London was a thrilling event which assumed symbolic significance as evidence that the war was really over at last, that a new era was about to dawn, and that (although meat rationing was to continue in Britain until 1954) good times were about to roll again. *Oklahoma!* was followed two months later by Irving Berlin's *Annie Get Your Gun* which I was taken to see at the Coliseum, now the home of the English National Opera. This was hardly less exciting and reinforced my image of America as a land of courageous individualists doing whatever they wanted to do, while we in Britain seemed to do mainly as we were told.

For many years thereafter my experience of America remained vicarious, nourished only by the dreams that Hollywood, Broadway and Tin Pan Alley chose to peddle. Apart from a few bits of classical music, the first records I bought as a teenager were of Fats Waller, Louis Armstrong, Ella Fitzgerald, Bessie Smith, Billie Holiday, Al Jolson, Eddie Cantor, Frank Sinatra, Bing Crosby, Fred Astaire, and Judy Garland. Having been nurtured on the tunes of Rodgers and Berlin, I was old-fashioned in my musical tastes. I had no time for Elvis Presley, who was then the rage among teenagers, but listened to the old standards again and again. I liked the tough, hopeful, grin-and-bear-it songs ('There's No Business Like Show Business', 'Pick Yourself Up', 'The Sunny Side of the Street'), but was even more susceptible to the melancholy, self-pitying ones ('Nobody Knows You When You're Down and Out', 'Buddy, Can You Spare a Dime') and to the vengeful ones ('Who's Sorry Now?', 'You're Nobody's Sweetheart Now'). I liked to play them gazing dreamily out of my window when I should have been doing my homework.

Although written for the most part by New Yorkers without much knowledge of the rest of the country, American popular songs reveal much that is true about the United States. One of their recurrent themes is the anguish experienced by people living far away from home. For the sake of a livelihood, Americans put thousands of miles between themselves and their roots. That is why so many of their songs are about places they miss—'Do You Know What It Means to Miss New Orleans?', 'Give My Regards to Broadway', 'Georgia On My Mind'. I found such songs extremely moving, which is hard to explain since at school at Eton and later at university in Cambridge I was never much more than an hour's drive from home.

As time passed, America came to seem increasingly glamorous and seductive, if a little frightening in its immensity. I was given my first Coca-Cola as a special treat by Aunt Rosemary, the wife of an Air Chief Marshal of the Royal Air Force who had represented the service in Washington for some years, and I still remember how exotic and delicious it tasted. I took up new American crazes like Hula-Hoops and slinkies. Then my sister Teresa, aged seventeen and six years older than I, went to New York to stay with an American couple my parents had got to know in China in the thirties: a hugely rich insurance tycoon called Neil Starr and his wife Mary, who lived in an elegant apartment on Park Avenue.

They coddled her and showered her with gifts, including, I was told, a mink coat. They took her to Sun Valley, Idaho, and had her taught to ski by handsome instructors. All this impressed me greatly, and I was impressed most of all by an enormous collection of books of matches which she brought back with her to England. I did not know that matches could come in books as well as in Bryant and May boxes, and I was even more astonished to learn that in America matches were given away free.

I was sixteen when I first set foot in the United States, though I only stayed in the country for one night. This was at a moment of high political drama when Britain and France had invaded Egypt to seize back the Suez Canal from Colonel Nasser, the Egyptian leader. Although at that age I had no interest in politics or international affairs, an awareness of the Suez crisis was forced upon me by the emotion it aroused in my father. We had just acquired a television set, and the first images I saw on it were of the British Prime Minister, Sir Anthony Eden, looking very pompous and grave.

Perhaps it was only to indulge his hatred of Eden that my father ever turned the set on. I don't recall seeing anybody other than the Prime Minister on television at that time. Eden, it later emerged, had lied to the House of Commons about the reason for our invasion of Egypt. He had claimed that Britain's sole objective had been to separate the Egyptians and the Israelis, who had already carried out a military incursion of their own. In fact it had all been a set-up. The Israelis had only gone into Egypt to provide the British and the French with an excuse for invading the country themselves.

As our dapper Prime Minister drawled on dishonestly about Britain's aims in Egypt, my father became furious and threw a glass of whisky at the screen. From this it was quite clear to me that Eden was a bad man, and that whatever he was planning to do to Egypt was not only a serious mistake but also, as my father said, a moral crime infringing a very important principle known as 'the rule of law'. The custodian of this principle was a fine organisation in New York called the United Nations to whose opinions Sir Anthony showed culpable indifference. President Eisenhower, however, was on the same side as my father and I. He refused to support the Suez operation and forced Britain and France into a humiliating withdrawal.

When I went back to Eton after the summer holidays of 1956, I was surprised to find that almost nobody there was on my side. The other boys had fathers too, who had persuaded them to adopt precisely the opposite point of view.

Everyone apart from me seemed to be baying for Johnny Gippo's blood. The spirit of Empire was still very much alive among the children of the ruling class, as was a burning resentment of the United States. I felt uncomfortably isolated, but every cloud has a silver lining. I was a regular reader of the *Daily Mirror*, a left-wing tabloid with a spectacular circulation then of around four million, which in the shallowness of its coverage of public affairs reflected my own interest in them. On Suez the *Mirror* was very sound. Its views could have been dictated by my father. They furnished me with ever more pious arguments to deploy against the militarists at school.

After the Suez débâcle, Eden was ill and exhausted and flew off to Jamaica to recuperate in a house called Goldeneye belonging to his friend Ian Fleming, the author of the James Bond books. Imaginative newspaper that it was, the *Daily Mirror* responded by launching a readers' competition. It asked for no more than two hundred words on how to solve the Suez crisis. The prize was a two-week holiday for two in a luxury hotel in the Jamaican seaside resort of Montego Bay, not very far from where Eden was staying. It was the beginning of winter in Britain, and the weather, despite the Gulf Stream, was miserable. I was too cowardly to enter the competition myself, but I mentioned it to my second sister, Susanna, who was then twenty years old and working as a secretary in London. She duly wrote a vigorous two hundred words about the United Nations, 'the rule of law', and Eden's wickedness. Her entry was one of seven thousand, and it won.

The *Mirror* wanted her to take a boyfriend with her to give the story some romantic impetus, but she decided prudently to take her younger brother instead. The coverage began at once, with daily front-page accounts of Susanna's preparations for her departure, including a touching photograph of her saying goodbye to 'her dog' (it was, in fact, my parents' Dalmatian which she didn't particularly care for). The *Mirror* insisted that she left immediately while public interest was still high, but I had to stay at school for another week until the Christmas holidays began. This allowed me my own private moment of tabloid glory. There appeared on the *Mirror*'s front page a large photograph of a pale youth waving feebly through a December fog at London airport and above it a huge headline, 'Another Etonian Leaves for Jamaica'. That was me. The first Etonian was the Prime Minister.

My journey to Jamaica was broken by a night in New York, but I never saw the skyscrapers. I was met at the airport by the *Mirror*'s North American business manager who drove me straight to his suburban home which was just as I had imagined such a home would be—a picket fence, a wooden porch, squirrels in the garden, and a Christmas wreath hanging on the front door. I knew from the cinema that Americans put wreaths on their doors at Christmas, but the sight of it made me uneasy all the same, for in Britain, so far as I knew, we only put wreaths on graves. We spent the evening listening to a new calypso record of Harry Belafonte, who was all the rage in America at the time and a favourite of the *Mirror*'s North American manager.

Next day I flew to Kingston, Jamaica, a town that Belafonte had been singing about. My sister came to meet me at the airport with a veteran *Mirror* reporter called Barrie Harding who was covering our reunion. His published account of it could not have been more luridly sentimental if I had actually been the boyfriend the *Mirror* had wanted my sister to take with her. 'Susanna and Alexander are together again,' it began—as if we cared. Barrie was the first real journalist I had ever met, and perhaps he contributed to my eventual decision to become a journalist too. I still remember him with affection. He was an easygoing, seen-it-all-before kind of man, and he spent a lot of time just lying in the sun on the terrace of the Sunset Lodge Hotel. Journalism, it occurred to me, was the ideal profession for the lazy person.

But I didn't then realise how hard it must have been for him to think up stories to write about a couple of young people just loafing about on a beach. He himself told me in a letter thirty years later that he had considered it a 'no-win' assignment, but I have to say that he acquitted himself brilliantly. By the time I arrived in Jamaica, my sister was already a celebrity in Britain. She had become 'Susanna' to the nation. Her photograph had appeared in the *Mirror* every day. She had been shown in a bikini drinking rum out of a pineapple. She had been photographed with the British colonial governor, Sir Hugh Foot. She had even been shown exchanging intimate smiles with the Prime Minister she had publicly reviled.

This was Barrie's greatest triumph. He had smuggled Susanna with the Press on to the tarmac at Kingston Airport as Eden was preparing to leave for home. He had placed her within inches of him and had them photographed together with no one else in the frame. The *Mirror* then published the photograph under the cheeky headline, 'Susanna Sees Eden Off'. This was pure tabloid genius, but Barrie, a modest man, refused to accept the credit. 'Susanna was one of the best sports I've met,' he said in his letter of 1986. 'Without her help it would have been impossible to get that front-page picture of her smiling gently at Sir Anthony and making him look the ass he was.'

Although Jamaica was then still one of our colonies, very few British people could afford to go there, and the residents of the Sunset Lodge Hotel were mostly elderly Americans. They had that comfortable, unhurried look that very rich people have, and they treated us kindly as interesting curiosities. But old Americans were not stimulating company for a twenty-year-old girl, on the lookout for fun, and her sulky younger brother. The holiday, in truth, was not a huge success. We both felt a bit tense and out of place, and it was especially odd to find ourselves alone together drinking rum out of pineapples on Christmas Day. But our stay had its memorable moments. We were taken up by

11

Adele Astaire, Fred Astaire's sister and famous dancing partner; and the mighty press baron Lord Beaverbrook, Sir Winston Churchill's friend, was scowling at the next table in the dining room when a calypso band serenaded me with 'Happy Birthday to You' on my seventeenth birthday. This was a surprise arranged by Susanna and for which I have never completely forgiven her.

It was many years before I made a proper visit to America. In 1964 I got married, left publishing, and joined Reuters, the international news agency to which my father had devoted most of his working life. I had met my future wife, Susanna, when we were working in the same publishing company for my brother John. For some reason, he was much irritated by our office romance, so we resigned together before he could get round to firing us. At the end of that year, six months after I had started working for the first time as a journalist in Fleet Street, Susanna gave birth to Eliza, the first of our two daughters. Our second daughter, Cecilia, was born nearly two years later after I had been posted as a trainee to the Reuters bureau in Paris.

We lived for a year and a half in Paris and then, from 1968, for five years in Rome, where I had been sent as bureau chief. I had always liked the idea of flitting about abroad, but it had never been Susanna's ambition. Having been brought up on a farm in Dorset, she'd always wanted to put down roots in the countryside, and in 1969, with a small sum of money she had been given, she bought an abandoned farmhouse in Tuscany and transformed it into a family home. Italy became part of her, and of me, but this was an accident of my career. Susanna had never wanted to settle abroad, and she had wanted even less to live abroad temporarily as a foreign correspondent's wife, though she loyally spent seven years in this uncongenial role. So when, almost two decades later, I was unable to resist offers to work first in Washington and then New York, it was understood between us that she wouldn't have to live that kind of life again. While I was in America, she stayed for most of the time at home in England or in Italy, and didn't share in most of my American life.

In Rome, however, we were together and got to know a number of American journalists and expatriates. The journalists were mostly decent and conscientious, but were discouraged by their newspapers back home from applying much subtlety to the interpretation of events. These papers were interested in only two subjects from Italy—the Communist Party and the Vatican—and they were not even very interested in those. American editors didn't like foreign news except from countries in which the United States was heavily engaged. A map of the world reflecting American priorities at that time would have shown Vietnam and Israel dwarfing every other place.

In 1973 we returned to London, and I was appointed Economic Affairs Editor of Reuters, coinciding with a speculative rush into gold and President Nixon's abandonment of the gold standard. I was sent to America to acquire some instant expertise in this matter, and, as so often happens to Europeans arriving for the first time in Manhattan, it was love at first sight.

> Ten thousand steamboats hootin'
> A million taxis tootin'—
> What a song! What a song!
> That dear old New York serenade!
> Just hear those rivets rattling—
> And hear that traffic battling—
> Come along, come along and hear it played.

The New York serenade was written by Ira Gershwin in 1927, and, with the exception of the hooting steamboats, which are long gone, the song hasn't changed very much. Europeans arriving in New York no longer get their first sight of Manhattan from the sea. They now alight at Kennedy Airport and are plunged into a mass of frantic, bustling humanity. The drive through Queens along the Van Wyck Expressway and Grand Central Parkway feels rather frightening when you do it for the first time. On each side of the swaying streams of traffic are miles of shabby housing, exuding menace.

Then, as you approach the Triborough Bridge, great clusters of skyscrapers loom into view from across the East River, and the heart leaps. It is a sight comparable only to Venice in its improbable beauty. That has been said before, of course. In fact, there have been so many attempts by visitors to sum up New York—how the air is electric, how the light is brilliant, how it looks like a giant asparagus bed—that I will try to be sparing with them. Europeans, as the late *New Yorker* writer Brendan Gill has pointed out, feel 'strongly inclined to tell us what America is like', and that is especially true of New York.

In any case, getting across the Triborough Bridge and on to the island of Manhattan is a moment of relief and exhilaration. Once surrounded by water, you feel as secure as the citizen of a fortified medieval town. You have entered a circumscribed, finite world, a teeming colony of ants who know and care about nothing beyond themselves. While London spreads out like a great ink blot across south-east England, Manhattan is neatly confined to its island, on which it can grow only upwards. In a country as enormous as the United States there is something a little comic, as well as exciting, in the spectacle of so many people battling over so little space.

Arriving in New York on a sunny afternoon in March 1974, I checked in at an old-fashioned midtown hotel and then went straight out on to Fifth Avenue to find a packet of English cigarettes. I hadn't walked very far when I was suddenly addressed by a voice from the crowd. 'What's the matter with you, for Christ's sake?' it said. 'Why the hell do you look so glum?' I looked up from the sidewalk and saw a pretty girl grinning at me. 'This is the first sun we've had this year!' she said reproachfully.

I said I was very sorry, had just arrived from England, and would make a point of looking less glum in future. This was my first encounter with a perplexing phenomenon—the fact that Americans never appear to be shy. Americans look you steadily in the eye and do not blink. If you ask them how they are, they are always very well and greatly enjoying whatever it is they are doing.

A few days later, I had to fly to the West Coast. That was when I learnt to admire American air stewardesses, the most positive thinkers of all. They were still called stewardesses then. Later, when they were renamed 'flight attendants', they became a little subdued and sullen. But when they were still stewardesses, they were eager and flirtatious. On that flight to Los Angeles, a very pretty blonde stewardess with a dazzling smile suddenly sat down beside me on an empty seat, pointed at my breakfast tray, and trilled, 'What's missing?'

There seemed to be nothing missing at all. In fact, the tray contained more breakfast than a glutton could dream of—sausages, bacon, egg, bread, butter, everything. 'I can't imagine,' I replied. 'Oh, go *on*!' she said, nudging me in the ribs. 'You *must* know. *Tell* me. What's *missing*?' I examined the tray with growing desperation, checking the salt, pepper, sugar, and so on. 'No, I really don't know,' I said finally. 'I really, *really* don't know. Please, *please*, tell me.' She paused for dramatic effect, and then squealed as if she had just won a prize on a game show, 'The maple syrup! We ran out!' Then, with a peal of laughter, she was on her way up the aisle.

I didn't see her again until, several hours later, I was leaving the plane in Los Angeles and she was standing by the door, bidding the passengers farewell with undiminished brightness. 'Enjoy the flight?' she asked. 'Yes, thank you, I did,' I said. 'Better than the wagon train!' she yelled. No wonder American millionaires fall for air hostesses and marry them, though only too often to ruin them by turning them into patrons of the arts.

I left Reuters that year, spent twelve months working for the ITN television news network, and was then made Editor of the *Spectator*, an old but failing political weekly (it was founded in 1828) which had been bought by a childhood friend of mine, Henry Keswick, when he returned home from Hong Kong with lots of money after fourteen years running Jardine Matheson, the great Far Eastern trading company. I was appointed, as Max Hastings, the future Editor of the *Daily Telegraph* and of the London *Evening Standard*, reported at the time, because I was 'the only journalist he knew'.

This was not very flattering, but it was true. Nearly all my journalistic experience had been as a news-agency reporter, and I knew nothing about political and literary magazines or about the kind of people who wrote for them. Still, I thought I would give it a go, especially since the *Spectator* was already close to death—its circulation had shrunk within fifteen years from 50,000 to around 11,000—and I didn't see how I could make things any worse.

The job must have seemed prestigious to the American Embassy in London, for after a while it sent me a letter proposing that I should visit the United States for a month at the expense of the American taxpayer. I was invited under the State Department's 'Important Visitor Program' which offered selected foreigners free travel anywhere within the United States and an allowance at that time of forty dollars a day. The only condition was that you had to start your visit in Washington, where you would meet your Program Officer and work out what you were going to do.

I accepted, of course, and in March of 1978 I flew to Washington, where I was allocated a program officer called Miss Buttermilk. Miss Buttermilk was very kind, but disconcerted by my lack of focus. Most visitors, she explained, had specific subjects they wanted to study—racial tension in the South, the decline of motor manufacturing in the Midwest—and it took her a little while to grasp that all I wanted to do was to spend as much as possible of the American taxpayers' money in the thirty days allotted to me. 'Think of me as Dr Livingstone,' I told her. 'I am here to explore a virgin continent.'

I paid a price for my avarice, for I spent so much time in the air, exploiting the free-travel opportunity, that I saw little of America from the ground. But I touched down in nine states and ended my journey with a full week in New York. Of my memories of this adventure, the most vivid is of a visit to North Carolina where I stayed in Winston Salem, a tobacco town, with a rich patron of the arts called Phil Hayes, to whom I had been recommended by my friend Auberon Waugh, the writer and journalist and Evelyn Waugh's eldest son.

Mr Hayes lived in a pretty eighteenth-century house that had been moved there plank by plank from somewhere else. His fortune derived from the charmingly named family firm of Hayes Dyeing and Finishing, and he had used it to transform Winston Salem into a centre of highly accomplished music-making, with a brilliant youth orchestra which spent its summers performing in Tuscany. I was astonished by the musical facilities in this modest town, which included a fine concert hall and several enormous organs. Such wealth so generously spent in such a way would be unimaginable in any equivalent town in Europe.

Mr Hayes's generosity was exceeded only by his enthusiasm. He took me up into the Blue Ridge Mountains and, during a long walk through the woods, suddenly took off all his clothes and leapt into an icy stream, urging me to do the same. Although horrified, I did as I was told. This is not the kind of thing we make foreigners do in England when we take them for walks in the country. We show them the cows and then take them to a pub. In America the countryside is treated as a giant outdoor health club, a place in which to ride and raft and canoe and be generally as physical as possible.

I was interested to read many years later in the memoirs

of the late and much lamented Joseph Alsop, famous conservative newspaper columnist and a White Anglo-Saxon Protestant if ever there was one, that naked bathing has a long tradition among the American gentry. One of his boyhood memories was of the 'men's swimming hole' at Avon, Connecticut, where his family lived and farmed. 'Throughout the hot weather,' he wrote in his autobiography *I've Seen the Best of It*, 'most of the male population of Avon went to the swimming hole every fine evening when the day's work was done. The swimmers ranged from five years old to upward of eighty. There might be three score of them on a good evening; and all left their clothes in heaps under the wide-branched willows on the bank and went in together.'

With Mr Hayes I toured Wilkes County, North Carolina, which used to call itself the world's centre of moonshine. Even then, hidden among the pine trees on the lower slopes of the Blue Ridge Mountains, there were said to be stills churning out the corn whisky. The beautiful countryside was inhabited mainly by small farmers. One or two of them, I was told, still bred cocks for illegal cock-fighting; but mainly they bred chickens. Beside each weatherboarded farmhouse stood a long and menacing new chicken shed in which thousands of chickens were passing their short lives in eternal twilight. With the decline of the cotton and tobacco crops, chickens had restored prosperity to the county.

I enquired about one particularly handsome farmhouse which had a wooden portico all the way around. It had been built, I was casually told, by the Siamese twins—*the* Siamese twins, the original Chang and Eng who were born in a Siamese fishing village in 1811 and lived for sixty-three years with their chests joined together at the breastbone. Chang and Eng are the most famous freaks who have ever lived. They were discovered in Siam in 1824 by a Scottish entrepreneur, Robert Hunter, who, with an American partner, Captain Abel Coffin, exhibited them triumphantly throughout the United States and Britain. When the twins were in London in 1829, they aroused such curiosity that even the Prime Minister, the Duke of Wellington, felt he had to go and see them. One newspaper reader, who thought prime ministers had more important things to do, expressed his disappointment in verse:

Thou Waterloo Hero! Thou Minister Prime!
Whose only delight is the Nation to please,
'Tis surprising to me that Your Grace should have time
A visit to pay to the young Siamese.

At the age of twenty-eight, having grown heartily sick of exhibiting themselves before a salivating public, the twins declared their independence and settled in North Carolina, where they managed two successful farms, owned twenty-eight slaves, and married two of the most sought-after girls in the neighbourhood, Sarah and Adelaide Yates, the daughters of a prosperous farmer. That these girls, twelve and eleven years younger than their husbands, could tolerate their deformity may have had something to do with the fact that their own mother was a freak—an enormously fat woman weighing more than 490 pounds.

Chang and Eng had a bed specially built for four, and between them they fathered twenty-one children, an astonishing achievement under the circumstances. After a bit, it is said, the two wives fell out. In any case, one of them moved out and established a new household one mile away. The twins went from one house to the other every three days. Chang was the master in one, Eng in the other. The system worked well, and the twins, who had meanwhile become patriotic American citizens, enjoyed the friendship and respect of all their neighbours. American society is hardly immune to bigotry, but the welcome given to the Siamese twins in North Carolina is proof of its remarkable openness in that place and time.

In New York, towards the end of my trip, I made a resolution, later to be broken, that I would never go and work

19

in New York for an American company. My friend Nigel Ryan, who had employed me at ITN, had left his job in London as a powerful television news executive to take up a highly paid position in New York at NBC Television News. I went to visit him one Friday evening in Rockefeller Center and was much impressed by the size of his office and the map of America on the wall, studded with little pins. But it quickly became clear that all was not well. Nigel revealed that his main responsibility at that time was for religious broadcasting—not a good sign—and that his immediate task was to organise the television coverage of the death of the Hollywood actor John Wayne, which was feared to be imminent.

While we were talking, a swarthy young fellow came into the room and asked how the John Wayne dying arrangements were going. He was a new top executive of NBC News, his predecessor—the one who had brought Nigel over from London—having recently gone because of some tiny fall in its ratings. The swarthy man probably didn't know why this slender, rather effete Englishman had been invited to New York in the first place. In any event, he exuded suspicion and hostility.

When Nigel told him what the John Wayne arrangements were, he said that they were not as he had ordered. He spoke in a slow, chilling monotone. 'I thought I told you, Nigel, that for political reasons I wanted Jim to anchor from LA,' he said (or something along those lines). 'Yes, I know,' replied Nigel, 'but it was impossible because . . .' 'Nigel,' this terrifying man broke in, emphasising every word, 'I will now leave this room. I will come back in ten minutes, and when I do so, Jim will be anchoring from LA. Do you understand?'

Nigel understood, and so did I. I was so unnerved that I tried to leave the room immediately, but Nigel insisted I stayed while he made a series of embarrassed telephone calls which resulted, of course, in the impossible being achieved. The swarthy man returned as promised, received the good news without a smile or a word of gratitude, and then walked out again. By now Nigel was very tense. He was frightened of missing a bus that was to take him out to Long Island for a fashionable country weekend, but he said there was just time for us to have a drink together in a nearby bar.

As if things were not bad enough already, we there encountered a classic example of the Great American Bore. The stools along the bar were all occupied by gentlemen with large bottoms, one of whom, hearing Nigel's British accent, turned round and offered him his seat. 'You British?' the man said. 'Be my guest. I will never forget what you guys did in the war. I want you to sit right here and have a drink on me.' So Nigel, increasingly worried about his bus, had to sit on his stool and talk to him about the war, while I stood aimlessly in the background pouring back the whisky.

John Wayne didn't die that weekend. Nigel returned to England not long afterwards, a chastened and wiser man. As for me, I still thought that New York was a wonderful place, but obviously not for the faint-hearted.

CHAPTER 2

The Gentleman Hack

The *Spectator* brought me closer to America through connections with the world of small magazines over there, and I made a number of new American friends—among them Michael Kinsley, the brilliant and acerbic young Editor of the *New Republic* in Washington. Rick Hertzberg, who also became a friend, was then a speechwriter for President Jimmy Carter and later succeeded Kinsley at the *New Republic*. He was to play his biggest part in my life nearly two decades later when we were both working for the *New Yorker* under Tina Brown. I did a fair amount of toing and froing across the Atlantic over the next few years, but never spent more than about a week at a time in the United States, and usually only in Washington and New York. Every visit filled me with the same feeling of liberation and excitement.

It was in the summer of 1975, just as I was starting at the *Spectator*, that I first met Tina Brown, a pretty, vivacious twenty-one-year-old just out of Oxford. I met her through Bron Waugh, who was then writing a provocative weekly column in the *New Statesman*—the left-wing equivalent of the *Spectator* and, at that time, a much better and more popular magazine. Bron Waugh was about the only person I already knew who was part of that little magazine world, and I took him to lunch at Bertorelli's restaurant in Charlotte Street to ask him how a new editor of the *Spectator* should set about his task. He replied that I should hire Tina Brown.

I had never heard of her, which was not surprising, given her youth, but it turned out she had already achieved a lot for her age. She had been the features editor of *Isis*, the Oxford University magazine; she had written a play that had actually been performed; and she had managed to get an article published in the *New Statesman*—an amusing, satirical piece about undergraduate high jinks on the River Thames at Oxford. Bron, as he confessed in his autobiography, had developed a weakness for Tina the moment he met her in 1973. She had invited herself to Combe Florey, his country house in Somerset, to interview him for *Isis*. 'It was plain that this extremely attractive young woman was going to go a long way,' he wrote nearly twenty years later in his autobiography *Will This Do?*

It was Bron who introduced her to Grub Street. He took her to the *New Statesman*'s sixtieth birthday party and to a lunch at *Private Eye*, the satirical magazine—events which she later said had altered the whole course of her life. Under pressure from Bron, I went with him to visit her in her two-room flat in Bloomsbury Street. I remember the flat being like that of a typical London girl of the period, with a Spanish bullfighting poster on the wall and a teddy bear on the bed, its only peculiarity being an unusually large expanse of mirror in the bedroom.

Tina tried very hard to get a job on the *Spectator*. She flattered and flirted with me. She said she was willing to do anything, make tea if necessary. But for reasons I cannot really explain, I failed to hire her. I think it may have been just timidity on my part. She was clearly very talented as well as ambitious, and I liked her a lot; but I may have feared that she would create too turbulent a whirlpool in the journalistic backwater into which I was then nervously dipping my toes. In any case, she soon got a job as a reporter on *Punch*, and I received a furious letter from Bron, beginning: 'You've lost her, you bloody fool, you've lost her!'

Before long, Tina was writing for the *Sunday Times*, then Britain's most admired newspaper, and so bewitched its editor, Harold Evans, twenty-five years her senior, that he subsequently left his wife to marry her. But Bron persisted for a while in his role as her mentor. They were together one year at a political party conference in Blackpool, where Bron was helping her find stories for a diary column in the *Sunday Times*. It was my misfortune to be within sight of them one night when I stumbled, drunk, into the indoor swimming pool of the Imperial Hotel while on my way to the bar to replenish my drink. Bron decided at once that this was a story worthy of dissemination. 'May Tina write about it in the *Sunday Times*?' he asked me. 'If not, I will write about it myself.' 'Let Tina do it,' I said; for Bron, despite his benevolence in everyday life, was a specialist in causing embarrassment in print, while Tina's record in this respect was still clean. As I recall, she did not deal with me unkindly.

Tina's road to glory in New York started in London at the *Tatler*, a Society magazine with a history going back to 1709. Still only twenty-five years old, she became its Editor in the same month that Margaret Thatcher became Prime Minister—June 1979. Both women set out with messianic zeal to transform the worlds they now controlled. While Britain was to be liberated by Mrs Thatcher from the shackles of old-fashioned socialism, the *Tatler* was to be liberated from the shackles of old-fashioned Society. Tina's decision was to mix hereditary grandeur with contemporary grooviness. She was inspired, she later claimed, by a joke made to her by the third Baron Hesketh, later one of Mrs Thatcher's junior ministers, that 'in 1979, the way to tell an English gentleman is by the quality of his drugs'. (Alexander Hesketh, who is a friend of mine, later disowned the remark, but I would have been rather proud of it if I'd been him.)

'I realised then that my struggle with the problem of how to reposition the *Tatler* as a Society magazine was over,' she wrote in the introduction to a book of her collected journalism, *Life as a Party*. 'I was going to let them all into the party—the debs and the Eurotrash, the sporting and the snorting. From now on the editorial policy was to mix the Queen Mother with April Ashley [a celebrated transsexual]—and make sure both of them had a good time.'

The new policy worked very well. The *Tatler*'s circulation quadrupled, and Tina was unwittingly establishing her credentials for her subsequent role as Queen of the celebrity culture in the United States. Although her own articles for the *Tatler* were sharp, observant and entertaining, they never failed to treat celebrity with respect. She was brought up with it. Her family background, she wrote, was 'flash', though not in a typically English way, for her father was a rare thing in England—a film producer. This made her, even as a child, 'a keen student of façade'. 'As far as I could see,' she wrote, 'castles were always plaster, money was always funny, and the nuns came off the set for a fag.'

She was also a girl who liked amusement wherever she found it. In the *Tatler*, she may have subjected the aristocracy to more mockery than it liked, but she had nothing against aristocrats provided they were capable of a good time. She formed, for example, a warm relationship with my cousin Colin Tennant (subsequently Lord Glenconner), the wealthy heir to a Scottish barony, whom puritans might have considered decadent, but whom Tina admired for having turned the West Indian island of Mustique into a fantasy pleasureland for the international jet set, including the Queen's sister, Princess Margaret. The only thing she couldn't stand, it seemed, was dinginess.

One might have expected her to look down on the *Spectator*, with its fusty conservative opinions and its instinctive urge to cut show-offs and celebrities down to size. But in fact she was a friend of the *Spectator*, would sometimes attend our lunches in the top-floor dining room of our clubby premises in Doughty Street, and continued to boost my morale with the occasional flattery. She once told me that I had the longest eyelashes of any editor in London, which was a clever compliment for, although she could not have known it, my eyelashes were about the only physical attribute of which I had always been proud. Maybe she saw the *Spectator* as having a certain kind of glamour; or maybe she just felt loyalty to her friends from earlier times—above all to Bron Waugh, who had by then moved with his column from the *New Statesman* to the *Spectator*.

Nevertheless, she did write a cutting profile of a type she called the 'gentleman hack', who was taken to be the archetype of a *Spectator* contributor.

High-Church Hugo is a gentleman hack [it began]. Please don't ever confuse him with a journalist. He is hostile to facts and even more hostile to investigation. His corner is very much the well-turned think piece, or well-cobbled Cobbett, published once a week in a range of ailing literary and political organs.

Although his prose style is seventy-five, Hugo himself is only thirty-eight. Physically, he does his best to catch up. He walks with a literary stoop and pushes aside a rumpled hank of prematurely grey hair. His dress tries to denote the aristocratic reach-me-down tradition—hence the goose-shit green corduroy trousers and deafening tweed jacket . . . The point of all this is to make self-made man feel overdressed. [Oh God, here I am, as I copy this out, wearing goose-shit green corduroy trousers!] The thing Hugo yearns for you to say is that he's a sort of eighteenth-century figure. After all, his theme is mankind, even if his house is in Stockwell. And his life embodies great eighteenth-century traditions—bad skin, old suits, and a black-and-white television.

But there is little evidence that Tina ever shared her husband's distaste for inherited privilege. Harry Evans, whom she married in 1981, was of working-class, north-country background and had risen entirely by his own efforts and on his own merits to become a highly successful editor of the *Sunday Times*, whence he was briefly and disastrously elevated by its proprietor Rupert Murdoch to what had traditionally been considered the grandest of all jobs in British journalism, the editorship of his daily paper *The Times*. He had been given a rough ride by the 'gentleman hacks' of *Private Eye*, who had sensed his vulnerability to criticism and played upon it mercilessly. It gave him the nickname 'Dame Harold Evans' for reasons that remain obscure even to the magazine's then Editor, Richard Ingrams, who thinks, however, that it may have had something to do with the fact that there was once a famous British actress called Dame Edith Evans. Harry Evans thought it suggested he was effeminate and threatened to sue.

He developed an understandable aversion to *Private Eye*, and he might have been expected to extend this to the *Spectator*, for the two magazines, having several contributors in common, were often portrayed—wrongly, in my view—as being osmotically linked, like Sinn Fein and the IRA. I was therefore surprised when he invited me to lunch at the *Times* in 1982 and offered me a job. He asked if I would like to be the paper's Paris correspondent; and when I said no, he suggested Literary Editor. 'I would like to have you on board in some capacity,' he said. But I stayed at the *Spectator*.

Shortly after this lunch, Harry mentioned me in a letter to Rupert Murdoch. The letter was published ten years later in a biography of Murdoch by William Shawcross. In it Harry reported to Murdoch on his efforts to recruit 'an intelligent polemicist'. Although 'intelligent polemics' had not been dangled before me as an option, the letter said, 'I did talk to Alexander Chancellor, but came to the conclusion he represents part of the effete old tired England.' So, there it was: ten years in Reuters covering plane crashes and football results had not been sufficient to wipe my slate clean. I do not deny that family connections of one kind or another had often played a part in my getting jobs, but I had hoped, after eighteen years in journalism, I might somehow have expiated my original sin. Yet even Mrs Thatcher, in 1976, had tried to get me removed from the editorship of the *Spectator*. It seemed I would never be acceptable to the new meritocracy.

Perhaps Harry didn't really mean it. Shawcross seems to suggest that he wrote what he did because he wanted to ingratiate himself with Murdoch, who was then showing clear signs of unease with his editorship of *The Times*. According to Shawcross, 'effete old tired England' was 'the class Murdoch most despised'. Maybe Harry wanted to show that he despised it just as much. Anyway, we were both to get sacked from our jobs —Harry that year and I two years later. Meanwhile, Murdoch, who was born to greater privilege than either of us (having inherited a newspaper and a small fortune from his Australian father), chose as Harry's successor the nephew of a former Conservative prime minister who had spent most of his political career in an unelected chamber, the House of Lords, as the 14th Earl of Home. The new editor of the *Times* was a friend and contemporary of mine, Charles Douglas-Home; and a good choice he turned out to be.

I left *The Spectator* in 1984 after discovering that Algy Cluff, the English oil prospector who had bought the magazine from Henry Keswick two years earlier, had secretly offered the editorship to Dr Germaine Greer, the Australian feminist academic. I was given this disturbing news by Richard Ingrams, whom she had consulted about it over a furtive tea at the Randolph Hotel in Oxford and who has claimed he was himself then offered the job when she turned it down. Another intimation of impending doom came from the *Spectator*'s then Washington columnist Christopher Hitchens who called me from the United States after hearing rumours that I was on the point of leaving.

At one of my regular lunches with Algy, I raised the question with him, and my departure was quite amicably agreed. The truth was that I didn't greatly blame him for wanting to replace me. It seemed natural that he should want his own person in the job rather than endure indefinitely a rather prickly editor he had inherited. In the end, my successor was, appropriately, Charles Moore, the magazine's gifted young political columnist who would later go on to become Editor of first the *Sunday Telegraph* and then the *Daily Telegraph*.

As soon as the details of the handover were settled, I decided to fly to America to say goodbye to friends and contributors in Washington and New York. Harry was then filling in time as a visiting professor of journalism at Duke University, North Carolina, having taken his revenge on Murdoch by damning him in a book of memoirs, *Good Times, Bad Times* (Weidenfeld & Nicolson, 1983). Tina, now aged thirty, was in New York embarking on a daunting mission—the resurrection, no less, of *Vanity Fair*. *Vanity Fair* had had a glorious past, but was having a wretched reincarnation. From 1914 until the end of the twenties, it had been one of the most delightful of all American magazines. In an editorial of March 1914, celebrating its purchase by the publishing tycoon Condé Nast, its new Editor, a polished New England gentleman called Frank Crowninshield, explained its objectives:

> *Vanity Fair* has but two major articles in its editorial creed: first, to believe in the promise and progress of American life, and second to chronicle that progress cheerfully, truthfully and entertainingly . . . Let us instance one respect in which American life has recently undergone a great change. We allude to its great devotion to pleasure, to happiness, to dancing, to sport, to the delights of the country, and to all forms of cheerfulness. Now *Vanity Fair* means to be as cheerful as anybody. It will print much humor, it will look at the stage, at the arts, at the world of letters, at sport, and at the highly vitalized, electric, and diversified life of our day from the frankly cheerful angle of the optimist, or, which is much the same thing, from the mock-cheerful angle of the satirist.

While dark clouds of war were gathering over Europe, this was the spirit at large in New York; and Frank Crowninshield was just the man to capture it in the pages of a magazine. He was so incurably cheerful that even the Depression failed to depress him, and *Vanity Fair* tripped gaily on into decline and finally death in 1936, when it was gobbled up by Mr Nast's more successful magazine, *Vogue*. It had been smart, but never cheap or meretricious. It brought together a remarkable group of young writers, some associated more often now with the *New Yorker*—Dorothy Parker, Robert Benchley, and Robert E. Sherwood, who were to form the nucleus of the Algonquin Round Table, as well as P. G. Wodehouse, Compton Mackenzie, Aldous Huxley, Edmund Wilson, and many others.

According to George H. Douglas's *The Smart Magazines* (New York, Archon Books, 1991), they were attracted to *Vanity Fair* not only by Crowninshield's amiability but also by his erudition and sense of style. He was a dapper man-about-town, a regular dinner guest of the Astors and the Vanderbilts, and a member of innumerable clubs; but he was also a bibliophile, an art collector, and a confident, carefree editor, certain of his own mind, who did not fear to upset readers or advertisers by being ahead of the times (in 1915, for example, he was already publishing features on Van Gogh, Gauguin, Picasso, and Matisse, which, according to the publisher Condé Nast, 'did us a certain amount of harm').

The New York of the eighties, in which Tina was to become a star, lacked the charm of Crowninshield's New York. The spirit that her *Vanity Fair* had to confront was one of rampant greed and success worship. The title *Vanity Fair* had lain dormant for decades, but in 1959 it had become the property of Samuel Newhouse, owner of America's largest newspaper chain, who bought the Condé Nast magazine business as an anniversary present for his wife. ('She asked for a fashion magazine, and I went out and got her *Vogue*,' he liked to claim afterwards.) Samuel Newhouse, the child of East European immigrants, had two sons—S. I. Newhouse (known as 'Si', pronounced 'sigh') and Donald Newhouse—who, on their father's death in 1979, inherited a publishing concern which grew into an empire worth billions of dollars.

They divided the empire between them. Donald took charge of the newspapers and the cable television; Si the magazines and the book publishing. In 1983, with a great flourish of trumpets, Si relaunched *Vanity Fair*. He wanted to cock a snook at the rich and complacent *New Yorker*, but instead burdened himself with a humiliating flop. He fired one editor and appointed another, but to no avail. So, in desperation, he turned to the bright young Editor of the *Tatler*, which he had added to his publishing empire two years earlier during a London shopping spree.

Tina was soon to deliver the goods, but when I saw her in New York that spring she had only been in the job for a matter of weeks and was still feeling nervous. She agreed to have dinner one evening and asked me to meet her at her office. When I turned up at the Condé Nast headquarters at 350 Madison Avenue near Grand Central Station, I was surprised to find that Tina was in a meeting and that her staff were still beavering away at their desks, even though it was well after 7 p.m., the lights were already twinkling on Broadway, and there was a month before the next issue of *Vanity Fair* was due to appear. I explained to these slaves to the work ethic how much more efficient we were in England. I told them that in London we had a magazine called the *Spectator* which came out not monthly but weekly, with a far smaller staff than theirs; but that this had never stopped us all disappearing into the pub when it opened at 5 p.m.

When Tina emerged from her office to greet me, she whispered fiercely in my ear, 'Don't speak until we are outside the building,' and then she led the way out of the office—briefcase in one hand, handbag in the other—to cries of 'Goodnight, Tina' or 'Goodnight, Miss Brown', depending upon the degree of intimacy each member of her staff dared presume. I attempted to say something to her in the lift on the way down, but was instantly silenced; and it was only when we were safely in the back of her chauffeur-driven limousine that Tina relaxed and started chattering away. She was very sweet that evening, venting her anxieties about her new job and being nostalgic about London and the friends she had left behind.

During dinner, she suggested I might write a regular 'Letter from London' for *Vanity Fair*. The idea came to her while I was describing a lunch I had had with the Queen at Buckingham Palace a few days earlier. A thick invitation from the Lord Chamberlain had 'commanded' me and my wife to attend a luncheon which the Queen was giving for the President of Italy. It had filled me with childish joy, for I had only once seen the Queen close up before—that was thirty years earlier when she attended a service in the College Chapel at Eton—and I had never been inside Buckingham Palace.

When Susanna and I arrived at the palace, the flunkeys at the door used all their powers of persuasion to get me to go to the lavatory—'There is plenty of time, sir. It is just around that corner'—and it required much strength of will to resist. I was later to hear that this is routine practice. One of the many unsettling effects that the Queen has on her subjects is that some of them lose control of their bladders when they meet her; and she has some very good carpets. I have even read somewhere that a hardened old British journalist, a veteran of many wars, was so confused by a surprise encounter with the Queen in Jordan that he sank into a deep curtsey before her. If some of the Queen's subjects find her odd, she cannot seem as odd to them as they must seem to her.

Before going to the palace, I had met my wife at the Ritz Hotel in Piccadilly and fortified myself with a dry martini, assuming—wrongly, as it turned out—that the Queen would offer her guests nothing but warm sherry. In fact, there was a variety of powerful American cocktails available in the upstairs drawing room. They were carried around on little silver trays by rather effeminate footmen whom I suspected—unfairly, I am sure—of planning to sell their stories one day to the tabloid press. Apart from members of the Royal household and the Italian and British governments, the guests comprised a small group of known Italophiles.

We were lined up in a row to be presented to the Queen on her arrival (by which time I had had two more dry martinis), and were lined up again for her to introduce us to the Italian President, Sandro Pertini (by which time I had had yet another), who was paying his first visit to Britain at the age of eighty-eight. For the second line-up we were placed in alphabetical order, which was the order in which the Queen had committed our names to memory, and she introduced us all correctly. A lifelong socialist, a hero of the Italian Resistance, and a politician of almost saintly integrity, Pertini was the most popular president Italy ever had. He was also notoriously informal and indifferent to protocol, which is maybe why he was so late for lunch and why I, therefore, had to drink so much. He was subsequently to cause a sensation in the United States by kissing young women in the streets.

After the lunch, which in the tradition of most long-established British institutions consisted of bad food but excellent wine, it was back to the drawing room for brandy and liqueurs served by the same footmen from silver trays. I had drunk too much by then to be inhibited by protocol and followed the Queen around wherever she went. But I never really got to talk to her; and when I tried writing about the event for Tina, as she insisted I should, I found I had very little of substance to report. So the piece became a series of whimsical reflections about the monarchy in which I concluded that I greatly envied the Queen her job. I called the article 'Closet Queen', and Tina, quite rightly, rejected it. After that, the idea of a 'Letter from London' was never revived.

Tina was not yet the great New York celebrity she was to become. But Society was already sniffing eagerly around her, and I became briefly in demand as someone who was reputed to be her friend. I was staying with my brother John, who had long ago left publishing and was then running an antiquarian book business in New York, and it may have been he who spread the word. In any case, I got invited to parties by people I barely knew who would say as a carefully prepared afterthought that, if I cared to bring Tina Brown along with me, she would be most welcome too. It was at one such party to which I had dragged her that I said goodbye to her before returning to London. She looked really sad to see me go, as if another link with England was being broken.

I had been accompanied to America on this occasion by my seventeen-year-old daughter Cecilia who had succumbed to persistent pressure from John Casablancas, the smooth-talking head of a celebrated model agency, Élite, who had promised her fame and fortune as a fashion model if she came to live for a year in New York. He had offered her lodging in an apartment next to his in a flashy skyscraper on the Upper East Side. This turned out to be a cramped little dormitory already containing two other aspiring models who were in constant competition for the bathroom mirror. We agreed that this wouldn't do, and I told Cecilia I would return next morning to take her away when neither Mr Casablancas nor his wife would be at home.

We were ridiculously nervous about this operation, having convinced ourselves, absurdly, that the poor Casablancases were Dickensian villains intent on condemning her to a life of exploitation. We had got her luggage ready and were about to leave when the doorbell rang. 'Who's that?' I asked over the intercom. 'The exterminator,' came the reply. We went cold with terror, since neither of us then knew that in New York an exterminator is a person who murders not people but cockroaches. After much anxious conversation on the intercom, I eventually let in a friendly man who went rapidly about his business, spraying the wainscoting with cockroach poison.

Cecilia moved into my brother's apartment on the corner of 63rd Street and Lexington Avenue, but the arrangement didn't survive for long. As a dealer in expensive rare books, John had to court New York's moneyed aristocracy for custom, and he seems to have hoped that his beautiful niece would be an asset in this endeavour. Cecilia's refusal to return telephone calls from a young man with the name of Vanderbilt was the last straw, and John told her to move out. She was generously taken in by our friends Alexandra and Taki Theodoracopulos, the *Spectator*'s 'High Life' columnist, and stayed in their house on the Upper East Side until eventually finding a flat to share with another model. But it was a little while before I completely forgave my brother for chucking my daughter into the street.

Cecilia's life in New York was very tough at first. For weeks on end she would do nothing but 'go-sees', which is model-agency jargon for visits to fashion editors and designers to solicit work. She would make several such visits a day, carrying her picture portfolio on the subway, to be casually inspected like a heifer in a market by the arrogant grandees of the fashion industry. It was, I suppose, a character-forming experience. It jolted her out of the gloomy introspection that had overcome her in London. It taught her to accept rejection, to take responsibility for her actions, to put a brave face on things, to become a trooper in the American style.

But I wouldn't have wanted it myself. New York is a frightening place if you don't know it, especially for a young girl. I still hate to imagine her struggling through the crowds, fending off approaches from strangers, and arriving with forced brightness at her appointment, only to be sent peremptorily on her way. But luckily it all paid off in the end. The work began to arrive, and within a year or two, Cecilia was one of the most successful models in the world, if not one of the most enthusiastic. If she did not become one of those famous 'supermodels', it was only because of her reserve, bred into her by her parents, and a natural reluctance to show off. Some American couturiers felt she didn't smile enough, but she was a huge hit in Japan, where smiling is not especially admired.

CHAPTER 3

The Smell of Beeswax

From the *Spectator* I went to the *Sunday Telegraph* as a writer and editor, but two years later I resigned to become the first Washington correspondent of a new British daily newspaper, the *Independent*. It was rather a foolhardy thing to do, since there was no guarantee that the *Independent* would be successful or even survive for more than a few weeks. But this was the first chance I had ever been offered of living in the United States, and I thought I should take it, even though it would mean spending some time away from my family. My spell in Washington started in September 1986, a month before the *Independent* was launched, and lasted for a year and a half. It began in an attic room of the Tabard Inn, a self-consciously old-world small hotel near Dupont Circle in the centre of town. It is the sort of place favoured by Englishmen who prefer 'character' to room service and by Americans who want to assert their individuality.

It wasn't the ideal place from which to establish a North American news-gathering operation, because there wasn't even television in the rooms to tell you what was going on; and I spent several days just sitting on my bed wondering what to do next. I had bought a map of the United States, and I would stare at it in horror for hours on end. America was so huge. Ten of the states were bigger—some of them vastly bigger—than the whole of the United Kingdom. Another nineteen were bigger than England; eleven were bigger than Scotland; six were bigger than Wales; one (Hawaii) was bigger than Northern Ireland; and only three—Connecticut, Delaware, and Rhode Island—were smaller than any of the nations of the United Kingdom.

There was another odd thing about the map. America didn't look as if it had evolved gradually and haphazardly like other countries. It looked as if someone had got out a ruler one day and crisscrossed it with straight lines to create states. The same straight-line fanatic had also drawn the street plans of New York, Washington and other cities. Both the scale and the shape of everything were very un-European. I felt like a Lilliputian come to Brobdingnag. As a first step, I decided to cut at least Canada out of my empire, which had been officially designated as the whole of North America. I was encouraged to do so by the very fashionable and sophisticated Canadian Ambassador, Alan Gottlieb, whose popularity in Washington owed much to the fact that he never mentioned Canada in social conversation. When I asked his advice at a dinner party, Mr Gottlieb, a former fellow of Wadham College, Oxford, said I would do well to jettison Canada because it was so much less interesting than the United States.

But there was still a lot of territory left to cover, and I wondered how I would ever find out what was going on in it. In fact, when I eventually moved into a dignified four-storey house on 33rd Street in Georgetown, an eighteenth-century port on the Potomac which had become the smartest suburb of the capital, and established an office on the top floor (which I shared with an old friend and new colleague, Peter Pringle), I discovered that Los Angeles and New York were to be covered by journalists on the spot; and if anything of interest happened anywhere else outside Washington, one would know about it soon enough.

There was no shortage of information. In fact, there was far too much of it pouring into our old Victorian house down television cables and telephone wires into computers and teleprinter machines, and filling the columns of those bloated East Coast newspapers—the *New York Times*, the *Wall Street Journal*, and the *Washington Post*—that were flung on to the doorstep early each morning. So much of our time was spent sifting and ordering this mass of material and stuffing paper into garbage bags that I began to wish I were working in a country where news was suppressed and foreign correspondents were obliged to ferret around for themselves. Excessive information creates its own form of blindness to what is actually going on.

When I got out of Washington, which was not very often, it was initially to report some manifestation of American spirituality. There was the cult of Elvis Presley, for example, which took me to Memphis, Tennessee, on the tenth anniversary of his death. There, in 1987, on a hot August night, I watched the faithful scrawl their devotional messages on the 'wailing wall' surrounding the Graceland Mansion, the rock singer's former home that had become his shrine. Then, when the gates were opened at 9 p.m., I watched them light candles and walk solemnly up the drive to the Garden of Meditation where Elvis and other members of his family are buried.

Elvis International Tribute Week was attended by about a thousand people from the British Elvis fan club, far the biggest in the world, for its 23,000 members were not confined to the British Isles but were spread around the world from England to China. I was proud of how down-to-earth the British fans were. None of them had ever seen Elvis in visions or been cured by him or believed him to be a saint. A 'Meet the Brits' party at the Airport Hilton Hotel on the eve of the anniversary was anything but spiritual. 'Come on, then, let's teach the Americans how to stroll,' said the North of England disc jockey imported for the occasion; and the fans flocked on to the dance floor, formed two long lines, and pranced gaily backwards and forwards.

The British are puzzled and usually shocked by the way in which the Americans manage to reconcile their spirituality with their materialism. In America, greed fails to dampen the religious spirit. A Gallup poll conducted during the late eighties showed that Americans are second only to the Maltese in their attachment to God; and 40 per cent said they were churchgoers, as opposed to 14 per cent of the British. Nine Americans in ten said they had never doubted the existence of God; eight in ten said they believed they would be called before God on Judgement Day to answer for their sins; and eight in ten said they believed God still worked miracles. Among those calling themselves Christians, 62 per cent said they believed in the Second Coming, 50 per cent said they believed in angels, and 38 per cent claimed to have been 'born again'.

In the spring of 1987 I had gone to South Carolina to visit Heritage USA, the 'inspirational' theme park managed by the husband-and-wife television evangelists Jim and Tammy Bakker, whose PTL ('Praise the Lord', 'People that Love') organisation had defrauded believers out of millions of dollars and paid $265,000 to silence a former church secretary called Jessica Hahn with whom Jim Bakker later admitted to having had a fifteen-minute sexual encounter. They were crooks, certainly, but not necessarily charlatans. Judging by the attitudes of their followers, I was prepared to believe that the Bakkers, who by then had fled in disgrace to California, were sincere in their religious convictions. Jim, said one of his followers admiringly, was a 'spiritual entrepreneur', and entrepreneurs were seldom perfect: his dalliance with Miss Hahn was of little significance compared with all the good he had done.

At that time, Heritage USA came third on the list of America's tourist attractions, beaten only by the Walt Disney theme parks in California and Florida, and it had earned $129 million the previous year. But apart from a much-derided water park containing the world's longest water slide and the world's largest wave pool, it was rather a puritanical place—no smoking was allowed anywhere within its 2,000-acre grounds—and the amusements on offer were nearly all of a quasi-religious character: tours of Billy Graham's childhood home which had been moved there from Charlotte, North Carolina; Bible seminars; counselling sessions; camp-fire singalongs; 'fellowship teas'; and meetings in the 'Upper Room' which was said to be an exact copy of the room in Jerusalem in which the Last Supper was held. People didn't go to Heritage USA to be amused. They went seeking solace, tranquillity and fellowship; and many found there in miniature the Utopia, the Shining City on a Hill, which had always been the America of immigrants' dreams.

There was a toy train for children running round the water park, and having nothing better to do I decided to take a ride on it. The only other passengers were also middle-aged—a schoolmaster and his wife from Komoko, Indiana. He was clearly an intelligent man with experience of the world—he had even taught for a while at a school in Kenya—but he had never been as happy anywhere as at Heritage USA. Komoko, he explained, was a grim and declining industrial town. 'I teach English,' he said, 'but none of the students care about their work. It is their apathy I hate most. I set them homework, but hardly any of them do it, and they don't even feel the need to explain why they haven't. Many of them are on drugs. Most of them get more money from their parents than I earn. They don't see the point of education. I try to tell them they'll need it to get jobs when they are older, but they aren't interested.

'The school is such an unfriendly place,' the poor man went on. 'The headmaster never speaks to me. I sometimes wonder if he remembers my name. But here everyone is so friendly. You meet any PTL minister for the first time, and he treats you like a friend.' The schoolmaster didn't reproach the Bakkers for their misdemeanours. He didn't even care if some of his dollars had gone into hush money for Jessica Hahn. Like most of the so-called 'partners' in Heritage USA, he didn't pay good money to spend sleepless nights wondering what should be done about Jim and Tammy. He paid it so that God would take care of such things.

Because they respect commerce almost as much as religion, most Americans don't complain when the two become entwined. It seemed perfectly normal that Pope John Paul II's tour of the United States in September 1987 should be exploited to the hilt not only by the hawkers of papal souvenirs but also by city governments and businesses touting for customers and investment. The New Orleans newspaper, the *Times-Picayune*, led its business section with an article about the Pope's likely impact on the New York Stock Exchange. It noted that, during his first visit to America in 1979, the Dow Jones Industrial Average reached its peak for the year. 'The Pope's charisma seems to put people in a more optimistic frame of mind, crucial for stock buyers,' it said.

I was one of hundreds of journalists who pursued the Pope around the United States in two chartered jumbo jets called Shepherd 2 and Shepherd 3 (the Pope's plane being Shepherd 1), and everywhere he seemed to generate the optimism stock buyers were reported to find crucial. Audiences, desiring only uplift, just ignored his sermons about the moral degeneracy of American society. In New Orleans, I ran into two drunk teenage girls in a restaurant one night. They were wearing little yellow-and-white Vatican flags in their headbands and had attended all the big papal events of the day. 'We're Poped out,' they giggled, ordering more drinks. They said they were Roman Catholics and loved the Pope, but spent the rest of the evening making obscene jokes about him. 'It's like liquor,' said a man a few days later on a pavement in Los Angeles. 'The more you drink, the drunker you get. I think we are drunk on the Pope.' The point of most religion in the United States is that, like liquor, it should make you feel good.

A year of lurid scandal in the television ministries substantially reduced their earnings, but it didn't damage them nearly as much as the liberal media had hoped. They continued to have great political influence. The National Religious Broadcasters' Convention held in Washington in February 1988 was attended by about a hundred senators, congressmen and government officials. Even President Reagan was there, offering reassurance. He attacked the media for 'taking the actions of an isolated few and portraying all broadcast preachers in that light'. 'You have shown that integrity is a cornerstone of your ministries,' he said.

No non-Christian has ever been elected President of the United States, and Vice-President George Bush, who was then running for the Republican nomination, informed the Convention that his own faith had 'lifted and comforted' him during crises in his life. Mr Bush had not always been so earnest about his religion. Eight years earlier, when he had been running against Mr Reagan for the Party nomination, he had made one of the best jokes of his political career when he told a Southern audience of born-again Christians that he seemed to be the only person there who had been born only once. The resurgence of fundamentalist Christianity in the meantime, and the success of the Rev Jerry Falwell's Moral Majority, a political movement of religious conservatives, had had the effect of making Mr Bush draw attention to his piety. He now assured audiences in the South that Jesus Christ was his 'personal Saviour'.

Washington is a much nicer place than it is generally reputed to be. It is often called a one-industry town because of its huge floating population of politicians, civil servants, lobbyists, journalists, diplomats, analysts, and students of every aspect of politics and foreign affairs; and it is perhaps true that there is little point in living there unless you want to put the world to rights. But Washington is also a beautiful city. It has a wonderful position between the rolling hills of Maryland and Virginia on a river of great splendour, the Potomac, and this gives it an air of almost rural serenity. It has no very tall buildings, but immensely tall trees teeming with birds and friendly squirrels.

Contrasting with the dreamy Southern atmosphere is the icy grandeur of Washington's monumental centre, which still astonishes visitors by its scale and presumption. The enormous Capitol building, in which the two houses of Congress sit, is doubly astonishing when one considers that Washington was only shakily established as a town—and the United States as a nation—when it was being built. Even in the eighteen-forties, Charles Dickens described Washington as a 'City of Magnificent Intentions . . . spacious avenues that begin in nothing and lead nowhere; streets miles long that only want houses, roads, and inhabitants; public meetings that need but a public to be complete; and ornaments of great thoroughfares, which only lack great thoroughfares to ornament . . .'

The Founding Fathers must have had a premonition that their poor, struggling country would one day become the world's top nation, for why, otherwise, would they have designed its new capital on such a scale? But their taste for grandeur did not extend to their own homes; the White House is famously modest, as are most American private residences built before the last quarter of the nineteenth century. Grandeur in the new American democracy was not for individuals but for the people's institutions—their elected chambers, their town halls, their libraries, their museums, their art galleries, their railway stations.

There are two Washingtons, of course: black and white. Blacks account for about three-quarters of the population and live in three of the city's four quadrants—North-East, South-East, and South-West. The other quadrant, North-West Washington, which includes Georgetown, is where the whites live. The segregation is as complete as anything ever accomplished in South Africa. I once got lost in my car in North-East Washington and stopped at a gas station to ask where I was. A dapper black man with a BMW said the question wasn't worth answering because it was obvious I shouldn't have come there in the first place. So instead of answering it, he jumped into his car, told me to follow, and led me for several miles back to the white colony in North-West. My home and my office were in Georgetown, and it was there that I mostly stayed. It was the pleasantest and prettiest place to be. Founded in 1751 by Scottish immigrants to Maryland, Georgetown had been a well-established town before the adjacent capital was planned; and it offers the only eighteenth-century architecture in the city. During the first half of the twentieth century, Georgetown went into decline. But now, as the Michelin Guide points out, its leafy residential streets 'bristle with refinement and respectability'.

The only black I knew in Georgetown was called Truman. He was an elderly chauffeur who drove a Cadillac for Evangeline Bruce, a Washington hostess of much elegance and beauty who lived just round the corner from me in a large house on 34th Street. I got to see two sides of Truman. When he was driving Evangeline, he was the quintessential old retainer. 'Did you wash the car today?' she would ask. 'Oh yes, ma'am,' he would reply, in his folksiest manner. 'Well, we know what that means, don't we, Truman?' 'Oh yes, ma'am. Dat means it be bound to rain.' But when Evangeline was abroad in Europe, as she was every summer, I would sometimes see Truman without his uniform on the sidewalks of Georgetown. Dressed for the streets, he looked natty and 'cool'—a man of the world if ever there was one.

I happened to be with Evangeline on the night that Truman died. We were having dinner at Joe Alsop's house on N Street. Joe, then in his late seventies, lived in a charming and beautifully furnished old Georgetown house in which he would frequently give dinner parties. On this occasion, there were only four of us at dinner: Joe, Evangeline, me, and Adam Platt, a young journalist who was helping Joe to write his autobiography.

Evangeline, who always went home early, had told Truman to be outside in the Cadillac at around 9.30 p.m. Leaving the house at that time, she found Truman slumped, unconscious, over the steering wheel. An ambulance was called, and Evangeline got into it to accompany him to the Georgetown Hospital. I was still drinking port in Joe's basement dining room, oblivious to the drama that was going on upstairs; and Joe, after seeing the ambulance off, returned to the table and, without mentioning anything, picked up the conversation where he had left it.

I knew nothing of what had happened until Evangeline telephoned from the hospital a little while later to ask if I could please drive over and join her there. She wanted some cash, having none in her handbag, and a magazine to read while waiting for news of Truman from the emergency room. Joe, unwilling to part with a new copy of *Country Life* which he feared might not be returned, looked around for a magazine he would be willing to part with and supplied me grudgingly with a very old copy of the *Economist*.

At the hospital I found Evangeline in a waiting room, looking shaken. She had used a payphone to call Truman's doctor and members of his family in North-East, and they had all been horribly rude to her. The hostility of black Washington towards white Washington had come as a shocking revelation, for she had never had to encounter it before. I gave her the old copy of the *Economist*, which was no kind of consolation, and we waited there tensely for quite a while until a doctor came out to say that Truman hadn't regained consciousness and there wasn't any point in us waiting any longer. I drove Evangeline home, and next morning I found that she had left a pair of high-heeled shoes in my car. Had this great lady been so distracted that she had walked up the steps to her front door in bare feet?

Truman died during the night, and the wake was held a few days later in Evangeline's drawing room. She asked me if I could be there to support her, but I had to be out of town on an assignment for the *Independent*. So Evangeline was alone in the company of black Washington to bid Truman farewell. Among the mourners were not only Truman's wife and family but several of his former girlfriends, for he turned out to have been a remarkable philanderer.

There was no doubting the genuineness of Evangeline's grief. She and Truman had been together for over fifteen years, and not only in Washington. In the early seventies he had been her driver in Beijing and Brussels, the last two diplomatic posts of her husband, David Bruce. Mr Bruce, an ambassador of great repute, had died in the mid-seventies, but Truman had stayed on to drive Mrs Bruce to the dinners and cocktail parties of which official Washington never tires. He had become well known to Washington society, which noted his death with regret. It was pointed out at dinner parties that the Cadillac had been beautifully and legally parked by Truman before he collapsed. This was typical of the man, people said. Just imagine what disasters might have occurred if he had died while driving the Cadillac down busy Pennsylvania Avenue! But no, not Truman: he would never have been as inconsiderate as that.

David Bruce was the only American to have served as Ambassador in all of the three top west-European capitals—London, Paris and Bonn. He was Ambassador in London throughout most of the sixties, and it was there that I first met Evangeline, who was a distant cousin of my mother. The Bruces were a famously rich, good-looking, and well-dressed couple. Evangeline's father, Edward Bell, was an American diplomat who died when she was very young. Her mother then married a British diplomat, Sir James Dodds, and they lived 'in just about every country you can imagine', she told *Vanity Fair* in an interview in 1995—Italy, Sweden, France, China, Holland, Britain, and Switzerland. With such a background—and with her gift for entertaining and her excellent taste—she was the ideal partner for the grandest American Ambassador since the war.

David Bruce was of an old Scottish family which settled in Virginia in the eighteenth century. Before Evangeline, he had been married to the only daughter of an exceedingly rich Pittsburgh industrialist, Andrew Mellon, who gave him one million dollars as a wedding present in 1926. This, prudently invested, made him a very wealthy man, and he wasn't asked to give any of the money back when he left his first wife for another. His wealth made him free to embark on a life of public service. He was to become closely associated with the so-called Wise Men who directed American foreign policy after the war. They all belonged to what Joe Alsop was to call the WASP Ascendancy, the East Coast élite who constituted the nearest thing in America to an aristocracy. It was a class which had much in common with the equivalent èlite in Britain, as Joe's memoirs make vividly clear.

According to Joe, the defining characteristics of an American 'gentleman' in the inter-war years were hardly different from those of an English 'gentleman' of the same period. He had his suits made in London and got his shirts from Charvet or Sulka in Paris. For formal dinners (and nearly all dinners were formal) he would wear a dinner jacket with a plain white shirt and handkerchief ('any fanciness introduced into the basic black-and-white pattern of a dinner jacket and trousers was grossly improper'); and at weddings he would wear 'as a minimum a top hat, a morning coat, striped trousers, dark socks and black shoes', though spring weddings also 'called for white linen double-breasted waistcoats and white linen spats'.

Gentlemen, meaning members of the WASP Ascendancy or persons who aspired to be members, did not wear brown suits in the city—I have never understood why [Joe wrote]. Dark-grey, navy-blue, or even black were required, albeit possibly with a discreet pinstripe, if desired. Black shoes also were essential in town—and no nonsense about it, except that with a dark-grey flannel suit, it was possible to wear brown shoes so repeatedly polished for so long a period of time that they all but counted as black. One also wore a silk handkerchief in the handkerchief pocket—and it was rather second rate to keep it just for show, instead of blowing your nose on it in case of need. To round it all out, in those days men still got boutonnires from the florist on festive occasions. I remember I used to buy a yellow carnation every Sunday in New

York after I went to work there—on eighteen dollars a week—and on Sundays too I would put a little Florida Water on my handkerchief, as my father had taught me.

Language was the most important social indicator—'the true empire of the dos and don'ts', as Joe put it—and in America, as in Britain, the Nancy Mitford snobberies applied.

> The rule was that the earliest English name for any thing or any occupation was desirable, and anything later was highly undesirable. So you were buried in a coffin, not a casket, and the coffin was supplied by an undertaker, never a funeral director and not (God preserve us) a mortician. Windows had curtains, not drapes or draperies . . . The unlucky had false teeth, not dentures; and when their lives ended, they died instead of 'passing' . . . (And WASPS really did say 'tomahto' as opposed to 'tomayto', though you seldom hear anybody pronounce it that way now.)

Here were plausible ingredients for a 'special relationship' between America and Britain, and I have sometimes wondered whether they were all it ever consisted of. In any case, the 'special relationship' declined as the WASP Ascendancy declined, until both terms became devoid of substance. By 1929, when the Wall Street Crash struck at the WASPs' power base—the banks and financial institutions of the East Coast—'this special group and its special place in American life had endured for no less than three centuries, which is a pretty good run by any standard', Joe wrote.

He claimed to be 'glad every day' that the WASP Ascendancy collapsed when it did, enabling the members of excluded minorities to become equal participants in American life. I always thought he was deluding himself about this. I don't mean that he didn't believe in equality of opportunity, but I feel he would have been happier if his own social class had remained on top. He now had to come to terms with people of power from unfamiliar backgrounds, some of whom, lacking charm or culture, he must have found uncongenial. The old assumptions and securities were gone, and his prejudices had to be suppressed.

I had first met Joe some years earlier, when he was already in his seventies, at a lunch given by the British Ambassador, Sir Nicholas Henderson, in honour of Yehudi Menuhin, the American violinist who was to become an English lord. I was staying in Washington at the time with my friend Michael Kinsley, and I had asked if I could bring him along. Mike, a former Rhodes scholar at Oxford and in those days a keen Anglophile, was delighted to set foot for the first time in Britain's great Lutyens palace on Massachusetts Avenue, with its huge portraits of British royalty and its dining-room chairs embroidered with the royal coat of arms.

After lunch, we gave Joe a lift home in Mike's car, and he urged us to come into his house to continue drinking. Mike, a well-brought-up doctor's son from Detroit, whose Anglophilia forced him to wrestle with his natural puritanism, agreed to this depraved suggestion, and we sat for an hour or two listening to Joe's drawling reminiscences and censorious judgements. I am sorry to say that my friendship with Joe was to some extent founded on a shared enthusiasm for alcohol and cigarettes; and after I came to live near him in Georgetown in 1986, I would visit him frequently for long sessions of both.

If Joe, as the title of his autobiography says, had 'seen the best of it', I was not to see the best of *him*. By the time I got to know him, it was twelve years since he had written the last of his newspaper columns, and he was a frustrated, cantankerous, heavy-drinking old man, given to serious attacks of ill humour. In his last years as a columnist, he had fallen far out of fashion because of his unshakeable enthusiasm for the Vietnam War, which he always believed America had been right to fight and had been capable of winning. In the words of John Kenneth Galbraith, Joe (along with President Lyndon Johnson) was 'the leading non-combatant casualty of Vietnam'—'From a much-feared columnist, warrior and prophet, he has become a figure of fun. It was the war that did him in.'

Yet my friendship with Joe was one of the great joys of my time in Washington—and also, when she was there, of my wife Susanna, for whom Joe had a particular affection. Even his cantankerousness seemed a virtue amid the blandness of Washington society. He hated being old and ill, and he once got much depressed comparing his appearance with that of Ronald Reagan (who was almost exactly the same age) after I had taken delivery at his door of a photograph showing them together at a White House function. But until the last few months of his life, when he had difficulty breathing, he was, for most of the time, charming, funny, affectionate, and full of deep, gurgling laughter.

He had a caricature of a face—a bit like Mr Punch's with pronounced chin and nose—and he had round, owl-like spectacles through which he peered intensely with an encouraging grin to make sure that his jokes had been properly appreciated. He was a bow-tie enthusiast and always immaculately dressed in tailor-made suits of the best material and assiduously polished shoes. He said in his memoirs that 'to this day, when I dress to go out to an old-fashioned luncheon party in Washington, I do my best to suggest a Morgan partner of 1928'. And, for all I know, he may have succeeded, but there were few people left who knew what a twenties New York banker was supposed to look like. His fine Georgetown house, too, reflected his nostalgia for his youth, for I am sure that it smelt like the old New England country houses he described in his book—'the secret was beeswax, rather lavishly used year round to polish floors and furniture, plus a great many flowers from the summer gardens'.

Joe liked to complain a lot about people, and one person about whom I never heard him say a good word was Pamela Digby Churchill Hayward Harriman. He particularly enjoyed telling a story which he attributed to Alistair Forbes, a famous London gossip. Someone had once said of her to Forbes, 'Pamela is beautiful, but it's a pity she has such a short neck,' to which Forbes is alleged to have replied, 'What do you expect, with her head screwed on so tight?'

Mrs Harriman was a very grand figure in Georgetown, but was resented by the surviving scions of the WASP Ascendancy. They probably considered her too ambitious and calculating, and also, I suspect, a bit of a parvenu, for her impeccably aristocratic English background did not make her an aristocrat in the United States. Daughter of the 11th Baron Digby, she married the journalist and politician Randolph Churchill in 1939; and, while he was off at the war, she moved into Number 10 Downing Street to stay with his father Winston, the one Englishman all Americans admire. (Joe was infuriated by her continued use, two marriages later, of the Churchill name.)

Leaping forward three decades, we find her in 1971 suddenly widowed by her second husband, the New York theatrical producer Leland Hayward, and embarking on a third marriage, to Averell Harriman, the very rich, very glamorous, and very powerful former presidential adviser and Governor of New York, who had been widowed himself only a short time earlier. Averell Harriman and Pamela Churchill had been lovers in London during the war. He was now eighty years old, and she was fifty-one. He was to live another fifteen years and to die just before my arrival in Washington.

It was at one of Joe's dinner parties in a room hung with his family portraits (copies, actually, for he had sold the originals) that I heard the bizarre story of Averell Harriman's funeral. It was told by one of his former close aides as an example of Mrs Harriman's lack of scruple. The Governor's funeral turned out to have been a sham. There had been a service at a fashionable church in New York City, conducted by the Episcopalian Bishop of New York, the Rev Paul Moore.

The family and mourners had then driven in a fleet of cars to Arden, the Harriman country seat north of the city, for his burial in the family graveyard. A hole had been dug next to the grave of his first wife, Marie. The Governor's coffin, surrounded by flowers, lay under an awning beside the hole as Bishop Moore committed his body to the ground, 'earth to earth, ashes to ashes, dust to dust'. But the hole was to remain empty. After the mourners had left, the coffin was quietly removed to a nearby funeral parlour and placed in cold storage, where it was to remain for many weeks.

I couldn't at first understand how the mourners had been duped into believing that the body had been buried. The key to this mystery lies in the American aversion to the realities of death, which was satirised by Evelyn Waugh in *The Loved One*. It is apparently quite normal at genteel American funerals for the mourners to be spared the sight of the coffin being lowered into the ground. Bishop Moore told the *Washington Post*, when it investigated the incident, that, so far as he was concerned, nothing irregular had happened. Even if Mr Harriman had not been physically buried, he had been buried 'liturgically'. 'It happens all the time,' the Bishop said. But not all of the Harriman clan were satisfied by this explanation. They suspected monkey business.

Mrs Harriman hotly denied it. She had simply been carrying out her husband's wishes, she said. He had told her before he died that he didn't want to be buried in the family graveyard, but in a romantic spot on a crag overlooking a lake three miles away, where she too one day would be laid to rest beside him. But the crag was of granite, and there hadn't been time to blast a hole in it before the funeral. One idea, it was explained, had been to inter the Governor temporarily beside his first wife, but the objection was raised that this might damage his coffin. So it was decided instead to put the coffin in cold storage until his chosen site could be made ready. Even so, Mrs Harriman had decided 'to go ahead with the normal conclusion of the Episcopal ceremony' because this was 'the most dignified thing' to do. But why, it was asked, did a hole have to be dug in the graveyard if no coffin was going to be put in it? This had been a mistake, came the reply. Estate workers at Arden had just gone ahead and dug it without being asked.

But would estate workers really have done such a thing on their own initiative? Joe's dinner guest thought not. Worse than that, Joe's dinner guest claimed to have been told by the Governor, shortly before his death, that he wanted to be buried in the family graveyard between his two wives. He had never been heard to propose anything else. But anyway, his body was eventually buried inside the crag, and now Pamela's lies beside it, just as she had wished. She died of a heart attack in 1997 after a swim in the pool of the Ritz Hotel in Paris, where she had served for four years as American Ambassador. Like her late husband, she was given a huge memorial service in Washington Cathedral, with the President making an address.

For all her blue blood and her links with the illustrious Churchill family, Pamela Harriman was, in American terms, an upstart. She was a first-generation immigrant who didn't even become an American citizen until she was over fifty; and her nostalgia, if she had any, would have been for the great country houses of England rather than for modest New England houses smelling of beeswax. Joe Alsop, her close neighbour in Georgetown, had lived in Washington since 1935; she, since 1971. While he spent the evening of his life contemplating the 'noble, congenial, curious old world' of the former WASP-run Washington and keeping the company of friends who remembered it too, she was an active player on the modern political scene—raising huge sums of money for the Democratic Party, picking out an obscure ex-governor of Arkansas as its coming man, and even, in a memorable social triumph, entertaining Raisa

Gorbachev to tea in her house on N Street. Her efforts were to reap their reward in 1993 when Bill Clinton sent her to Paris as his Ambassador.

She was said to have hoped for more—perhaps a position in Mr Clinton's cabinet. (After his election as the first Democratic president since Jimmy Carter, she had said that having waited twelve years to have a Democrat in the White House she wasn't suddenly going to leave Washington.) But rumour had it that Hillary Clinton didn't want her in the neighbourhood, and so she was sent to preside over America's largest embassy abroad, in a city where she had lived for several years between her first two marriages and enjoyed some notable romantic attachments—to Gianni Agnelli, Elie de Rothschild, and Prince Aly Khan. In a cover story entitled 'Queen Mother of the Clinton Court', coinciding with President Clinton's Inauguration, *New York* magazine put her in her place. 'Hers', it said, 'is a unique immigrant's tale.'

I barely knew Mrs Harriman, though she was charming and polite on the two or three occasions I met her and I thought her a wonderful advertisement for the plastic surgeon's craft. My only friends among the Georgetown hostesses were Evangeline and Susan Mary Alsop, the ex-wife of Joe. Both lived alone in palatial houses, like royal widows, and they had an almost royal sense of their social obligations. I don't know to what extent they actually enjoyed Washington's predictable social rituals, but it would not have occurred to them to wonder. Entertaining was their profession, and they did it like professionals, without complaint. They also did it very well.

Evangeline was famous for the Sunday brunches she would give in her large, pretty, sun-filled drawing room— oysters, smoked salmon, dainty sandwiches with delicate fillings, and crystallised bacon. The bacon was prepared to her own particular recipe, and she was proud and possessive of it. It was always a talking point among her friends, with opinion sharply divided about how good it actually was.

She was in her late sixties then, but looked twenty years younger and quite natural in the girlishly short skirts she sometimes wore. Like all good hostesses, she preferred listening to talking, and she would move gracefully about the room, soliciting opinions on the latest social and political scandals in America and Europe. Washington power and money were always strongly represented among her guests, but more by Democrats than Republicans. The Reaganauts, like the Thatcherites in Britain, were generally too earnest for such frivolities. Nevertheless, they recognised Evangeline's unofficial status as a kind of royal personage, and Nancy Reagan would visit her once a year for lunch.

Susan Mary Alsop, who lived only a few streets away, had a larger dining-room table and so gave larger dinner parties. She and Evangeline were old friends, but had a slightly tricky and competitive relationship. Susan Mary was irritated by Evangeline's habit of always going home very early after dinner. On one occasion, when Evangeline was about to leave before the coffee after a star-studded dinner party, Susan Mary told her huffily to stay; and Evangeline responded by sitting stonily in a corner of the drawing room until the last guest had left at around 1 a.m.

Evangeline was very thin, but Susan Mary—a heavy smoker with no appetite—was even thinner. She, too, had been a beauty. She was, however, of more distinguished lineage, being a direct descendant of John Jay, an eighteenth-century statesman who helped negotiate the peace with Britain after the American Revolution. Joe married her after the death of her first husband, Bill Patten, an old schoolfriend of his who had been an American diplomat in Paris in the immediate aftermath of the Second World War. Susan Mary had been close at that time to the British Ambassador, Sir Alfred Duff Cooper (later Viscount Norwich), who had been Churchill's information minister during Britain's darkest hour.

Joe was fifty years old when they got married. He had never felt the urge to marry before, but he had grown a little lonely in middle age and was feeling the lack of an immediate family. He set up house in Georgetown with Susan Mary and her two children, shortly after his friend and hero John Kennedy had been elected President. Theirs was the only private house in Washington that President Kennedy visited regularly while he was in office. He and his wife Jackie dined with the Alsops once every six weeks, and the President would also come often to see them on his own when Jackie was away during the summer. It was an exhilarating time for the Alsops, whose closeness to the Kennedys brought them great social success, but their marriage did not last. According to Joe, they 'irritated one another far too often for a really successful partnership'. They divorced in 1975, but more than ten years later they were still playing host and hostess at each other's dinner parties in their separate large houses only four blocks apart.

In fact, Joe was a reluctant, secret homosexual, and his life was once almost ruined when the KGB attempted to expose him. They had set him up in a Moscow hotel with a handsome young man and had them photographed together in a state of undress. Joe contemplated suicide. He left a letter with the American Ambassador, Chip Bohlen, with instructions for it to be opened a week later if he hadn't made contact in the meantime. The Ambassador, who was one of Joe's oldest and closest friends, opened the letter at once. In it, Joe said he felt he had betrayed his country and his family and had therefore decided to kill himself.

The Ambassador managed to track down Joe and talked him out of suicide, but the crisis did not end there. The KGB sent prints of the photograph to several of Joe's known political enemies in the United States, including other journalists, but, to their eternal credit, they all destroyed them; and Joe continued to live and write his newspaper column. As far as I know, he never confessed his homosexuality to any of his friends (except, presumably, Chip Bohlen); but he did tell Susanna and me after dinner one evening at the Hay

Adams Hotel how a friend of his, a famously heterosexual English nobleman, had once taken a bet on the matter and tried, unsuccessfully, to seduce him on a sofa. Joe was clearly proud of having resisted these advances and, surprisingly, harboured no resentment against his friends. Perhaps he permitted special licence to English aristocrats.

CHAPTER 4

Cigarettes and Whisky

When Joe's lung cancer was diagnosed, he was in the care of one of Washington's leading society doctors, Richard Perry, who also looked after Susan Mary Alsop and Evangeline Bruce. On Evangeline's recommendation, I went to see him in December 1987 because of an excruciating pain in the forefinger of my right hand. Washington was then deep in snow, through which I trudged for a mile to visit Dr Perry at his surgery. The cause of the pain turned out to be a splinter, though it was not Dr Perry but Susanna who immediately discovered this when she arrived from London a couple of days later on one of her periodic visits to Washington. Dr Perry, being an American doctor, was less concerned with the finger than my overall health and sent me off for a check-up that made the finger problem pale into insignificance. For such an easygoing man, accustomed to the incurably bad habits of a patient such as Joe, he wrote me a surprisingly severe and technical letter:

The ventilatory study shows that you were able to inspire and then expire 85 per cent of the air predicted, based on your height and age. However, there is a significant reduction in the speed with which you can expire this air, measuring only 38 per cent of predicted normal in mid-expiration. This is consistent with obstructive lung disease caused by the two-pack-a-day thirty-year history of smoking. Unfortunately, after breathing the bronchodilator, there was no measurable change, so some of these changes are probably irreversible at this point.

The main findings, then, were as follows. It is imperative that you stop the smoking now. There is measurable lung disease without improvement following the bronchodilator. We can at least arrest this damage at this point and hope for some improvement as time goes by, but this won't happen unless you can stop smoking. The Smoke Enders group have an excellent program, and they can be reached by phone through the Yellow Pages.

I found Smoke Enders in the Yellow Pages and enrolled in their six-week course. This cost $300 and required me to attend a two-hour class every Thursday evening in a deserted office building close to the White House. This wasn't easy for me, because I had to be out of Washington most of the time, covering the presidential election primaries for the *Independent*. But giving up smoking seemed to be a very good idea, not only for the reasons given by Dr Perry but also because the habit had begun to seem more trouble than it was worth. My colleague Peter Pringle clearly didn't like me smoking in the office, though he did his best to tolerate it; and his otherwise admirably tolerant wife Eleanor, a journalist on the *Washington Post* at that time, was then, like many middle-class Americans, going through a phase of almost hysterical aversion to tobacco smoke. One summer's night, when her large and airy house had all its windows open, I had lit a cigarette in the dining room after she had gone upstairs to bed, and a few minutes later she came down to say that the smoke was disturbing her.

Such horror of smoking struck me as odd, not to say ungrateful, in a country which owed so much to tobacco. Where would the early settlers in Virginia have been without their tobacco crops? The plant was their economic salvation; and without it Virginian farmers like Thomas Jefferson and George Washington would never have been rich enough to concentrate their energies on revolutionary policies. When Congress in the eighties adopted the rose as the floral emblem of the United States, I felt that the tobacco leaf would have been much more appropriate.

But the anti-smoking movement, which started to gather momentum in the sixties, had grown so powerful over the next twenty years that smoking had come to be regarded as extreme anti-social behaviour. With a proliferation of studies purporting to show that smokers not only damaged themselves but also put the health of non-smokers at risk, its wickedness was widely taken to be proven; and the Reagan administration, in the person of its formidable Surgeon General, Dr C. Everett Koop, was firmly of that view.

Dr Koop, a bearded conservative prophet of terrifying moral certitude, had announced that it was his goal to make America totally smoke-free by the end of the century, and he was making good progress. The strident government health warnings, the ban on television advertising of tobacco, and the ever-widening restrictions on smoking in public places had reduced the number of adult male smokers from 53 per cent to 35 per cent within the space of two decades, and the trend was continuing. It was only in the company of Joe Alsop and of one or two unreformed British journalists, like Christopher Hitchens and Andrew Cockburn, that I was able to smoke in Washington without guilt. I had thought of emigrating to North Carolina, where I had noted some years earlier that cigarettes were always abundantly available in private houses and that smoking seemed to be regarded as a local patriotic duty. But I decided that it was probably a better idea just to give up.

The Smoke Enders' class was conducted as an evening job by an employee of the government's environment protection agency, whose name was Kirby Biggs. Mr Biggs's method was seductive. He taught that giving up smoking should not be an exercise in will-power or self-denial, but a positive pleasure. You should learn how to enjoy every cigarette you didn't smoke, just as you used to enjoy—or misguidedly believed yourself to enjoy—every cigarette you did smoke. Giving up smoking was something you had to learn, just as, once upon a time, you had had to learn how to smoke. You should not feel guilty about having taken up smoking in the first place, for it had not been your fault. 'You were tricked, and you were victimised,' Mr Biggs said. People had urged you to smoke, and they had told you of the pleasures it would bring, but they had not disclosed the eventual costs—cancer, heart disease, emphysema, personal repulsiveness, and so on.

All but one of us stayed the course. The drop-out was a pot-bellied man who had deeply impressed the class during our first meeting by saying that he smoked seven packets of cigarettes a day. Even Mr Biggs blanched a little when he heard this. When this remarkable man failed to attend future meetings, we all wanted to know what had happened to him. Not wishing to admit failure, Mr Biggs claimed he had switched to another Smoke Enders course nearer to where he lived, but nobody believed this. After six weeks, during which I had flown back to Washington every Thursday from various corners of the United States, 'Graduation Day' arrived.

We were invited to bring our loved ones along for the ceremony, and I happened to have my Uncle Robin (a committed smoker himself) staying with me at the time, so I made him come. I was the last person to be called by Mr Biggs to the front of the class and, being the only non-American graduate, received especially polite applause. My 'Certificate of Graduation', printed in Gothic script, read as follows: 'Greetings. Be It Known That Alexander Chancellor, having smoked an average of two and a half packs a day for the past thirty-one years, has with great pride and wisdom stopped as of 12 February 1988.' To my shame, I was later to take up smoking again in New York. But thanks to Kirby Biggs, I did survive cheerfully without cigarettes for almost five years. Mr Biggs bade us farewell with a final 'power idea'. If ever we were tempted, he said, we should repeat to ourselves: 'I'm a puff away from a pack a day.' He was perfectly right, and I should have heeded him.

Evangeline and Susan Mary were much homelier than the word 'hostesses' suggests, and I would often see them on their own or at meals with one or two of their old friends, like Joe Alsop or Katharine Graham. I particularly enjoyed those small domestic gatherings in which they humanised Washington with their gossip and reminiscences, making it seem a cosy, old-fashioned Southern city instead of the scary breeding ground for men in suits which it had become. I would sometimes go to the cinema with Susan Mary, who was always keen to see the latest film, and I would occasionally accompany Evangeline to parties and first nights.

I went with her in a snowstorm to the Washington première of *Les Misérables*, the British musical based on the Victor Hugo novel, which I loathed but she adored. 'I like anything revolutionary,' she said in the interval. It was a remark I thought comic from a rich Washington widow, but I later discovered that she had been quietly working away for years on a book about revolutionary France— *Napoleon and Josephine: An Improbable Marriage*—which was eventually published to considerable acclaim in 1995 shortly before she died. For after a party in New York to celebrate the book, she suddenly and inexplicably went blind and died soon afterwards of a heart attack. I and my sister Teresa were surprised and touched to find ourselves beneficiaries of her will, for she left us jointly a painting of a mutual ancestor which used to hang over the mantelpiece in her Georgetown dining room—an eighteenth-century portrait by Francis Cotes of a certain Dr Charles Chauncey of the county of Hertfordshire where we had been brought up.

Susan Mary was a writer too, who had already published one book—a biography of Lady Sackville, the mother of Vita Sackville-West—and was a regular contributor to the magazine *Architectural Digest*. In April 1988, Susan Mary kindly gave me a farewell dinner in her house. I brought along Richard Ingrams, who had come to America for the first time in his life to attend a conference on 'humor' in Philadelphia. It was symptomatic of American humourlessness, he thought, that such a conference should be held at all.

The dinner was notionally for me to say goodbye to my friends, but, though I am sure Susan Mary wasn't aware of it, she and Richard Ingrams were practically the only people there I had ever met before. Richard was intrigued by a little silver bell beside our hostess's plate which she would ring when she wanted to generalise the conversation and solicit contributions from particular guests. It was his initiation into the American addiction to speechmaking and mutual congratulation. Five years later, I was to write in the *New Yorker*'s 'Talk of the Town':

> Of all the noises New Yorkers have to endure—the honking of horns, the roar of pneumatic drills, the crackle of gunfire, the yapping and howling of police cars and ambulances—one little sound may have come to be more widely dreaded than any other: the gentle ping-ping of a spoon on the side of a glass.

Among those I met for the first time at my farewell dinner were Henry and Jessica Catto—he a former ambassador, she a Texan heiress—who were close friends of George Bush. When Mr Bush was elected President later that year, he sent Henry Catto to London as his Ambassador; and I invited him to a lunch party at the *Independent*. In accordance with American custom, I tapped my glass with a spoon and made a short speech of welcome, in which I described the circumstances in which we had first met. I explained that it was common in the United States to meet brand-new people at farewell parties, and that the Ambassador had so much enjoyed meeting me as I was leaving Washington that he had decided to follow me across the ocean to London in order to get to know me better. Mr Catto cannot have been listening to this nonsense, for he sat back in his chair, nodded solemnly, and replied with some thoughtful words about Nato and the 'special relationship'.

Richard Ingrams seemed to enjoy his first experience of America rather more than he had expected and was, like me, much impressed by its size. This continued to strike me as the most significant thing about it. The countries of Europe are, generally speaking, similar to each other in scale. Town follows town at the same kind of reassuring interval. The countryside is orderly and domesticated, a comforting patchwork of woods and fields. In America, on the other hand, towns are separated by great stretches of half-tamed wilderness. While the English dream of escape to rural seclusion, Americans are frightened that the wilderness may swallow them up. So they seek security in close-knit communities or, if they live in the countryside, in houses as close as possible to roads.

Georgetown is a close-knit community for Washington's grandees. Their houses are mostly in walking distance of each other, though they travel between them in limousines. To leave Georgetown is to go into exile. Joe Alsop once asked me to a farewell dinner for Alice Acheson, the widow of Dean Acheson, President Truman's Secretary of State, whom, needless to say, I had never met before. Well into her eighties, she had decided to leave the Georgetown house in which she had lived for as long as anyone could remember. It was a solemn occasion. Memories were exchanged. Last farewells were made. Only later did I learn that Mrs Acheson had moved into an apartment only a few hundred yards away. But since the apartment was on the other side of Rock Creek Park, which divides Georgetown from Washington proper, she might as well have emigrated to China.

* * *

My time in Washington was to culminate in an incident which could have prevented me from ever returning to America again. I was arrested in Atlanta, Georgia, for being drunk at the wheel of a car. This is a criminal offence, of which I was undoubtedly guilty. Had I been convicted, as I should have been, I would have been sent home and barred indefinitely from entering the United States. But, as I will explain, I was extraordinarily fortunate.

The problem wouldn't have arisen at all if I had not insisted, to the considerable annoyance of the *Independent*'s Editor, Andreas Whittam Smith, upon going to Atlanta in July 1988 to attend the Democratic Convention at which Michael Dukakis, a dull and now forgotten man, was to be appointed as the Party's presidential candidate. There was no professional reason for me to go there, since I had already been back in London for a couple of months and was supposed to be concentrating all my energy on planning the new *Independent Magazine* which was to be launched in the autumn; but having covered the presidential campaign from its beginning, I was determined to attend at least one American party convention, just to see what it was like.

The previous eighteen months had been an unsettling time in American politics. It even looked for a time as if the Americans might turn against their president, Ronald Reagan, because of his fumbling, distracted performance during the Iran-Contra affair. But their affection for him survived the scandal, and he was allowed to fade with dignity into retirement and senility

British people could never understand Reagan's popularity in America. This was not only because he had been a second-rank Hollywood actor, though that played a part in it. It was mainly because of the apparent banality of his thought and his endless repetitiousness. British people do not understand that the principal challenge facing any candidate for the presidency in the United States is to become known and recognised throughout that enormous country.

This involves saying one or two simple things and saying them again and again.

Ronald Reagan, although lost without a script, had the actor's gift of delivering the same lines with apparent spontaneity every time. I don't know how many times, for example, he began a speech with the same joke: 'As Henry VIII said to his six wives, "I won't detain you long".' I don't know how many times he referred to the United States as the 'shining city upon a hill', but in his farewell address to the nation in January 1989 he said:

> I've spoken of the shining city all my political life, but I don't know if I quite communicated what I saw when I said it. But in my mind it was a tall proud city built on rocks stronger than oceans, windswept, God-blessed, and teeming with peoples of all kinds living in harmony and peace, a city with free ports that hummed with commerce and creativity, and if there had to be city walls, the walls had doors and the doors were open to anyone with the will and the heart to get here. That's how I saw it, and see it still.

Winston Churchill wouldn't have quite got away with that even during the darkest days of the Second World War, but the Queen Mother might have. It is the rhetoric not of a politician but of a monarch, the personification of dreams. 'We've polished up the American dream,' Reagan claimed in July 1987, and that is just what he had done. Meanwhile, the battle was on for the succession.

The eventual winner, Vice-President George Bush, lacked Reagan's charisma and his campaigning skills, but he had the general idea of what's required to get elected President. He replaced the 'shining city upon a hill' with an even more meaningless slogan representing America as 'a thousand points of light'. There were one or two little question marks over Bush's war record, whereas his Republican opponent, Senator Bob Dole, still had a paralysed right arm to show for the war wounds in Italy which almost killed him. But Dole, being a subtle and ironic man, was saddled with a reputation for 'mean-spiritedness', while Bush, who was in reality no less mean-spirited, maintained a blander façade and was less damagingly characterised as a 'wimp' and 'looking like every woman's first husband'.

'While common in England, class has rarely come so close to the surface in American presidential politics,' said a writer in *The New York Times* about the Dole—Bush contest, which was, indeed, curiously reminiscent of the British general election of 1964, in which Harold Wilson, a man of provincial lower-middle-class origin, constantly baited his opponent, Lord Home, about his privileged background. Dole, who started out making ice-cream sodas at a drugstore in Kansas, did the same to Bush, a Yale-educated relic of the old East Coast establishment whose father was a senator and grandfather a New York banker. 'I don't want to get into class, but all of us have different backgrounds,' Dole said in one campaign speech. 'I didn't start at the top. I started at the bottom.' In America, in contrast to Britain, it was the man who started at the top who won.

On the Democratic side, the initial front-runner was Gary Hart, who had in common with Nancy Reagan that he lied by one year about his age. But Hart was forced out of the race after he was photographed in Florida cavorting on a yacht called *Monkey Business* with a model named Donna Rice. To the astonishment of British reporters, the *Miami Herald*, which broke the story, was much criticised for staging a round-the-clock watch outside Senator Hart's house in Washington to record Miss Rice's comings and goings. Accused by all and sundry of scandalous invasion of the Senator's privacy, the newspaper stated in its defence that its car had at all times been legally parked.

I ended my assignment in America by covering the New York Democratic primary in April 1988 which secured the Democratic nomination for Michael Dukakis. Although the campaign had been a source of endless interest and excitement, I had by then grown somewhat disillusioned by America's way of electing its president. Candidates who had gone beyond vapid sloganising had been dispatched to oblivion. George Bush, who had been weak even on sloganising, had finally responded to demands that he display some 'vision' by announcing that he would wish to be remembered as 'the education President'.

This was how he explained it: 'When I'm in a motorcade in the cities, I'll look up sometimes and see the lights in the homes and the apartments. Now and then I'll see a student with his head bent down, reading something in the glow of a lamp. And I'll think, that child—that's what it's about. Because that child in the light, that's America.' Although this raised questions about what it is in fact possible to see of the insides of people's apartments from a vice-presidential motorcade, it did not prevent Mr Bush winning the Republican nomination. He was elected because of his dumb loyalty to Ronald Reagan and his trick of appearing to be Mr Reagan's adopted son. Like the Indians of Asia, but unlike the British, the Americans revere political dynasties. We have a hereditary monarchy to revere instead.

Democracy cannot work properly on such a vast scale because unknown candidates require months, even years, of tireless campaigning to achieve even name recognition. Without money and strong media interest, they are doomed. And, under a voting system of mind-boggling complexity, the media decide on the basis of their own whimsical expectations which polls matter and which don't. The Iowa caucuses, because they were the first test of electoral opinion in the country, used to be credited with make-or-break significance for the candidates. But they were the clumsiest of democratic exercises.

Poor, dear, dull Iowa, land of modest, law-abiding farmers, of rich black earth and tree-lined river beds in which the grandest edifices are the vast grain silos which rise out of the fields every mile or so. Nothing of note appears to happen there between presidential elections, not even crime, and it is signally lacking in tourist attractions. But once every four years, thousands of journalists descend upon the state capital, Des Moines, to witness American democracy at work. In February 1988, I attended two of the 5,000-odd caucuses (or 'carcasses', as they pronounce them there), one Republican and the other Democrat, held one after the other in the same high-school building. The Republican ballot was theoretically secret, though Elizabeth Dole, the candidate's wife, was there canvassing voters while they sat openly at tables, marking their ballot papers.

The Democratic voting ritual was even more surprising. To participate you only had to prove you were resident in the precinct and declare an allegiance to the Party, if only for the evening. Participants did not vote, but formed up in groups for the different candidates. The groups supporting three of the candidates, among them the Reverend Jesse Jackson and Al Gore, were declared 'not viable' because they comprised less than 15 per cent of the caucus-goers. There followed frantic efforts by the 'viable' groups to get the non-viables to join them. Following prolonged negotiations, the Al Gore group moved *en bloc* into the camp of Senator Paul Simon. Two bewildered black women who had supported Jesse Jackson found themselves dragooned into the all-white camp of Congressman Richard Gephardt, one of whose supporters, an elderly lady with a blue rinse, said she had wanted to be with Michael Dukakis, but her friends had said they wouldn't give her a lift home unless she backed Gephardt.

After the New York primaries, which established at last who the presidential candidate of each party would be, all that remained for me to do was to attend Mr Dukakis's enthronement by the Democratic Party in Atlanta in July before he engaged in battle with George Bush. The *Independent* was represented there by five journalists lodged in a small hotel twenty miles from the centre of the city. Peter Pringle, who had succeeded me as Washington correspondent, knew a fun-loving woman reporter on the *Atlanta*

Constitution, the local newspaper, whom he had recruited to entertain us on our first evening there. He and she were almost to be my undoing. While three of our colleagues prudently decided to return to the hotel after dinner in a restaurant, I was persuaded to go with Peter and his friend to a dance hall where huge men with beer bellies performed country-dance steps with mesmerising nimbleness.

By about 2 a.m., although urged to keep partying, I decided it was time to go to bed and set off in my rented car for the hotel along one of those many-laned, empty American roads with ridiculously low speed limits. Suddenly a police car was wailing behind me. I stopped, got out, and was spreadeagled over the car to be searched for weapons. Failing the breathalyser test by a substantial margin, I was taken off to a police station and flung into a cell. Through the bars in the next cell a black man was moaning and sighing inconsolably. We were in the South: perhaps he was pining for the River Jordan. His immediate problem was that he had been charged with a drugs offence.

Officer Underwood was a policeman who had somewhere acquired strong feelings against the British, or perhaps against foreigners in general who came to his country and broke its laws. He was cold and aggressive throughout my interrogation and the humiliating rituals of fingerprinting and photograph-taking. But he passed me a telephone through the bars to enable me to make the one telephone call a prisoner was allowed. I used it to awake John Lichfield, one of my *Independent* colleagues at the hotel, who selflessly drove down to the station in the early hours with the $500 in cash that were needed to bail me out.

Next day my friend Nicholas von Hoffman, the syndicated columnist, impressed upon me the gravity of my predicament and urged me to get a lawyer without delay. I was recommended a woman attorney called Jane E. Jordan of the firm Elrod and Thompson on Peachtree Street, and I made an appointment with her at once. She proved an inspired choice. Not only was she a lover of Shakespeare who visited Stratford-upon-Avon every year; she was determined to do everything in her power to get me off. This appeared an impossible task, given the strength of the evidence against me, but two weeks later she rang me in London to say she had succeeded.

She had gone before a judge 'in the Recorder's Court of Dekalb Country, City of Chamblee', and, on my behalf, pleaded *nolo contendere*, which is something less than an admission of guilt but not a claim of innocence either. 'Mr Chancellor,' she explained to the judge, 'is a distinguished journalist who at home in Britain commands universal respect for his moderation in all matters. But he had never before visited the state of Georgia or been exposed to the legendary warmth of Georgia hospitality. The experience, your honour, was more than he could handle. He was not equipped for it. This is an exceptional case which cries out for leniency on your part.'

She continued in this absurd vein until the judge, increasingly amused, interrupted her. 'Can we get this straight?' he asked. 'What is it exactly you are saying? Are you saying that what Mr Chancellor did is actually *our* fault?' 'Well, in a way, your honour, yes, I am,' Ms Jordan replied. The judge then burst into laughter and issued an order that 'justice would be best served and this court's judicial discretion would be properly exercised' by letting me off scot-free.

But for Ms Jordan I might never have returned to America again, and her bill was only $800.

CHAPTER 5

Eat Here Now!

Four years later, in July of 1992, I went to New York to cover another Democratic National Convention, at which Bill Clinton was chosen to take on George Bush in that year's presidential election. To widespread astonishment, Tina Brown had just been appointed Editor of the *New Yorker*, and I telephoned her partly to congratulate her, partly out of nosiness, and partly to determine if there was any small part of her doubtless enormous editorial budget of which I might somehow be able to partake. We met for breakfast on a swelteringly hot day in the self-consciously fashionable restaurant of the Royalton Hotel just across the road from the *New Yorker*'s offices on West 43rd Street.

I proposed over my bacon and eggs that I should write her an article about Tuscany, but her mind was on more important things. Her appointment had caused great alarm within the American literary establishment. One reason was that she was British; and Joseph Epstein, Editor of the *American Scholar*, reflected the view of the American literary establishment when he wrote in the *Times Literary Supplement* that 'it does seem a bit odd to have someone who is English edit the *New Yorker*, this most peculiarly American of institutions'.

Another reason for its alarm was that her background had been in glossy, gossipy magazines, first as Editor of the *Tatler* in London, and then as Editor of *Vanity Fair* in New York. She had been hugely successful in both jobs, but not everybody liked her tone. Mr Epstein certainly didn't. He called Tina's *Vanity Fair* 'simultaneously readable and disagreeable'. 'The world Miss Brown projected in *Vanity Fair* was a transatlantic one, made up of clothing designers, secondary royalty, youthful Hollywood actors, middlemen in the arts, and the very rich behaving themselves very badly,' he wrote. 'Always promising vastly more than it delivered, the magazine's articles left one with the intellectual equivalent of a hangover.'

The *New Yorker*, by contrast, had traditionally projected 'an easy but unpretentious elegance and a world filled with amusements, where people were charming in their idiosyncrasies, everyone had a clear notion of fair play, courage and decency, and life held an endless interest'. Tina was keenly aware of this kind of criticism, but seemed to regard it with contempt. Again, she reminded me of Mrs Thatcher, by portraying herself as prey to hostile, reactionary forces over which she would have to triumph if her mission were to succeed.

She called these enemies 'them' in a non-specific way which could have meant anybody from her new colleagues on the magazine to all of the people of the United States. Mrs Thatcher used to refer disparagingly to the members of her own government as 'them', as if she and they were quite unconnected; and Tina too conveyed the impression that whatever was to be achieved at the *New Yorker* would be the result of one woman's struggle against petty, nit-picking opposition.

The destination, however, was not altogether clear. She talked eagerly about breaking old *New Yorker* taboos by introducing photographs and colour illustrations. She talked about making the magazine more topical and relevant, of giving it an informative contents page, and of making the articles shorter. She talked of restoring the spirit of Harold Ross, the *New Yorker*'s Founder-Editor, who in the twenties and thirties had created a brighter, wittier, less self-important magazine than what it was to become in its glory years after the war. At any rate, something had to be done, she said, for the *New Yorker* was now losing $10 million a year, and that could not go on (though it turned out it did).

Then Tina discussed 'The Talk of the Town', the celebrated diary section of the magazine which, since the very first issue of 21 February 1925, had always been adorned by a drawing of the *New Yorker*'s mascot, a period fop known as Eustace Tilley wearing an absurdly high collar and reading a manuscript disdainfully through a monocle. She said she wanted to hire an editor to brighten up the section, but could not think who it should be. Then she paused, looked winsomely at me and said, 'Of course, you would be perfect for it.' This astonished me. 'But I've never lived in New York,' I said, not wishing to dwell on all the other reasons why I might, in my own and other people's eyes, be less than perfect for it.

'Oh, that doesn't matter. You've lived in Washington. You know America. You have good contacts here. And, anyway, you could get other people to do the reporting for you and then run it through your typewriter.' 'How many journalists work for the section?' I asked. 'Oh, I'm not sure. About fourteen or fifteen, I think,' she replied. That was almost as many people as the entire staff of any magazine I had ever worked for in London. The prospect of writing an overpaid article from Tuscany was now replaced in my imagination with the more alluring picture of me as Eustace Tilley tripping gaily along the avenues of New York, dining in the best restaurants, and enjoying the deference which the editor of such a prestigious column must surely command. It was a pleasing fantasy, and I decided to look interested. 'We would pay you well,' Tina added; and she mentioned a sum far larger than anything I had ever been offered in all my working life.

Tina had much work to do, so the breakfast was not long, and I was soon prancing foppishly back to my hotel, the Helmsley Palace behind St Patrick's Cathedral, whose owner-manager, the legendary Leona Helmsley, was then languishing in prison in Connecticut for massive tax evasion. Her eighty-four-year-old husband Harry, who owned the Empire State Building as well as a chain of Manhattan hotels, had had the skyscraper's floodlights turned off to express his sorrow at her incarceration. On the cover of a hotel brochure, adorned with her ghastly face, she was still threatening to extend a personal welcome to all her guests. But I was comforted by the certainty that there was no risk of my bumping into her.

In that July of 1992, New York was not at its most appealing. Not only was the weather miserably hot and humid, but the city had been inundated with sweaty provincials attending the Democratic Convention at Madison Square Garden. To escape the cheap staginess of the Convention, I went to a real theatre to see a matinee performance of a revival of *Guys and Dolls*, Frank Loesser's brilliant 'musical fable of Broadway', based on the Damon Runyon stories. I counted eight US senators in the first few rows: 8 per cent of the world's most powerful legislative chamber lost in happy fantasies on a weekday afternoon.

Guys and Dolls cast New York in a most beguiling light, but, back in London, I decided all the same to decline Tina's offer. Although I was in a mood for adventure, I was actually quite happy where I was, and a move to New York seemed too drastic an upheaval. Furthermore, I might make a complete fool of myself, for I hardly knew New York at all. But I had a nagging desire to go there all the same. One reason was the comic improbability of the proposal. It would, I thought, be a spiritless response to turn it down out of hand.

I was also intrigued by Tina's recklessness in making it. Why should she wish to stir more controversy by bringing another British editor on to the magazine? Her own appointment as Editor-in-chief was being widely seen as a climactic event, an assault on one of the great citadels of American literary culture; and my appointment could only strengthen this perception. So why should Tina want to take this risk? As I dithered, she suggested that maybe I would be willing to come for just a year; and this suddenly sounded a good idea.

It was not emigrating. It was not pulling up one's roots. One could have one's adventure and then come home, and, with luck, everything would be the same. It would be a low-risk adventure, yet the plan also smacked of boldness. So I agreed to a year in New York. I got the *New Yorker* to include eight return flights to Europe in my contract, so I would be sure to see something of my family. I agreed with *The Times* (of London) to write them a weekly column from New York while I was there. And, finally, I agreed to a proposal that I should write a little book on my return—its working title, *A Year in New York*.

When I arrived in the city that autumn, the *New Yorker* had sent a limousine to meet me at Kennedy Airport. The driver was waiting for me outside the customs hall in the British Airways terminal. Wearing a proper chauffeur's hat and uniform, he was much the smartest of all the drivers there and had placed himself a good distance away from the rest of them, as if to emphasise the distinction. He was holding a spotless white placard with the name Chancellor printed very neatly on it in large capital letters. When I greeted him, he looked perplexed and disappointed, and later I discovered why. He had mistakenly assumed that the Chancellor he was going to meet would be the pipe-sucking American television pundit, John Chancellor, who for years had been the principal anchorman and commentator on NBC News, and therefore a national celebrity.

The driver, a handsome black man named Aaron, had brought with him a book by John Chancellor hoping to get him to sign it. It was a portentous book called *Peril and Promise: A Commentary on America*, and Aaron was a great admirer of it. It was, he said, the first book he had ever read. He had started reading it two years earlier, in his fifty-first year. This was the year in which he had become a driver for the Manhattan Limousine Company, an event which had changed his life. Before that he had driven a bakery van, delivering bread in the early mornings to shops around New York. Now he met important people at airports.

Aaron had started reading books to kill time while waiting for passengers in his car. If his passengers were important enough, he would get them to sign his book. *Peril and Promise* had been signed by several media celebrities, though not by its author, the late John Chancellor, whom Aaron had still failed to meet. The signatories included Dan Rather and Connie Chung of CBS News. They even included Tina Brown, confirming her status as a full-blown American celebrity. I was able to boast to Aaron that I knew John Chancellor. Whenever I visited New York, I would have lunch with him at the Century club, of which he was a pillar, and I was to lunch with him there a couple more times during my spell at the *New Yorker*.

On one of these occasions, after a couple of dry martinis, I tried to become more intimate. 'I have noticed,' I said, 'that your friends tend to call you Jack. Would you like me to call you Jack?' John Chancellor pondered the question for a while and then said, 'In fact, I'm a bit picky about who calls me Jack, Alex. But you can call me Jack if you want.' 'Thanks,' I replied. 'By the way, only people I don't know well call me Alex. My friends always call me Alexander. But you can call me Alexander if you want.' This seemed to confuse him. He made no reply, but afterwards went on calling me Alex, so I went on calling him John. We seemed to have decided that John and Alex suited our relationship best, even if they were not the names most people called us.

I told Aaron that I would arrange for John Chancellor to sign his book, and I did later mention the matter to the great pundit; but, to my regret, I failed to see it through. Aaron had finished reading *Peril and Promise* and was now on to a novel by P. D. James. He was an even greater fan of hers. 'I've learnt a lot about England from her,' he said. 'I now know about sirs and lords. Most Americans don't know about those things because they haven't had a Shakespearian education.' As we drove into the city, we passed a group of Japanese on the sidewalk. 'There's a word for them,' Aaron said. 'I think I read it in P. D. James, but I can't remember what it is. It's something like "enmatic".' 'Enigmatic?' I suggested. 'Yes, that's it,' he said.

Aaron's knowledge was wide, especially about England (he had even heard of John Major), but it didn't extend to the geography of New York City. He had a lot of trouble finding the Algonquin Hotel, even though it could hardly be better known and is centrally located in Midtown Manhattan. But New York taxi drivers are notorious for their ability to lose their way in a city laid out according to an almost childishly simple plan. Aaron was one of 32,000 drivers of what are called 'livery cars', the kind of taxis, like London's minicabs, that can only be hired by pre-arrangement. New York also had more than eleven thousand of the famous yellow cabs which were allowed to pick up fares on the streets. In addition, there were countless unlicensed cabs plying their trade illegally, beyond the control of the New York City Taxi and Limousine Commission.

My brother John once told me with an air of great authority that the average waiting time for a New York taxi was two and a half minutes. This could not have been true. In the rush hour or in the rain, it was just as difficult to find a cab in New York as it was in London. But at quiet times of day the taxis came swaying and jostling down the avenues like shoals of fish, swerving violently towards the kerb at the smallest suggestion of a raised hand. Then, unlike the complacent taxi drivers of London, they would roar off as fast as they could in the approximate direction of where you wanted to go.

What most New York taxi drivers seemed to lack, with the notable exception of Aaron, was the slightest pride in their work. One told me once that he wasn't really a taxi driver but a comedy trumpeter. He only drove a taxi because there was so little work nowadays for comedy trumpeters. A comedy trumpeter, he explained, was someone who could produce funny noises from his trumpet and make balloons come out of it and burst. While London taxi drivers were conceited to a fault, those of New York were gloomily aware of being near to the bottom of the social heap. Because it was easy to obtain a badge—you only had to be over nineteen, possess a clean driving licence, and pass a simple proficiency test in English—a large percentage of New York taxi drivers were new immigrants to the United States.

Increasing numbers of them were from the Indian subcontinent. Of the applicants for yellow cab licences in 1991, 21 per cent were Pakistanis (the largest single group), 10.2 per cent Bangladeshis, and 10 per cent Indians. Only 10.5 per cent were American citizens. These new immigrant taxi drivers were a generally dissatisfied lot. Most of them said they disliked America and planned to return where they came from. Far from yearning to breathe free in the United States, they appeared to yearn for home. This was not what immigrants to America used to feel. America was created by fugitives from crueller worlds wanting to start new lives. They would typically turn their backs on the past, forget their roots, and assume a new American identity.

The melting pot is an idea as old as the Republic itself. In his *Letters from an American Farmer*, the eighteenth-century French immigrant Hector St John de Crevecoeur wrote:

What then is this American, this new man? He is an American, who leaving behind him his prejudices and manners, receives new ones from the new mode of life he has embraced, the new government he obeys, and the new rank he holds. The American is a new man who acts upon new principles . . . Here individuals of all nations are melted into a new race of men.

Two hundred years later, books were being written warning that a new explosion of ethnic separatism was threatening to tribalise American life.

In *The Disuniting of America*, the historian Arthur Schlesinger said that 'the point of America was not to preserve old cultures, but to forge a new American culture' and complained that the new ways history and language were taught in schools—'to build a sense of self-worth among minority children' by extolling minority cultures—were creating an ever more divided society. In *Culture of Complaint: The Fraying of America*, the Australian writer Robert Hughes blamed both conservatives, with their ideological commitment to 'culture war', and radicals, with their encouragement of 'separatism', for the deepening ethnic divisions:

> America is a collective work of the imagination whose making never ends, and once that sense of collectivity and mutual respect is broken, the possibilities of Americanness begin to unravel. If they are fraying now, it is because the politics of ideology has for the last twenty years weakened and in some areas broken the traditional American genius for consensus, for getting along by making up practical compromises to meet real social needs.

The new immigrant taxi driver was representative of the new ethnic separatism. He usually spoke little English and was in no hurry to learn more, preferring to remain cocooned in his own cultural world. He would work for a cab company organised along ethnic lines and conduct radio conversations with his controller in their native tongue. He might even be tuned into a radio station broadcasting in that language—Arabic, Creole, Urdu, or whatever—so that the passenger in the back, if his language was English, would feel sadly isolated and inadequate.

The lot of New York taxi drivers was generally not a happy one. Fares were held low, so that they had to work very hard to earn a living wage, and theirs was one of the most dangerous jobs in America. In London, if anybody was ever frightened in a cab, it was usually the passenger. In New York, it was the other way round. The National Institute of Occupational Safety said that taxi drivers were more likely to get killed on the job than workers in any other American industry.

The Algonquin was the base camp from which I set out to conquer New York, or at least to prevent it from conquering me. I didn't want to go mad, as some do, and stand on street corners screaming resentment against the city and forecasting its doom. The most important thing, if you are to stay sane, is to find somewhere decent to live. It is essential in New York to have a tranquil place of escape. To this end, I spent days looking for a flat with the help of an enthusiastic young 'realtor' (estate agent) from Uruguay called Cecilia. Most of the flats we saw were small, neat, and bleak, and ruled over by tough, suspicious landladies. They looked as if they had been made to be let to transients. But Cecilia would have given anything to live in any of them. She was a starry-eyed immigrant, in love with New York, who dreamed only of moving to the island of Manhattan from the shabby borough of Queens. I was sad that I could not share her enthusiasm for these places.

While most of the flats themselves were much alike, Cecilia was always discussing the different degrees of 'niceness' of the buildings they were in. Since the buildings were usually pretty similar as well, with their spotless lobbies and uniformed doormen, I was never quite clear what made one building nicer than another. Perhaps, when Cecilia talked about niceness, she had in mind the social standing of the residents. Many New York apartment buildings are condominiums whose occupants club together to vet would-be tenants or purchasers, thereby exercising one of the few remaining forms of racial and sexual discrimination against which the victim has no appeal.

There were one or two apartments available in Greenwich Village which had a certain amount of charm, but I didn't feel I could quite face the self-consciously colourful street life and decided in the end to settle for the solid bourgeois respectability of the Upper East Side. Regretfully, I left Cecilia unrewarded for her efforts, for it was privately through a friend that I eventually arranged to rent a two-room flat on East 63rd Street. This fitted my Eustace Tilley fantasies very well. It wasn't exactly grand, but it had high bohemian elegance, and I could not have hoped to be in a smarter neighbourhood.

It lay between the grandest stretches of Madison Avenue and Fifth Avenue, only a couple of minutes on foot from Central Park. It looked across the street to the north and was consequently rather dark, but that was its only major defect. It occupied the *piano nobile* of a brownstone house of 1876, which happened to be the year in which our house in Hammersmith, west London, was built as well—a reminder that New York, despite its many skyscrapers, remained, like London, essentially Victorian in character.

From the mid-nineteenth century onwards, property developers covered New York with rows of brick terraced houses faced with thin slabs of 'Jersey freestone', a reddish-brown sandstone from New Jersey which became dark-chocolate-coloured with time. Lots of these brownstones were quite small and depressing-looking, but I was glad to see it confirmed in the *AA Guide to New York City* of the American Institute of Architects that in this particular house and its two neighbours on 63rd Street 'the brownstone is elevated to mansion status, unlike the endless rows east of Park Avenue'.

It did have a certain faded grandeur, and the two rooms I was to occupy on the second floor were large and high and square, both with handsome working fireplaces. The whole house, I was told, had once been owned by Jolie Gabor, the mother of Zsa Zsa, which gave it a certain raffish glamour in my eyes. The former Miss Hungary had reputedly lived on my floor and her mother on the floor below, and I imagined that there must have been a lot of emotional comings and goings and shouting in Hungarian on the stairs.

The floor above me had been let for a while to the French fashion designer Jacques Fath, one of whose slim, square-ended neckties I sometimes wore in the early sixties. Zsa Zsa Gabor, having reached the age of seventy-four, was seldom in the news by the time I arrived in New York, but then her puffy face did appear in 1993 on the front page of the *New York Post* over a report that she and her husband, Frederick Von Anhalt, had been ordered to pay $2 million in libel damages to the fifty-two-year-old actress Elke Sommer for saying that she was penniless and balding and looked a hundred years old.

This was their revenge for remarks made by Ms Sommer about the size of Ms Gabor's bottom. Having been brought up to believe that America was a free country in which you could be rude about anybody with impunity, I was shocked that a Los Angeles court should have seen fit to penalise Ms Gabor in this way. In Britain, however, the law of libel is much fiercer, and you cannot even get away with criticising people's bottoms.

It was many decades since the Gabors had lived in 63rd Street, and the flat I was to rent now belonged to a European couple called Gregor and Beatrice von Rezzori. Much of the mail that arrived for them would be addressed to the 'Baron' or 'Baroness' von Rezzori, and these titles, whatever their origin, suited them well, conveying exactly the right impression of Central European courtliness. Gregor, known familiarly as Grisha, was born in 1914 in the Bukovina, an area which was ruled successively by Turks, Austrians, Romanians, and Russians, and then split in 1947 between the Romanians and the Russians.

In 1952, the Romanian half of the Bukovina, the part from which Grisha came, was simply abolished, making him an unusually stateless person by any standard of statelessness. Grisha, who died in 1998, was a writer of autobiographical fiction whose best-known book, *Memoirs of an Anti-Semite*, was originally published in the *New Yorker*. He was exceedingly charming and very popular with women, but sometimes—perhaps because of this—less popular with men, though I greatly liked him. Unlike me, he would have made a perfect Eustace Tilley. He was a serious dandy with an enormous wardrobe, a small portion of which was kept at 63rd Street and which I was generously invited to borrow when I was living there as his tenant. The main part of it, including a collection of shoes that Imelda Marcos would have envied, was at the Rezzoris' farmhouse in Tuscany, together with their six pug dogs.

Beatrice, who was quite a lot younger than her husband, was half-Italian and half-Armenian and still beautiful. In the sixties she had run a modern art gallery in Milan, and the flat on 63rd Street contained several abstract works of art of the period, the two principal ones in the sitting room being entirely white. While in New York, she would make regular expeditions downtown to the art galleries in SoHo (which stands for 'south of Houston Street' and has nothing to do with London's Soho, which, having once been a hunting field, was named after a hunting cry, 'So-ho!'). Grisha would mock her enthusiasm for fashionable New York art and liked to say, though I never quite understood the joke, that the word 'art' should be spoken out of the corner of the mouth and pronounced 'arrrt'.

The Rezzoris must have been reasonably well off because, in addition to the house in Tuscany and the flat in New York, they had a house on a Greek island; but Beatrice always seemed eager to earn money, which she did mainly by setting up features for American glossy magazines. For several years she worked for the magazine *House and Garden*, using her excellent contacts to obtain access for its writers and photographers to the homes of the rich and famous. But in 1993 Si Newhouse, having purchased its principal rival, *Architectural Digest*, suddenly closed it down (he was to reopen it a couple of years later), and she started carrying out similar assignments for *Vanity Fair*. Editors were quite nervous of her, for she was famously persistent about getting what she wanted, but she was good-hearted and generous and sufficiently capable of self-mockery to make her assertiveness acceptable.

I obtained the flat quite cheaply because it was agreed that the Rezzoris could throw me out whenever they visited New York, which was not, however, to be very often. Tuscany was their home; and while they left it frequently, they did so to visit all kinds of places, for they were tireless travellers. They seemed to have friends everywhere, and to feel instantly at home in any city. Given the rarity of their visits to New York—they came about twice a year—the flat felt remarkably homely.

The modern art was old enough to have acquired a period charm; and while Beatrice was an aesthete who prided herself on her taste, she was as keen on comfort as she was on beauty. In the sitting room was a huge sofa, and in the bedroom a colossal double bed, both of them piled high with cushions. There were pretty Afghan rugs on the floors, nice old pieces of furniture, *objets trouvés* from all over the world, shelves full of books in various languages, piles of old magazines, and—presumably to make the rooms look bigger, but creating a slightly louche atmosphere—several large expanses of mirror. If everything had been less tasteful, I could have imagined Zsa Zsa and her sisters feeling quite at home there.

Although they had only two rooms, the Rezzoris liked to entertain, and the broom cupboard in the hall contained several folding tables which would be brought out for dinner parties that could include as many as two dozen people. The tables would be laid in the sitting room and bedroom. Grisha's glass writing table would be transformed into a bar, with a French barman behind it, and Alicia, the Peruvian daily, would put on a smart white apron to receive guests at the door and take their coats and hang them in the broom cupboard.

The cooking would be mainly done by Grisha in the tiny kitchen sandwiched between the two rooms. The kitchen was so small that two people could hardly get into it at the same time, but it contained—as every American kitchen must—a refrigerator at least twice the size of any you would find in an English kitchen and a substantial gas stove. On these occasions, you would meet an assortment of writers, publishers, editors, artists, and art dealers, and a smattering of what New Yorkers like to call 'Eurotrash', Europeans who live in New York merely to posture, embellish their pasts, and divert themselves in ways that would be frowned upon at home. When I lived in the flat, I never actually cooked dinner for anybody, but I was inspired by the Rezzoris' example to give a few drinks parties with Alicia and a French barman to help me, though these never quite had the air of sophisticated informality that the Rezzoris could effortlessly create.

After accepting me as a tenant, the Rezzoris stayed on in the flat for a few more weeks before returning to Italy, so I had to take up temporary residence in a hotel. The Algonquin was too expensive, and I ended up in the Barbizon on Lexington Avenue at 63rd Street. This was in one of the few bits of New York with which I was already familiar. It was close to my brother's former flat and to a café called Eat Here Now! in which I had often eaten in mindless obedience to its name. It was also only two blocks away from the flat into which I was poised to move.

The Barbizon Hotel, originally the Barbizon Hotel for Women, used to be the place in which the daughters of the provincial rich would be forced to stay when they went to live in New York. Sylvia Plath, who lived there for a month in 1953, renamed it the Amazon in her novel *The Bell Jar* and said it was for parents 'who wanted to be sure their daughters would be living where men couldn't get at them and deceive them'. Grace Kelly, Liza Minnelli and Joan Crawford had all stayed there in their time. Several years before I was there it had been restored and reopened as a hotel for both sexes, but it retained an atmosphere of quiet respectability and still had many single women among its guests.

It was a delightful, romantic brick building of 1927, with exuberant stone Gothic excrescences. I had two small corner rooms on the sixteenth floor with fine views in two directions, and I had only to cross the road to take the subway direct to 42nd Street and the *New Yorker*'s offices, a ride of about fifteen minutes. But since the hotel had no liquor licence and no room service—I had to buy an electric kettle to make tea and the porter refused even to deliver *The New York News* to my door on the ludicrous grounds that it might get stolen—I was impatient for the Rezzoris, much as I liked them and would miss them, to return to Europe and allow me to take possession of their flat.

When the great day finally came, on a Saturday in mid-December, New York was enduring a snow blizzard. Snow is particularly inconvenient for the rich and famous because they would never dream of travelling by subway. The night before my move, there had been a sold-out charity premiere at the Brooklyn Academy of Music—followed by an immense caviare banquet in Grand Central Terminal with two thousand candles and a male choir in red bow-ties—of a modern version of *The Nutcracker* by the avant-garde choreographer Mark Morris. It was supposed to start at 7 p.m., but the curtain didn't go up until after seven-thirty; and even then the theatre was only partly filled and some dishearteningly weak sounds emerged from the orchestra pit, reflecting the fact that the Brooklyn Philharmonic was still missing a good many of its players. Among those who had not yet arrived was my hostess, Tina Brown, whose limousine, together with scores of others, had set out from the Upper East Side more than an hour and a half earlier and was still crawling miserably through the wet towards the

Brooklyn Bridge. I, on the other hand, had boarded a subway train at 6.40 p.m. and got to the theatre at seven.

The subway was of no use to me next day. I had several immensely heavy suitcases, full of books and papers, and was desperately in need of help. I found it in Helena D'Arms, a young niece of my old friend Bron Waugh, whose sister Teresa, her mother, was married to an American classics scholar, Professor John D'Arms, then at the University of Michigan in Ann Arbor. The D'Armses were old friends as well, and I had recently spent the Thanksgiving holiday with them there. John played jazz piano in his spare time, and on his grand piano in the sitting room had been one of those nostalgic songs that immigrants from Eastern Europe were so good at writing about an America they had never known—this one by Irving Berlin, who was born in Siberia: 'Oh, how I wish again I were in Michigan, down on the farm.'

Helena was, like me, out to conquer New York, but finding it uphill work. She was down on her luck and out of a job, so I bribed her modestly to help me move. We got a taxi, filled it with luggage, and slithered west for three blocks to our destination. New York houses are like fortresses compared with London ones. They have very heavy doors and very complicated locks. We pushed and heaved and staggered up three flights of stairs, repeating the performance several times until finally I was bolted safely inside my new home and made us both a cup of tea.

CHAPTER 6

The Talk of the Town

I have not yet confessed that until I came to New York I had rarely read the *New Yorker*. I had seen it often and admired it greatly, but seldom actually read it. I couldn't but admire it for its beauty and its charm and its aura of wealth and sophistication. Its cartoons were better drawn, and its advertisements more elegant, than those to be found in any British magazine. The articles were presumably brilliant like the rest of it, but they were very long and it didn't seem strictly necessary to read them.

It was enough to flick through the magazine to get the idea that over there, across the Atlantic, there was a city— New York—more bright and splendorous than anything we would ever know. When I announced in the summer of 1992 that I was going there to work, the designer of the *Independent Magazine*, Derek Birdsall, who idolised the *New Yorker*, gave me some early copies of it. In one dated 19 May 1928, three years and three months after the magazine was founded, 'The Talk of the Town' opened with the following item:

We received some blotters the other day from the vice-president of a bank. He had sent them to us because we had let drop just the merest hint that we needed them. This clears up an old question which has been stewing and stirring about in our mind for many a fiscal period, namely—what do vice-presidents of banks do? Obviously one of their duties is to be watchful and search out persons needing blotters; and having found such a person, send him some.

This would be my model, I thought. I would try to make 'The Talk of the Town' like that—airy, unpretentious, and cheerfully mocking. Since then it seemed to have grown a bit long-winded and writerly. I would try to recapture the freshness of the early days. Flicking on through the same issue of the magazine, I came across a humorous piece by Donald Ogden Stewart, entitled 'How to Be Presented at Court':

> This is the time of year [it began] when the subject of presentation at Court is uppermost in the hearts and minds of many of our young American lassies, and hardly a night goes by these days without the following conversation taking place in some Park Avenue home: 'Papa!' 'What?' 'Papa!' 'What?' 'Papa, can I be presented at Court?' 'Phyllis, you eat your caviare or Papa will be very angry.'

Phyllis is sent to bed 'without any liqueurs', but Mama decides over Papa's protests—'Aren't we in the rotogravure section almost every Sunday?' he pleads—that she really ought to be presented at Court. The rest of the piece consists of satirical advice on how to achieve this objective and how to behave at Buckingham Palace when you get there. 'The first step, if you wish to have your wife and daughter presented, is to write to your congressman and explain to him what it is you want,' says Mr Stewart, warning that this must be done 'rather tactfully' with 'a mixture of social and political diplomacy'. He suggests the following letter to a senator as a model:

> Dear Sir,
> Probably you do not remember me but I am the man who contributed two million dollars to your campaign fund

last June and I was wondering how things were going down your way. It has been very warm here, unusually, for this time of year, although the nights are generally cool and we always get a breeze in our East windows. I think, though, that we shall probably have to go to Europe soon and while we are in London, we expect to see many interesting sights. They tell me that the King and Queen are to be there next month and that many Americans are desirous of being presented to them at Court. That probably is a pretty difficult thing, I suppose, unless one has the right kind of 'pull'. My wife and daughter are going with me, and they join me in extending to you our best wishes.
Sincerely yours,

'That kind of letter,' the author explains, 'will quite probably bring about the right sort of results, and before long you will receive an invitation from King George and Queen Mary asking that your wife and daughter be presented to them.' There follows a discussion about what to wear for the occasion, with a long and ludicrous passage about how to catch an ostrich to obtain the obligatory 'three ostrich plumes which protrude pleasantly above the head, giving to the wearer the appropriate appearance of something out of English history, like the Gunpowder Plot or the loss of the Royal George'. Then comes the great moment when Mama and her daughter reach the 'throne' and curtsey to the King:

This is a really crucial moment, because Mama's knees will probably crack quite audibly and her face will get quite red, and there will be an anxious moment or two when it will be extremely doubtful whether or not she can make the grade. But if she doesn't, there are plenty of men called 'Beefeaters' who are there to help her up, and then she has the choice of either repeating the same performance before the Queen or going home mad. And incidentally, there is no necessity of saying anything to either George or Mary, and even well-meant remarks like 'Well, Your Majesty, if you're ever in St Louis—' are not at all expected. And don't, under any circumstances, use this time for the asking of such personal questions as 'Do you know the name of a good dentist?' This is really about all there is to the 'presentation'—except, of course, the distribution of photographs of yourself in 'Court dress'.

The piece is still funny more than seventy years after it was published; and, even though presentation at Court was abolished by the Queen in the fifties, there are still many rich Americans who would happily line up to be presented if they could be and who have the same perplexed, awe-struck view of the British monarchy as Phyllis and her parents. On the whole, though, it is now more common for people in search of social kudos to cross the Atlantic in the other direction, especially British royal princesses with large wardrobes and tiaras.

The breeziness of the early *New Yorker* suggests editorial offices full of laughter and gaiety and comradeship, but that is an illusion created by most lively magazines. The reality is usually rather less fun. In his enjoyable book, *Here at the New Yorker*, Brendan Gill described what it was like when he got his first and lifetime job there in the thirties:

To me in the early weeks and months on the staff of the *New Yorker*, the most startling fact was the total absence of any camaraderie in the office. Among my family and friends, I was accustomed to a continuous manifestation of high spirits in the form of badinage, laughter, and intermittent bursts of song and whistling. At the *New Yorker*, I perceived that a show of high spirits was out of the question; it was not merely unwelcome but impermissible. The custom was to speak as little as possible, and then as dourly as possible. One never touched an-

other person except by accident . . . At the magazine, it
was plain that any ordinary show of friendship was
thought to invite bad luck. No one invited me to pass the
time of day with him. The editors and other writers on
the staff appeared not to see me; against my will, I had
become invisible to everyone except the elevator men.

In one of Brendan Gill's anecdotes, a new member of the
magazine's staff, a well-mannered young man from the
Midwest, found himself one 2nd of January standing by an
office water fountain next to a legendary *New Yorker*
writer, Wolcott Gibbs. 'Did you have a nice New Year's,
Mr Gibbs?' he asked. 'Fuck you,' replied Mr Gibbs.

I was never to suffer anything as dispiriting as that, but
the tradition of non-conviviality seemed to have survived
the *New Yorker*'s first sixty-seven years more or less intact.
It was not that people were unfriendly. Actually, they were
usually very friendly when you forced them to talk to you.
It was just that the custom of keeping oneself to oneself was
still very much alive and encouraged by the *New Yorker*'s
celebrated indulgence towards its writers and editors by
providing each of them with his or her own private room.

Curiously, one of the few people who could be guaranteed to stop you in the corridor for a chat was the one
member of the staff who could not see you, the blind Indian
writer Ved Mehta, Despite his blindness, Ved was furnished
with a radar system which could identify any approaching
object over a considerable distance. To my lasting shame, I
once attempted to take advantage of his blindness while we
were standing at adjoining urinals in the gentlemen's lavatory by choosing not to greet him until I had finished my
business. Next day, when I bumped into him in a crowded
elevator, he publicly rebuked me for my bad manners.

More representative of the old-fashioned school of *New
Yorker* etiquette was Roger Angell who never acknowl-
edged my existence at all, however boldly I greeted him.
This was a little disappointing, for Roger Angell was not

only a fine writer and editor, and a person much liked and admired about the office, but a living part of the *New Yorker*'s history, being the son by a first marriage of Katharine White, who, with her husband E. B. White, did more than anyone else to define the character of the magazine in its early days. I took comfort in Brendan Gill's assurance in his book that there was never anything personal in this kind of behaviour. And, indeed, it seems there wasn't in Roger Angell's case, for I did once extract a friendly letter from him.

It related to an episode which I described as follows in one of my regular columns from New York for the London *Times*:

Here I am in New York, minding my own business, thinking of Britain only in terms of what I like about it and what I miss, and I receive this letter, forwarded to me from London. 'Dear Mr Chancellor,' it begins. 'I am writing a book, *Crushes and Comrades*, on the history of homosexuality in boarding schools. This builds on the work done for my PhD at the University of Essex on changing perceptions of homosexuality. The book will hopefully contain a section of comments, either by interview or letter, from Old Etonians.'

As I recover from the shock of the writer's presumption, I begin to feel a little sorry for him. His crass choice of title would seem to doom the project from the start, and the idea that Old Etonians might want to write him letters about their adolescent experiences is clearly absurd. But, as the letter continues, my pity turns to indignation. After asking for my opinions about the prevalence, or otherwise, of homosexuality at Eton in my day, and the attitudes of boys and masters towards it, the writer goes on: 'My second purpose in writing to you is to ask if you have any amusing anecdotes about close friendships or homosexuality at Eton that I could quote. I aim to include a little light relief for the reader—ex-

amples of schoolboy humour, the embarrassing intercep-
tion of *billets doux*, pep talks by one's housemaster—that
sort of thing.'

Here, it seems to me, we have the worst aspects of the
British class mentality at work. The writer clearly believes
that children born into money or privilege are devoid of
all sensitivity, and that what for others are the torments
of adolescence can be categorised, in the case of the upper
class, as 'light relief'. In Britain, privilege is assumed to
produce heartlessness, which is one of the reasons why
the royal family gets such a raw deal. Even so, one might
expect a man who got his doctorate in homosexuality to
have cottoned on to the fact by now that homosexual
attachments are sometimes more than just jolly good fun,
that they can even involve pain.

Also, why is he so fixated on Eton? If homosexuality
exists there (and I refuse to tell him whether it does or
doesn't), it must surely exist in every other boarding
school. Yet Eton is the school which particularly interests
him. This, surely, is because he regards Eton as the po-
shest of public schools, the one which the richest and
most privileged boys attend, and therefore the one in
which homosexuality is likely to be treated with the
greatest sophistication and nonchalance, and therefore
the one most likely to yield 'amusing anecdotes'.

Perhaps I would be less startled by the attitude of this
English scholar if I wasn't reading a new book by Calvin
Trillin about a contemporary of his at Yale in the fifties
who committed suicide two years ago. The book, *Remembering Denny*, describes a kind of American equivalent of the Eton swell, a young man of extraordinary
intellectual and athletic gifts and of dazzling good looks,
whom all his classmates revered and who they liked to
imagine would probably end up one day as President of
the United States.

Instead, after being featured in *Life* magazine as one of
the country's most promising graduates, and then going

on to Oxford as a Rhodes scholar, Denny settled for a lacklustre academic career and ended up as a professor at the Johns Hopkins School of Advanced International Studies in Washington DC. After he killed himself, Calvin Trillin set out to discover why. The suicide note mentioned agonising back trouble, but the real reason seems to have been that Denny had always been a secret homosexual and could not live with the shame. Not a very amusing anecdote, I'm afraid.

But then, in this era of AIDS, which in this country (America) takes its heaviest toll among gay men, homosexuality is not generally thought of as a source of jokes. One may mock some of the posturings of gay rights activists. One may laugh at the fix President Clinton has got himself into over the issue of gays in the military. But, on the whole, there is little scope for light relief. There is far too much fear and suffering involved.

Before writing the column, I sent to Roger Angell, as a product of the American equivalent of an English public school education, a copy of the letter and asked him how he would have responded to the questionnaire. He replied as follows:

Dear Alexander:
Well, if someone had sent *me* a letter and a set of questions like this, I wouldn't answer and I wouldn't give the matter a moment's further thought. Yes, the letter is flip and rather silly, if you ask me, and it doesn't give me any confidence that the sender would be a man to trust with material of this nature. I suppose there's a potentially interesting book or article on this subject, but I doubt that a promise of anonymity is worth much. Clearly, you are too responsible and admirable to give this the treatment it deserves. And if you quail at using your wastebasket, mine is always available.
Best, Roger

In the peculiar climate of the *New Yorker*, friendships blossomed slowly and discreetly, for the staff had no collective watering holes and there were no regular opportunities for them to meet together except in pairs, crouched over galleys. There were plenty of opportunities for that, though, since the manner in which the *New Yorker* was produced involved a great deal of crouching over galleys. Never in the history of magazines had so many galleys been circulated by so many to so few.

Once an article had been accepted for publication, four sets of galleys would be produced, and all eventually would land on the desk of the editor in charge of the piece. One galley would go to this editor, another to the author, another to the fact-checking department, and another to Miss Gould. Eleanor Gould, always known as Miss Gould, was of advanced years and stone deaf. She had joined the *New Yorker* nearly fifty years earlier, but was still the magazine's chief copy editor, its house grammarian, the custodian of its style and traditions, and the one person who read absolutely everything.

Like every other editor, I would, as the one in charge of 'The Talk of the Town', read and mark my set of galleys for this section, but I would also have to read all the other sets and approve or delete every amendment that anyone else had proposed. The various sets, covered with marks, would then be sent to the collating department to be fused into one. The next stage would be the transformation of the galleys into page proofs that would go on the same rounds and arrive, once again, with fresh marks on them, on my desk.

The process, it seemed, need never end, and possibly *would* never have ended if there hadn't been an ultimate deadline by which copy had to be delivered to the printer. At every stage, there had to be negotiations between the various people who had attached their marks to the galleys or page proofs; and it was another *New Yorker* tradition that you conducted these in person rather than on the telephone. So you spent much time walking backwards and forwards down long corridors, seeking the appropriate people in their offices. Since they were often out walking too, for the same purpose, they would usually be absent.

The only person you could be sure to find at her desk was Miss Gould. I always enjoyed my sessions with her. Since she could not hear, you had to present your arguments in writing on pieces of paper. 'What is wrong with a semicolon here? Why do you prefer a dash?' I would write; and she would reply in her firm harsh voice, explaining the *New Yorker* style. She always prevailed. The *New Yorker* rules, strange though they sometimes were, existed to be obeyed. One rule for which I never obtained a satisfactory explanation was the spelling of 'theatre' in the English manner instead of the American manner, 'theater'. This did not apply to 'centre', which was always spelt 'center', as one would expect.

This was just one of the many little ways by which the *New Yorker* sought to differentiate itself from all other magazines, American as well as British, and so perpetuate its mystique.

Before its move in 1999 to the new Condé Nast tower in Times Square, the *New Yorker* filled the sixteenth, seventeenth, and eighteenth floors of an imposing office building on the south side of West 43rd Street between Fifth and Sixth Avenues. Tina Brown and her editorial executives were on the seventeenth floor, sandwiched between the businesspeople on the floor above and the writers on the floor below. Although I suppose I was a kind of editorial executive, I had chosen to appear humble and be on the writers' floor; and, as it happened, I ended up appearing very humble indeed, for my room was almost as far from the seat of power—Tina's office—as it was possible to be. The distance didn't bother me particularly, even though it meant my corridor-pacing was more extensive than most people's, but

I felt a nagging sense of grievance over the smallness of my room and its pitiful outlook.

From the other side of the building, the one facing south over 42nd Street, there were exhilarating views of the Empire State Building and other great skyscrapers across Bryant Park, the only decent piece of green in Midtown Manhattan. It was there, on the south side, that the editorial grandees and star writers had their offices—and that I had originally been promised one. During Tina's first year as Editor there was much shuffling of office space. But despite energetic lobbying, I was never allowed to move out of my 'temporary' room. The problem, I imagine, was that I, too, was temporary. There must have seemed to be no point in allocating an enviable office to someone who was going to leave after a year.

My room contained a telephone and a typewriter, but at first neither of them worked. An office 'Mr Fixit' arrived and said he would sort things out. 'I don't like to be beaten by machines,' he explained. 'I never give up. I try one thing. I try another thing. I go on until it works. Call me any time for anything. You need a chair? Call me. You need your typewriter mended? Call me. Call me as often as you like.' The man, whose name was Eric, was hardly ever possible to reach, but eventually I had a working telephone, and the broken typewriter was replaced by a functioning desktop computer.

The room had no view of consequence, but looked north across 43rd Street at the grimy windows of the old *New Yorker* offices which had been abandoned nearly two years earlier and had remained empty. They were rumoured to be full of ghosts and rats, which made them difficult to let. The new headquarters had none of the romantic dirt and clutter of the old. It resembled a very expensive private psychiatric hospital with its long corridors, soft neutral colours, and polished linoleum floors. It also had the sleekness of a corporate headquarters, and the image of Eustace Tilley was displayed everywhere, even on doorknobs, to remind us of our corporate identity.

'The Talk of the Town' had been dumped in an area previously occupied by accountants; and apart from a couple of offices, including mine, which had doors that shut, it consisted of five three-sided cubicles in which accountants had till recently been crouched over their calculators. Now all but two of the cubicles were empty. One was occupied by Vanessa Friedman, the personal assistant I had been allocated; the other by a reporter, Helen Thorpe.

The large staff of eager reporters which Tina, in good faith, had told me I would find at 'The Talk of the Town' didn't actually exist. There was only Helen, who had been hired shortly beforehand from a gossipy weekly, the *New York Observer*. Helen, whose speciality was news about the media, was diligent in pursuit of stories, but she was not a graceful writer. The idea, I think, had been that she should deliver raw nuggets of hot news which I would try to make elegant and amusing. This didn't work, because I didn't like rewriting Helen's stories, and she didn't like me doing it either. I didn't blame her for that, but the result was constant polite friction, which was painful because I liked her.

I was especially charmed by her seriousness. On two occasions she formally approached me in her librarian's spectacles to 'declare an interest' in stories she was writing. The 'interest' in each case was that she had had an affair with the person the story was about. To spare her the embarrassment of any further such disclosures, I suggested we assumed that she had had affairs with everybody.

I had hoped to identify among the *New Yorker*'s group of gifted writers a few who would enjoy contributing to 'The Talk of the Town' and to form them into a kind of gang. This too was not to be—even though Tina, in her eagerness to revitalise the section, had insisted in the contracts of new arrivals that they should write for it from time to time. One obstacle may have been suspicion of me, the implanted foreigner; but, even if that was a problem, it was certainly not the only one.

Several potential contributors, I discovered, were unwilling to appear anonymously. They would write for the section if their names were attached to their pieces, but otherwise not. But I was determined that 'The Talk of the Town' should remain unsigned. If it was not to remain the collective voice of the magazine, setting a modest, cheerful introductory tone, I couldn't see what the point of it would be.

But many *New Yorker* writers clearly felt too grand to commit any part of their talents to a collective enterprise. Tina could have been partly to blame for this, for she liked to turn them into celebrities and feed their vanities with extravagant compliments and bouquets of flowers. At the same time, she would grumble privately about their big-headedness and dwell upon the virtues of the flexible British journalist who would quickly and competently turn his hand to anything in return for no more than a modest fee.

British journalists are not permitted to give themselves airs. They are too numerous, too dispensable, and too despised. If any of them get above themselves, they are crushed by the mockery of their peers. American journalists are on the whole more diligent, conscientious and high-minded, as befits their exalted concept of their constitutional role, but they consequently lack the cheerful solidarity and subversive urges of their colleagues across the ocean.

The family of *New Yorker* writers and editors, which was enormous by the standards of any comparable British publication, ranged in age from the very young to the remarkably old. Soon after I arrived there, I received a telephone call from Emily Hahn. I knew of Emily Hahn from my parents, who had been friends of hers in China in the thirties. She had scandalised the Europeans in Shanghai by becoming the concubine of a Chinese poet called Sinmay Zau, and then scandalised them again, on the eve of the Pacific War, by falling in love with Major Charles Boxer, a married British officer in Hong Kong. Shortly before Pearl Harbor, she gave birth to Boxer's child, a daughter named Carola, and after the war, they got married and had a second daughter, Amanda. From the late forties until her death, aged ninety-two, in 1997, she and Charles Boxer lived apart for most of the year—he was at Berkhamsted near London and she in New York, where she had joined the staff of the *New Yorker*. Every summer she would go to Berkhamsted for ninety-one days—the longest time she could be there without paying British taxes. Meanwhile, she wrote more than fifty books and innumerable articles for the *New Yorker*, of which her dispatches from China in the forties were the most celebrated.

She asked me on the telephone if I remembered her; and I said I remembered my parents talking of her, but could not recall if we had ever met. She told me that we had met when I was ten years old—I had brought her a drink in my parents' house in London—and that she would like to see me again. Although it was now some time since she had had anything published in the *New Yorker*, she still had her own office there along the corridor from mine, and I went immediately to see her. She greeted me wamly, with the charming observation that I hadn't changed at all in the past forty-three years. I asked her when she had started writing for the *New Yorker*, and the answer was astonishing. It was in 1927, four years before the Empire State Building was built. When Emily Hahn died, she had been with the magazine for seventy years.

I warmed to the *New Yorker* for allowing her to stay on even though she was in her late eighties and had contributed nothing to the magazine for a considerable time. It must have been comforting for her to have her little office to come to, even if she felt somewhat isolated in it. She told me she was puzzled by all the changes that had been going on at the magazine and no longer knew whom to approach with suggestions for articles. She asked me if I would be her conduit and subsequently sent me a couple of ideas which I knew, alas, would have no chance of being published. According to her obituary in the London *Times*, her last article, about her daughter Amanda's dog, appeared at the time of her death in the British publication *Dogs Today*.

By comparison with Emily Hahn, Brendan Gill and Philip Hamburger were recent arrivals. Although hovering around the eighty-year mark, they were several years younger than she was and had joined the *New Yorker* only in the late thirties—Brendan in 1937 and Philip in 1939. Philip had been put in the same office as Brendan when he arrived, and they had been close friends ever since, calling each other (for reasons they claimed to have forgotten) Uncle Brendan and Uncle Phil. They were still very active contributors to the magazine—especially Brendan, who had exceptional energy—and they both enjoyed Tina's enthusiastic support. I doubt if any new broom would have dared to sweep them away, but Tina would not have wanted to anyway. She valued them not as historical relics but for their continuing usefulness.

Unlike so many of their younger colleagues, these two old men still regarded journalism as fun. They had been trained at the *New Yorker* under Harold Ross who had a horror of waffle and pretentiousness—'Never go cosmic on me, Hamburger,' he had once told Philip—and who warned all his young writers not to hope for glory. 'Don't expect literary fame,' he had told Philip again. 'It's like lightning, either it'll strike or it won't.' Neither Brendan nor Philip felt there was any loss of face involved in writing short pieces quickly on demand, and neither had any objection to writing anonymously for 'The Talk of the Town'. They also still wrote to a consistently high standard.

New Yorker writers of the old school tended to dress as if they had just dropped into the big city from the country; the younger ones as if they were on their way to the gym. Philip Hamburger always looked tweedy and countrified and wouldn't go into the street without a hat. I don't remember if he ever smoked a pipe, but he certainly looked as if he should have. Brendan Gill was leaner and nattier—tweedy but always with a flamboyant touch, such as a brightly coloured baseball cap. While they were quite different in character—Philip gentle and folksy, Brendan taut and driven—they both appeared to believe that, thanks to the *New Yorker*, they had led altogether perfect lives. To judge from their writings and their conversations, it would seem that they had experienced nothing but gaiety, happiness and personal fulfilment.

Such perfect contentment is hard for an Englishman to take. Even if an Englishman felt wholly satisfied with his lot, which would be most unlikely, he would consider it improper to admit to it. And I have to say that, while I much enjoyed and admired Brendan's book of *New Yorker* reminiscences, I did become gradually demoralised by the sheer heaven of everything. Envy gave way to suspicion, and I began to look for chinks in the man's armour of perpetual bliss. This was a mean thing to do, but my peace of mind depended on it. On closer inspection, Brendan seemed to me to have his fair share of life's frustrations, even if he concealed them from himself as well as others.

He had become quite famous as theatre critic of the *New Yorker* and as a public-spirited citizen of New York with a passionate interest in the conservation of its old buildings and institutions. He deserved a lot of credit for this last activity, for he gave himself unsparingly to it without remuneration, and he wasn't a rich man. He believed himself to live in the greatest city in the world (a perfectly plausible point of view) and he also believed himself (quite plausibly again) to have an enormous circle of interesting and affectionate friends on both sides of the Atlantic.

For all that, I felt there was some little demon of discontent gnawing away inside him. The thought first occurred to me when he came to a cocktail party I gave in my flat for my daughter Eliza and her husband, Alexander Waugh, when they visited New York. Introducing my son-in-law to Brendan, I pointed out that he was Bron Waugh's son and therefore a grandson of the novelist Evelyn. Brendan immediately launched into a vituperative attack upon Evelyn Waugh, which was odd of him—not to say, rude of him— under the circumstances.

He repeated most of what he had already written about Evelyn Waugh in a book of biographical sketches, *A New York Life: Of Friends & Others*. In a chapter on Alec Waugh, Evelyn's elder brother who had spent his last years living in New York and had become a good friend of Brendan, he wrote:

> Alec was charming and kindly without, as the British say, 'side', while Evelyn was a viperish and pretentious snob. Alec was content to be an upper-middle-class Protestant; Evelyn would have liked to be a member of the ancient Catholic gentry. Lacking that (to him) enviable ancestry, he produced an imitation that deceived no one and that cost him much of his humanity.

To my son-in-law Alexander, Brendan added something which he had not written in his book and which was patently absurd—that Alec had been also a much better writer than Evelyn.

I wondered why an old man should talk to a young man about his grandfather in this way, especially as Brendan did not appear to nurse any personal grievance towards Evelyn Waugh. 'He [Alec] had always liked coming to America as much as his brother Evelyn had disliked coming here—or claimed to dislike it, even when he was handsomely paid for doing so,' Brendan wrote (failing to acknowledge that it is, of course, perfectly possible to dislike something one is handsomely paid to do). Perhaps even an American as urbane and well travelled as Brendan Gill found it hard to stomach an Englishman who openly disliked America.

Reading *A New York Life*, I became gradually aware that

its author was somehow trying to put down nearly everybody he wrote about, though usually in the form of an os-
tensibly affectionate anecdote. The picture he left us of Alec
Waugh, for example, was of a shrunken old man in an enormous overcoat shuffling off each morning to a pornographic
film. His portrait of Joe Alsop, to whom he also devoted a
chapter, was of a self-indulgent 'aristocrat' who had squan-
dered his family inheritance upon himself while claiming
hypocritically to wish to preserve it for his male heirs.

Even of Sir John Betjeman, the late British Poet Laureate
and good friend of Evelyn Waugh, Brendan had a patronising (though entertaining) anecdote to tell. This was that
the morning coat, waistcoat and underclothes of Henry
James, which Betjeman had bought at an auction in Oxford
and found, to his delight, to fit him perfectly, had not really
belonged to the great novelist at all, but to a nephew of the
same name. Brendan had learnt this from James's biogra-
pher, Leon Edel, who had urged him to keep it a secret so
that Betjeman might 'go on believing something so appropriate to his nature'.

In *Here at the New Yorker*, Brendan Gill even snipped
away fiercely at the reputation of the magazine's founding
Editor, Harold Ross, and I couldn't help wondering what
it was all about. Brendan was at root a generous and enthusiastic man. But perhaps, for all his successes as a journalist, he had not quite lived up to his own expectations of
himself as a writer of fiction. Perhaps he had felt a little
jealous of his more famous contemporaries on the magazine—James Thurber, E. B. White, S. J. Perelman, Joseph
Mitchell, Robert Benchley, and so on—of whose doings he
had appointed himself the chronicler. But I can only spec-
ulate. It is just as likely that he had buckled under the strain
of having to appear positive about everything, which is
what America seems to require of all its citizens and which
is, to be fair, one of the country's charms.

Being English, and therefore inclined to be negative and
to blame all my own difficulties on others, or at the very

least on circumstances beyond my control, I resolved before coming to New York that I would have to change my ways. I would just get on cheerfully with whatever was asked of me. I would not complain. I would be a 'can-do' person in a 'can-do' society. If things became tough, I would keep on smiling and, of course, the whole world would smile with me. If anything went wrong, I would pick myself up, dust myself off, and start all over again. That was the kind of person I intended to be.

CHAPTER 7

Down in the Street

In the meantime, there was an incident on West 44th Street. It happened within a few weeks of my arrival in New York and was immediately recognised by everyone who had it described to them as a mugging, even though I had found it a good deal less frightening than going to the top of the Empire State Building. This is because what happened to me on West 44th Street was not in reality a mugging at all. I know this because I looked up 'to mug' in the Concise Oxford Dictionary, which said it meant to 'thrash, strangle, rob with violence, especially in a public place'. I also looked it up in Webster's Dictionary, which offered a less dramatic definition but nevertheless recognised that a mugging should involve at least some degree of violence.

It was in December on a Friday evening, the time each week when 'The Talk of the Town' got sent off to the printers in distant Kentucky, and I was getting bored hanging around in the office waiting for the final corrections to the pages to be made. It would be another half an hour before they would be ready for me to pass them, so I thought I would sneak out and get myself a drink. I had a cheerless dry martini in the gloomy little bar in the Algonquin Hotel and then ambled off towards Fifth Avenue on my way back to the office.

It was only 8.30 p.m., but the street was almost deserted. I think I was musing rather dolefully about the meaning of life. In any case, I can't have been paying much attention to what was going on around me, for suddenly a young black man materialised in front of me, blocking my path.

He addressed me in an urgent voice. 'I am unemployed,' he said. 'I am desperate. Please give me money.' I was taken aback, but not at first particularly alarmed. People in New York in 1993 were always wanting money. But it quickly dawned on me that there was something tense, almost frantic, about him. I couldn't decide how to respond, and within seconds he had become angry. 'I am *talking* to you,' he said with sudden aggression. 'I am *talking* to you.'

I reached into a trouser pocket and pulled out a banknote which turned out to be a ten-dollar bill, much more than I would have wished to part with. But the situation being what it was, I handed it over to him with a friendly smile. He was not to be so easily placated. He put his hand inside his black leather jacket and said, 'I know you have money in your wallet. I have a knife. Don't make me use it on you. Take out your wallet. Give me *all* the money in it—*all* of it—and there will be no problem. You will go your way and I will go mine.'

He was right. There *was* money in my wallet. I had just extracted two hundred dollars from a cash machine for the weekend. I did as I was told. I took out my wallet and gave him all the money it contained. True to his word, he took it and went on his way. I also went on mine, feeling a little shaky, but above all grateful that he hadn't also deprived me of my driving licence and credit cards. I even began to feel I had struck a rather favourable bargain.

When I got back to the office, I told everybody what had happened. The reaction of my colleagues could not have been more gratifying. I had definitely been mugged, they insisted, and I had acted with great wisdom and foresight in handing over all my money. But hadn't I been a bit of a coward? I suggested. After all, I hadn't seen any knife, and quite possibly the man hadn't got one. He had also been much smaller than I. Oh no, they said. You could never be too careful. He was probably a crack addict.

On reflection, I think it highly unlikely he was a crack addict. I even doubt if he had a weapon. He may well have been just a spur-of-the-moment beggar who only decided to pose as a mugger when he realised he might get more money that way. One can hardly blame him, given the conventional wisdom of the New York middle class. This was that you always handed over all the money you had to anybody who asked for it in an even slightly menacing way.

On the whole, this might have been good advice. In those pre-Giuliani days, there were certainly lots of brigands in New York with whom it would have been rash to seek a confrontation. On the other hand, they were greatly outnumbered by perfectly harmless beggars, even polite, old-fashioned ones who said 'God bless you, sir' if you handed them a quarter. They proliferated in the grander parts of town, hoping to prick the consciences of the rich. They squatted in the doorways of the expensive shops on Madison Avenue. They hung out reproachfully outside the fashionable restaurants with cardboard begging cups in their hands. They slept in the lobbies of banks where the cash machines stood, so you had to climb over them to fill up your wallet. They were everywhere, so you were never allowed to forget about them for a moment.

More often than not, I enjoyed my encounters with beggars. Most of them were black, but there were lots of white ones as well, including a very scruffy, bearded, thin man of indeterminate age who used to hang around the corner of 63rd Street and Madison Avenue close to my flat. I met him for the first time soon after I had moved in. He had a long face and a long overcoat almost down to his ankles, an impersonation of Fagin. 'Look at me,' he said. 'I am disgusting. I am dirty. My clothes are horrible. I don't want to be like this. All I need is twenty bucks. Give me twenty bucks, and it will all be different. I will shave. I will clean up. I will get new clothes. I will get a job. When you next see me, I will be another man.'

So I gave him twenty dollars. Thereafter, almost every day for a year, I would meet him in the street, and he would make the same pitch. Every day, I would point out to him that I had already given him twenty dollars and was awaiting the promised transformation. He would look bored and puzzled and move on. After a bit, I couldn't stand him. This was not because he had broken a promise, but because he could never remember having seen me before.

One freezing night in the winter of 1992, I had borrowed from Grisha's wardrobe a very heavy sheepskin coat and a pair of very thick sheepskin gloves. On my way to a restaurant on Central Park South I was hailed by a beggar with a cardboard cup. He appeared a friendly fellow, and I would have liked to give him something, but there was nothing I could do. My gloves were far too thick to get into any pocket. I waved my hands in the air to demonstrate the problem. 'Never mind,' he said cheerfully. 'I want you to know, anyway, I just love the coat.'

On another occasion, I went with my friend Lynn Wagenknecht, the lovable restaurateur, to a cinema in Harlem, on 125th Street, next door to the famous Apollo Theatre. There was a notice at the door of the cinema saying that guns should not be brought inside. I was surprised the instruction was considered necessary, especially as we also had to go through a metal detector so sensitive that it could pick up the silver strand round a packet of cigarettes. There were no other white people in the cinema and no white people in the bustling street outside when we came out after the film. I was a little frightened when a big man came up to me and demanded money. Maybe I had a suicide wish, for I only gave him a quarter and stood back expecting to be murdered. But he took the coin, bowed slightly and said, 'Thank you, sir,' in a most deferential manner.

Five years earlier, when I was living in Washington DC, I had an experience which made a far deeper impression on me than my 'mugging' in New York. It was in the evening at around the same time, and I was walking down a dark and empty street in the middle of the city—19th Street, I think it was. Approaching me from the opposite direction on the same sidewalk was a very large black man. I wanted to cross the road to the other side, but felt ashamed at the very thought. The man had done nothing to arouse suspicion. He was probably a splendid man, a pillar of his local community, a regular attender at church.

Even so, as I continued to walk in his direction, and he in mine, I found that my heart was racing. I told myself there was nothing to fear, and yet my anxiety grew. His footsteps grew louder, my heart beat faster, until finally we came face to face. Then, with great suddenness, he waved his arms violently in the air and let out a terrifying roar. I thought my heart would stop, but he did not even pause. He just walked on by, chuckling contentedly to himself. When I got home, I poured myself an enormous glass of Scotch and lay down on my bed to reflect on the experience.

The man had frightened me almost out of my wits, but I couldn't feel angry with him. What would it feel like to be a black in Washington, striking fear into every white you passed? You might at first be deeply insulted to find that your mere presence on the street aroused such alarm. Then, perhaps, you might begin to relish the power this gave you. You had no other power over 'whitey', but at least you knew that you could frighten him, and this was a power you could learn to enjoy.

In 1993, anxiety about crime and violence had reached almost panic levels across the United States, and for the first time it was being openly acknowledged that blacks were disproportionately responsible for it. From the pulpit of a church in Memphis, Tennessee, where Martin Luther King had preached for the last time before his assassination, President Clinton described violence among young black people as a 'great crisis of the spirit that is gripping America today'. 'I tell you, unless we do something about crime and drugs and violence that is ravaging our country, it will destroy us,' he said. Then, imagining Dr King resurrected at his side, assessing the civil rights achievements of the quarter-century since his death, Mr Clinton pictured him saying, 'I fought to stop white people from being so filled with hate that they would wreak violence on black people. I did not fight for the right of black people to murder other black people with reckless abandonment.'

The President would probably not have dared address the problem so directly if the Rev Jesse Jackson had not already blazed the trail. For months Mr Jackson had been travelling the country on a crusade he called 'the new frontier of the civil rights movement', urging blacks to take responsibility for the carnage on their streets instead of explaining it away as a response to white oppression. He said he could not remember a time when so much of black America had been in such deep danger and despair.

But panics usually go as quickly as they come. By the end of 1993, Rudolph Giuliani had been elected Mayor of New York and launched a war against crime which was to yield spectacular results. And across America, crime and violence were soon in decline. There were still, of course, far more murders in the United States than in any other Western country, and the blacks were still bearing the brunt of them, but the 'great crisis of the spirit' was over, and America was no longer fearful of being destroyed.

CHAPTER 8

The Quest for Truth

My assistant Vanessa worked in the cubicle directly outside the door of my office, but shielded from my sight by one of its three sides. This was an irritating impediment to communication which caused me, from time to time, to suspect conspiracy. I am now certain that Vanessa never did any conspiring at all. Her only crime was to be young, which to me seemed like a conspiracy in itself. She was an intelligent, nice-looking girl whose mother, it had been repeatedly murmured to me, was 'important in publishing'. The implication seemed to be that I should try not to upset her.

Vanessa was part of the *New Yorker*'s youth mafia which was dedicated to its members' advancement in the world of journalism. There were a couple of dozen of these young people, mostly graduates of Ivy League universities, working either as fact-checkers or personal assistants to editorial executives (boys being at least as common as girls in those secretarial positions). Virtually all of them were eager to contribute to 'The Talk of the Town', which they saw as a launching pad for their journalistic careers. Vanessa was keen to contribute to it herself, but was hardly less enthusiastic in advancing the interests of her friends.

I wish I had been more receptive, but encouragement of the young was a luxury which I felt I couldn't afford. They might become brilliant journalists in time, but they were not yet deft enough to confer charm or originality on the generally predictable story subjects they proposed. Meanwhile, Tina was aching for results. She wanted 'The Talk of the Town' to be instantly brilliant in vindication of her risky decision to entrust it to an Englishman. I, of course, wanted the same, but what constituted brilliant and how to achieve it were never very clear to either of us.

I was perhaps a little kinder to these ambitious young people than I have suggested, for I did commission—and usually rewrite—a number of pieces by them; but the results were seldom wholly satisfactory. This did not bother them. They had the simple objective of accumulating press cuttings which they could use in subsequent job applications, and they pursued this aim with single-minded determination. I found that my habitual method of rejecting a piece— 'Very interesting, but'—was usually ineffective. The supplicant would latch on to the words 'very interesting' and insist on having reasons why anything so described could be considered unworthy of publication. If I was bold enough to suggest that a piece was not in fact interesting at all, the riposte might be (though much more politely put than this) that I, as a newcomer to New York, was in no position to judge.

Where did this infuriating obstinacy come from? I once asked that question of a long-serving *New Yorker* editor who said that the trouble with young American university graduates of today was that they believed their degrees had qualified them for any kind of work, including writing, and that they had nothing more to learn from anybody. But anyway, writing was not what they were presently employed to do. Many of them worked in the fact-checking department. This celebrated institution had been created by Harold Ross and was later widely imitated by other American magazines. In its founding manifesto of 1925, the *New Yorker* had promised to be gay, witty, satirical and sophisticated, but also to print 'the truth and the whole truth without fear and without favor'.

To fulfil this promise, a special department was formed to verify everything in the magazine that could be categorised as fact; and it would assiduously check not only the journalistic articles but also the fiction pieces and cartoons which might have real people and occurrences lurking within them. Ross's quest for unassailable truth gave birth to a culture of high pedantry at the *New Yorker* of which the fact-checking department was the hub.

In the novel *Bright Lights, Big City*, Jay McInerney draws on his own experience as a former *New Yorker* fact-checker in a chapter entitled 'The Department of Factual Verification'. Here he is ordered by the magazine's Editor to pester the White House for permission to change the word 'precipitous' to 'precipitate' in a quotation from a speech by the President of the United States warning against 'precipitous action'. The Editor thought the President had misused the word 'precipitous' in this context. In the end, he approved publication of the original quotation after it was found that the third edition of Webster's Dictionary, unlike the more finicky second edition, listed the two words as synonyms.

In McInerney's book, the head of the fact-checking department is a woman called Clara Tillinghast with 'a mind like a steel mousetrap and a heart like a twelve-minute egg'. Its head in my day, who had held the job for twenty years, was Martin Baron, a man of almost impossible gentleness and courtesy. However busy he was, and he was usually very busy, he would always rise to his feet when I entered his room, invite me to sit down, and offer me a cigarette. Only his chain-smoking suggested that he might not be as calm within as he appeared without.

Martin was a middle-aged man in charge of some fifteen fact-checkers, most of whom were in their twenties. I cannot imagine that he ever instilled terror into any of them. If Miss Tillinghast resembled 'a fourth-grade tyrant, one of those ageless disciplinarians who believes that little boys are evil and little girls frivolous, that an idle mind is the devil's playground, and that learning is the pounding of facts, like so many nails, into the knotty oak of recalcitrant heads', Martin resembled the kind of trusting, well-intentioned schoolteacher around whom rings are run.

I found Martin less plausible than the fictional Miss Tillinghast, for I could not imagine how a person working in such a frenzied city and on such a driven magazine could be as courtly and old-fashioned as he was. His way of trying to please me and make me feel at home was to bring England into the conversation whenever he could. He would tell me of his dealings with the British Information Service in New York and say how pleasant the people there were. He would try to remember all the British writers who had contributed to the *New Yorker* over the years and extol their qualities. He could broach no subject of any kind without struggling to find a British aspect to it.

A year after I had left New York, I went to see him on a return visit and found him looking alarmingly thin and unwell. He had been very ill, he told me. I asked him what had been the problem. He wouldn't say, but confided that his disease, whatever it was, had been named after an English physician. I found myself confusedly apologising for this, but Martin clearly wanted me to feel that this represented yet another bond between our two nations. Luckily, he was to make a full recovery, and Britain's shame was expunged.

The American fact-checking system is a source of fascination to British writers and journalists who come into contact with it. The novelist Julian Barnes, who wrote a 'Letter from London' for the *New Yorker* for five years, from 1990 to 1995, later collected them in a volume with a preface marvelling at the magazine's elaborate editing procedures. He described the fact-checkers as 'young, unsleeping, scrupulously polite and astoundingly pertinacious'. Then, coming over all robust and American, he added, 'They bug you to hell, and then they save your ass.'

Well, yes, often they do; but sometimes they simply exasperate you to no useful purpose. They don't merely check dates and names and spellings; they try to corroborate practically every statement a writer makes. This can mean checking a description of a restaurant by eating in it, or verifying the facts in a film review by going to see the film. It also means checking with people that they hold the opinions attributed to them in articles; and while this is supposed to be done without divulging the exact words used in a quotation, it gives them an opportunity to deny or amend views that they wish with hindsight they hadn't publicly expressed.

These enquiries are made, of course, in the interests of accuracy and fairness, but they do not automatically achieve either. Despite every effort to prevent mistakes, they still slip through. For example, in one issue of the *New Yorker* published soon after my arrival, the British Army was twice described as the 'Royal Army', as if it were a single military body like the Royal Navy or the Royal Air Force and not (as it in fact is) an assemblage of regiments, both royal and non-royal. One could hardly reproach a young American fact-checker, ignorant of this distinction, for failing to telephone the British Army to verify its royalness.

Immeasurably more threatening to the reputation of the *New Yorker* was a libel action brought against the magazine and one of its most admired writers, Janet Malcolm, by a psychiatrist, Jeffrey Masson, who had once been curator of the Freud Archives in London. The case, which came to court in San Francisco just a few months after Tina Brown had become Editor, referred to an immensely long and unflattering two-part profile of Mr Masson which had been published in the *New Yorker* nearly ten years earlier under the fastidious and high-minded editorship of William Shawn, Ross's successor.

Mr Masson's principal complaint was that Ms Malcolm had sought to put him in a bad light by changing or making up quotations she attributed to him. It also emerged during the trial that the writer had combined quotations spoken during many different interviews in different meeting-places and given them a single setting. In an early draft, this had been a pier in Berkeley, California. For the final published version, the scene was moved to a restaurant nearby.

Ms Malcolm insisted upon the accuracy of all the quotations she used, even though the most contentious ones had been neither tape-recorded nor jotted down in her notebooks; but she admitted to combining quotations spoken at different times and in different places into a single monologue in a single place, claiming that this had been necessary for turning months of interviews and impressions into a coherent narrative.

The trial revealed that the *New Yorker* under the legendary Mr Shawn had been rather less meticulous and literal in the pursuit of accuracy than people had imagined. Not only did it turn out that the member of staff whose job it had been to edit Ms Malcolm's articles was her husband, Gardner Botsford, whom one wouldn't expect to be her most impartial critic; but it also emerged that Mr Shawn himself had made a deposition before his death five months earlier, in which he had said that Ms Malcolm's compression technique was perfectly acceptable, so long as it was never done 'to distort anything or deceive anybody or done to the disadvantage of anybody'. Mr Shawn's deposition was read out in court by a television actor, Stephen Bradshaw, who said he would try to read 'in a patrician manner' to evoke the eminence of Mr Shawn.

The case, which ended confusingly with the jury finding Ms Malcolm responsible for the libel but exonerating the *New Yorker*, generated fewer doubts about the magazine's basic integrity than about the value of its fact-checking techniques. No fact-checker, however assiduous, could possibly have verified the accuracy of Ms Malcolm's quotations without listening to them all on tape, and they hadn't all been taped. And it would have been futile for a fact-checker to have verified the description of the restaurant in which her conversation with Mr Masson had reportedly been held when she had talked to him in various locations. The literary licence which Mr Shawn had granted to his most trusted reporters was obviously in conflict with the *New*

Yorker policy of insisting upon the verification of every mundane detail published in the magazine.

The trial was worrying to Tina Brown because, although she was blameless in the affair, it had focused media attention on the *New Yorker*'s journalistic standards. Reporters, hoping to find evidence that these were really a sham, constantly called up with questions about present fact-checking arrangements and seeking her views on the ethical issues raised by the Masson case. Her policy, which she imposed on the rest of the staff, was to say nothing; and this policy continued even after the trial had ended. Her public relations director, Maurice Perl, who had been elevated to the position of Vice-President of the company, issued a press statement after the verdict saying, 'Because the case is still in litigation, we cannot at the moment comment on any specific aspects of the trial or the verdict or the issues they raise. We look forward to a time when we are free to do so.'

In the meantime, Tina took precautions to protect herself from outside criticism by increasing the staff of the fact-checking department, which became larger than it had ever been. I felt sorry for Martin Baron at this time. He was under intense pressure to ensure that the magazine was free of errors. I think he must have got depressed, for on one occasion he sadly confided to me, 'I sometimes have a nightmare that my work is redundant, and that the magazine might actually contain fewer inaccuracies if my department didn't exist.'

It was sad that he should think that, but occasionally I had the same thought myself. One reason for thinking it was the excessive reliance that some contributors to the *New Yorker* seemed to place on the fact-checkers. They had to some extent corrupted the system by using these young and inexperienced graduates to discover facts rather than just check them. The letters TK had traditionally been used at the *New Yorker* to fill blanks in copy, indicating that further information was 'to come'. In my time, they were being widely used by writers as instructions to fact-checkers to unearth information which they couldn't be bothered to discover for themselves.

In Britain, where the roles of editor and fact-checker are usually combined, the writer knows he has no secure safety net. If he is conscientious, therefore, he will assume greater responsibility for the accuracy of his story than an equivalent contributor to an American magazine. In America, the writer may not feel the same necessity to be conscientious. Relying on the fact-checking system, he may make little effort to verify his facts himself, so generating more errors to correct and more to slip through.

Even the *New Yorker*, with all its built-in safeguards, has to accept that the final responsibility is the writer's. There are statements which cannot be checked, questions which cannot be verified, and in these cases the fact-checker has to admit defeat and rely on the writer's word. To show where responsibility lies, he scribbles OA—'on author'—in the margin of the proof.

Most British journalists would argue that fact-checking is a quixotic quest, for the overall accuracy of a story is in no way guaranteed by the accuracy of its details. A story may also be essentially true, even if many of its details are wrong. As well as encouraging pedantry, the system can degenerate into an expensive and time-consuming obsession with trivia. These criticisms are not wholly unfounded.

For 'The Talk of the Town', I once wrote a whimsical item about a dinner-dance given in Washington by the British Ambassador, Sir Robin Renwick, in honour of two distinguished men named Powell—General Colin Powell, Chairman of the United States Joint Chiefs of Staff; and Sir Charles Powell, the former Chief Foreign Policy Adviser to Margaret Thatcher and John Major. My little piece dwelt on the different pronunciations they used for their identical name. I began: 'There are at least two ways of pronouncing the name Powell. You can rhyme it with "bowel" or you can rhyme it with "bowl". In this country "bowel" is generally preferred. In Britain, there is an unfathomable snobbish prejudice in favour of "bowl".'

A fact-checker with furrowed brow came to see me in my office. There was a problem, she said. She had telephoned the British Information Service in New York which had told her it was unable to confirm the existence of a snobbish prejudice in Britain in favour of any pronunciation of Powell. I told her she had better take my word for it. Obligingly, she wrote 'OA' in the margin.

If I was often irritated by the system, I was only once angry with any of the fact-checkers, for they generally did their jobs as they had been instructed, with good humour and to the best of their abilities. I lost my temper with one of them only when he told me haughtily that, in a piece I had written, I had compromised the *New Yorker*'s 'integrity' by quoting from an article in *The New York Times Magazine* by a journalist, Raymond Bonner, whom Tina Brown had sacked. I hadn't known about this alleged event, for Mr Bonner had left the *New Yorker* before my arrival there, but that was entirely by the way.

The charge was not only insulting; it was pure humbug. Much of American journalistic self-righteousness is wrongheaded or hypocritical, but this seemed to me to be the limit. It should have been obvious even to a young fact-checker that to excise an appropriate quotation from an article simply because its author had once fallen out of favour with the Editor of the *New Yorker* would have been a grotesque thing to do. The young man seemed to have no idea what 'integrity' meant. Anyway, he subsequently apologised to me, and I forgave him; and the piece was published in 'The Talk of the Town' in its original form and with Tina's strong approval.

I have perhaps become a little too condemnatory. The fact-checking system may be flawed and frustrating and sometimes silly, but it *does* catch errors in almost every article the *New Yorker* publishes. More importantly, though, it is a reflection of American idealism. Americans not only believe that the Press ought to try to tell the truth; they believe that, with sufficient objectivity and diligence, the truth can be achieved. We in Britain are more sceptical, but I often wish we weren't.

Now, as a digression, I will publish again here the item that I wrote for 'The Talk of the Town' in February 1993 and which caused my little quarrel with a fact-checker. It confirms that even the United States is not without its pigheaded bureaucrats. The piece was published under the headline 'Key Largo'.

Pianists tend to be passionate about their pianos. 'My piano is to me what a ship is to the sailor, what a steed is to the Arab,' Franz Liszt once wrote. 'It is the intimate personal depository of everything that stirred wildly in my brain during the most impassioned days of my youth. It was there that all my wishes, all my dreams, all my joys, and all my sorrows lay.' The piano that Liszt most liked to play was an instrument from the once great Parisian house of Érard. The Israeli-American pianist Ophra Yerushalmi, who is a devotee of Liszt, would like to play an Érard piano, too.

She fell in love with one she discovered last June at the Bibliotèque Polonaise in Paris. It was a beautiful, sweet-toned rosewood grand, built by Érard in 1920 when the company was still at the height of its glory. Six months later, she returned to Paris and bought it, for a bargain six thousand dollars—the same amount that it cost her to transport it by plane to the United States. 'God sent it to me,' she says. 'I am a Lisztian, you see.' Yet it languishes in a back room of her apartment on Riverside Drive, unplayed and unplayable, a useless, mutilated object. For, on the orders of the Fish and Wildlife Service of the Department of the Interior, the ivory has been stripped from its keys and sent back to France.

This act of butchery against a charming seventy-three-year-old French piano can be understood only in the context of the international hysteria described in last week's [*New York*] *Times Magazine,* in an article entitled 'Crying Wolf Over Elephants: How the International Wildlife Community Got Stampeded into Banning Ivory'. Its author, Raymond Bonner, described how public opinion, whipped up by alarmist press propaganda and lurid advertising from the wildlife charities, persuaded governments to impose a worldwide ban on trade in ivory in defiance of some of the best expert opinion in the conservation field. The American response was the African Elephant Conservation Act of 1988, which allowed for fines of up to $25,000 and jail sentences of up to one year for the importation of African elephant ivory, new or old, worked or unworked, without the prior permission of the Secretary of the Interior. No exemptions were to be granted, not even for musical instruments or works of art, unless the article in question was more than a hundred years old.

On January 17th, Ms Yerushalmi was notified that her Érard piano had arrived at Kennedy Airport from Paris aboard an Air France cargo plane, but that customs clearance had been refused by the Fish and Wildlife Service, which, in support of its decision, cited the Elephant Act and also the Convention on International Trade in Endangered Species (CITES), which, in October 1989, formally put the African elephant on its endangered list. (The piano had been accompanied on its journey by a CITES form pointing out that it contained ivory keys derived from the *Loxodonta Africana,* or '*éléphant d'Afrique*'.) Ms Yerushalmi was distraught. After what she describes as 'days of nerve-wracking effort', she finally got an official of the Fish and Wildlife Service on the phone and pleaded, 'I am a pianist. This is not a luxury. This is not a piece of furniture. This is my work.' But the answer was uncompromising. The law was the law. Either the piano would have to be sent back to France or it would have to have its ivory keys removed.

Early on January 29th, the brothers Gabor and Karoly Reisinger, who own Klavierhaus on East 79th Street, and are specialists in the restoration of old European pianos, accompanied Ms Yerushalmi to the Air France warehouse at the airport, with the utmost reluctance, to mutilate the Érard. 'What was done to that piano is what they don't want to do to elephants,' Ms Yerushalmi says. Before the Reisinger brothers dismantled the piano and, using steam irons, unglued the ivory from each key, she gave a little impromptu Chopin concert to an audience of about a dozen warehousemen. Karoly Reisinger reports that the men put down their burdens to listen. 'It was very moving,' he says. 'When we told them what we had to do, they were all indignant at the stupidity of the law.'

Every piano made in or imported into the United States now has to have plastic-coated keys, and, according to the Reisingers, there is no longer any second-hand ivory available for use in the repair or restoration of old pianos. Not only is it an outrage to put modern plastic on an instrument as fine as Ms Yerushalmi's Érard, Karoly Reisinger says, but it makes the instrument more difficult to play. 'Ivory has pores,' he says. 'It absorbs moisture from the fingers, and that means they can slide easily over it. Fingers can stick on plastic keys.' As for Ms Yerushalmi, she has been slowly recovering from her heartbreak while practising on a Yamaha in her front room for a Chopin Birthday Celebration Concert, which she is giving at the Kathryn Bache Miller Theatre at Columbia University on Monday, February 22nd.

'I love to run my fingers o'er the ivories,' goes a line from Irving Berlin's famous song in praise of the piano. But 'I Love a Piano' was published in 1915.

CHAPTER 9

He is an Englishman

When Tina Brown became Editor of the *New Yorker* in the summer of 1992, the magazine's marketing strategy changed, and she herself became its principal selling point. A new direct-mail subscription card contained phrases like 'First offer with Tina Brown as Editor' and 'For only 32 cents an issue, the *New Yorker* brings you the best cartoons, humor, fiction, reporting, and Tina Brown . . . the best magazine editor in the country.' It was on her name and her record that the marketing people proposed to rebuild circulation and advertising revenue after a period of decline. It followed from this that Tina's reputation was a precious asset needing serious protection. This task was entrusted to the *New Yorker*'s new Director of Public Relations, Maurie Perl, who had done the same job for Tina at *Vanity Fair*, having been lured there from the employ of Barbara Walters, the celebrated television interviewer.

Maurie, a small, fast-talking woman of ferocious energy, ran a busy three-woman office just a few yards away from mine. She was a cheerful and friendly neighbour who had in her cupboard a little store of pretzels—not, alas, my favourite cookies—from which she was always offering me one. Although officially she handled public relations for the magazine as a whole, there was never any doubt that her main job was to represent Tina personally and make sure that she was given the credit for whatever went right at the *New Yorker* and spared the blame for whatever went wrong. This may have been resented by some people on the magazine, but it made sense. Not only was Tina's reputation genuinely important to the *New Yorker*; it was also under sustained attack.

Her harshest critics were to be found among the little handful of writers who resigned in disgust over the mere fact of her appointment. The best known and most outspoken of these was Garrison Keillor, an old *New Yorker* hand, who never missed an opportunity to excoriate her in public. His remarks to the *Columbia Journalism Review* in the spring of 1993 were typical of his many utterances on the subject of Tina. 'I left because I love the *New Yorker* and because she is the wrong person to edit it,' he said. 'I didn't want to be on the premises to watch it suffer under her hand.' (Tina claimed he left because she had hired James Wolcott, a journalist who had once been critical of him in *Vanity Fair*.)

The *New Yorker* is a glorious and dear American institution [Keillor went on] but Ms Brown, like so many Brits, seems most fascinated by the passing carnival and celebrity show in America. Fiction, serious reporting, the personal essay, criticism, all that made the *New Yorker* great, do not engage her interest, apparently. She has redesigned it into a magazine that looks and reads an awful lot like a hundred other magazines. The best writing to appear in Ms Brown's *New Yorker*, in fact, was the section of tributes to William Shawn [who had recently died], which read like an obituary for the *New Yorker*.

The article in the *Columbia Journalism Review*, for which both Tina and Garrison Keillor had given interviews, was by Eric Utne, founder and Editor of the *Utne Reader: The Best of the Alternative Press*. Mr Utne had been sitting one day, waiting for an appointment, in a reception area at the *New Yorker*, when he caught sight of Tina for the first time. This is how he described what he saw:

At 5.22 p.m. the clickity click of two-inch pumps caught my attention. Looking up, I recognised Herself, led by a little woman hurrying backwards, just ahead of Tina Brown, talking non-stop. Brown looked surprisingly tall (or was the talking woman exceedingly short?). Brown's camel-coloured wrap was shapeless and limp. She gripped three bags: a big, black Gucci-like handbag with an over-sized gold chainlink shoulder strap, and two big shopping bags. The little woman [who turned out, of course, to be Maurie Perl] never stopped talking until the elevator door closed between them. Brown had not said a word.

I had been told by one of Tina's detractors that, because of her obsession with public relations, she spent four hours every day with Maurie Perl. This was demonstrably an exaggeration, but she did spend a lot of time with her and allowed her privileged access to her office. It was obvious that Tina took her public relations extremely seriously; but sometimes I wondered why she bothered with a PR adviser when she was so accomplished at PR herself. But she couldn't have asked for anyone more loyal than Maurie.

I was sitting in my poky office one day when Maurie stormed in and demanded with great urgency that I give her a photograph of myself. I said I hadn't got one and asked her what she wanted it for. 'I need it to give to *Newsweek*,' she said. 'They want to publish a picture of Tina, but I can't let them do that over the shitty story they are planning to write. I want them to print your picture instead.' The story, it turned out, was about a rather painful controversy which had erupted over the publication in 'The Talk of the Town' of a piece about the trial in Berlin of the eighty-year-old former East German dictator Erich Honecker, who was accused of the manslaughter of thirteen people who had died trying to escape from his wretched republic.

The article had been sent unsolicited to Tina, who had passed it on to me. Although it was vastly too long for my section, I thought it was exceptionally interesting and well written; and I tried to get it placed uncut in the body of the magazine. But there was no room for it there, and I was asked instead to cut it right down and put it in 'The Talk of the Town'. This presented an unusual problem. I checked the credentials of the author of the piece, the novelist Irene Dische, and was told that she had contributed to the *New Yorker* before and was recognised on the magazine as a writer of repute. But she also happened to be the American wife of Nicolaus Beeker, a Berlin lawyer who was leading Erich Honecker's defence at the trial.

She had been quite open with me about this fact, and we would certainly have revealed it to the readers of the *New Yorker* if the article had been published under her name. But 'The Talk of the Town' was (it no longer is) a miscellany of unsigned pieces, purporting to represent the collective voice of the magazine. In this context, it was impossible to identify Ms Dische as the author; and because I was very keen to see her piece published, I persuaded myself (with hindsight, rather too easily) that this didn't matter.

Irene Dische had used her special position as the defence lawyer's wife to get into the trial as a member of his legal team. Since the trial was being held *in camera*, this enabled her to write the only eyewitness account of it—a scoop for her, and also for the *New Yorker*. And she insisted to me that her opinions were her own, not her husband's, and that she had followed the trial with the eyes and ears of a free and independent spirit. Tina, who was very supportive of me during the subsequent furore, commented that 'the issue is the integrity, not the identity, of the writer'. The magazine was nevertheless accused in the *Columbia Journalism Review* of 'a fundamental breach of ethics' and was solemnly reprimanded for this in several prominent magazines and newspapers, including the *Washington Post* and the *Wall Street Journal*.

The censure from journalists on the Right was especially fierce—less because of any 'breach of ethics' by the *New Yorker* than because Irene Dische had been broadly sympathetic towards Honecker. She credited him with being sincere in his Communist convictions, and she sided with the defence in wanting the trial stopped on the grounds that he was terminally ill with liver cancer. Her article dwelt comically upon the gruesomely detailed medical evidence produced by the defence to show he was unfit to stand trial. When later the court agreed to stop the trial and let him go into exile in Chile, I prayed that he would die very quickly to show that we (and the Berlin court) had not been taken for a ride. He did eventually die, but he took an unconscionable time about it.

Meanwhile, Maurie arranged that I should answer all media enquiries about the affair while she listened to my replies from across my desk. I told her it would be quite pointless to send *Newsweek* a photograph of me because they would never publish a picture of an unknown, white-haired Englishman in his fifties. They would put in a picture of Tina in any event. 'But they *can't* do that,' protested Maurie. 'I haven't allowed Tina to *say* anything. They can't publish her picture if she hasn't *said* anything.' 'Yes, they *can*,' I said. 'Oh, maybe you're right,' she replied. 'I'll prepare something for Tina to say.' The photograph of Tina duly appeared in *Newsweek* above a statement in her name saying how fervently she believed in ethical journalism (or something along those lines).

The *New York Observer*, a lively alternative weekly, was often critical of the magazine and talked in one article of a widely voiced opinion in New York 'that the *New Yorker* has been utilizing the "Talk" section to settle personal scores, and that it has been using the section's tradition of printing articles without bylines to cover up questionable conflicts of interest between writer and subject'. The *Observer*'s first example of such alleged score-settling was an item published in 'The Talk of the Town' in October 1992, just before my arrival in New York. This particular piece was not sheltering behind anonymity, but was signed by its author, the *Guardian* columnist Francis Wheen.

It concerned the biography of Rupert Murdoch by William Shawcross, which Wheen derided as a hagiography. He wondered how such a book could have come from the same pen as that of the author of *Sideshow*, an exposé of Henry Kissinger's destruction of Cambodia which was widely admired on the Left. He concluded not only that Shawcross had drifted far to the Right since *Sideshow*, but that he had also been completely seduced by Murdoch's legendary charm. Tina, who had personally commissioned the piece, was quite shaken by the reactions to it. She received a stream of furious letters from Shawcross and his friends, accusing her of trying to discredit his book because it had shown her husband, Harry, in a poor light.

Though the charge of score-settling was a plausible one, I don't actually believe that Tina was consciously doing any such thing when she commissioned the piece. She explained to me later that she had been desperately looking for something with which to fill a gap in 'The Talk of the Town', and that the 'hot' new Shawcross biography of Murdoch had seemed an obvious theme. That explanation is consistent with Tina's normal enthusiasm for articles about media celebrities. She should have foreseen the brouhaha, but she often appeared oddly puzzled and hurt by predictable examples of aggressive human behaviour.

In this instance, I was almost as surprised as she was by the violence of John le Carré's reaction. He described the Wheen item as 'one of the ugliest pieces of partisan journalism that I have witnessed in a long life of writing'. In a letter he subsequently made public, he told Tina: 'Within weeks of taking over the *New Yorker*, you have sent up a signal to say that you will import English standards of malice and English standards of inaccuracy . . . God protect the *New Yorker* from the English!'

This fierce public attack on Tina by an English writer of world renown fuelled the controversy about her in New York, and prompted a headline in the *New York Times* which read: 'Tina Brown Accused of Misusing New

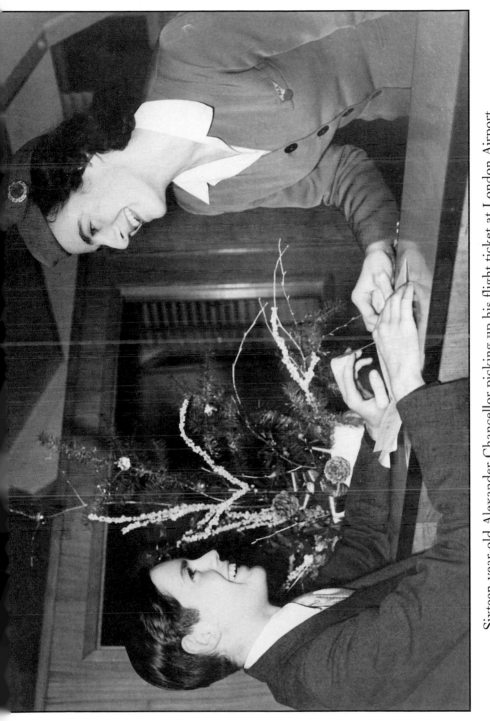

Sixteen-year-old Alexander Chancellor picking up his flight ticket at London Airport to fly to Jamaica and join his sister Susanna who won the *Daily Mirror* prize.

Tina Brown in 1978.

Tina Brown in her office at *Vanity Fair* magazine, 1 July 1992. Boxing gloves, originally owned by Marvin Hagler, were a gift from Annie Leibovitz.

Tina Brown, soon after she resigned from her position at the *New Yorker* on 8 July 1998.

Peter Pringle pointing at Alexander Chancellor's
house on 33rd Street in Georgetown, 1987.

Joseph Alsop and Evangeline Bruce with Chancellor, spring 1988.

American Ambassador David Bruce and his wife Evangeline Bruce, 1961.

Alexander and Susanna in Tuscany.

Susanna in Tuscany.

Brendan Gill and Jackie Onassis.

Brooke Astor, 1990.

River House. Germantown, New York.

Chairman and CEO of the Walt Disney Company Michael D. Eisner, center, joins Tina Brown, chairman and editor-in-chief of *Talk* magazine, and Ron Galotti, the magazine's president and publisher, at the inaugural party on Liberty Island, New York, August 1999.

Yorker'. 'Misusing', indeed! This was an early-warning signal for Tina. She lived for months thereafter in fear of the *New York Times*. There was in her mind's eye—or so I imagined it—a grey young man sitting behind a desk somewhere on that newspaper's vast and gloomy editorial floor on West 44th Street assembling material for the great attack.

He would be looking for errors in every issue to prove that, under Tina, the *New Yorker* had ceased to care about checking its facts; he would be compiling examples of alleged 'ethical' lapses of the Honecker variety; and he would be clipping articles on film stars, fashion models, and fly-by-night social celebrities as evidence that the *New Yorker* was 'dumbing down'. Then, when he had got enough of all this stuff, Pow! He would write an article proclaiming from a great height that Tina Brown of Britain had singlehandedly destroyed a monument of American civilisation. But luckily the dreaded article was never written. On the contrary, the *New York Times* seemed to bend over backwards to be fair to her.

'The Talk of the Town' was sometimes charged with being too 'hot and snappy' and sometimes with not being hot and snappy enough. But the most persistent criticism may be summed up in the question: 'What on earth is an Englishman doing editing "The Talk of the Town"?' It would often crop up obliquely in ordinary conversation, as when the historian Arthur Schlesinger, whom I love and admire, would introduce me to people at parties with the unsettling words: 'May I present Alexander Chancellor, who has come all the way from London to tell us about New York.' I didn't blame readers for being on the look-out for signs of British ignorance and naivety about their great city. But occasionally I found the criticism unfair.

I once published an item by David Remnick, who five years later succeeded Tina as Editor, about an old-timers' basketball game at Madison Square Garden. It was a nostalgic event at which a few of the Knicks of the golden era turned out to play. Most of them, wrote Remnick, had gone to fat.

> The one player who seemed unchanged from his playing days was Walt Frazier [he continued]. Clyde [Frazier's nickname] is still trim, still wears disco muttonchops, and, as an announcer for the Knicks, indulges in a baroque sixties patter. 'The luminaries are really illuminating the Garden now!' Frazier informed his listeners. Cool to the end, he had sensibly chosen the microphone over a stint in short pants: Clyde did not play.

But, as I was subsequently informed by a reporter from the *New York Post*, Clyde not only did not play; he was actually on holiday in Florida at the time, having pre-recorded a video for showing at the event. Remnick—who could blame him?—had not realised this, and had assumed that Clyde was broadcasting his message live at the Garden. 'Were you aware that Walt Frazier wasn't there?' the *Post* reporter asked me when he called. 'No, as a matter of fact I wasn't,' I replied. 'Perhaps you had better talk to the person who wrote the story.' David Remnick later revealed that the reporter in question told him that his current assignment from the Editor of the *Post* was to find examples of errors, misjudgements and general incompetence committed by British journalists in New York.

David freely admitted that the error was his, but that did not deter the *Post* from leading its 'Page Six' gossip column next morning with an account of how this supposed-to-be-so-brilliant British editor of 'The Talk of the Town' had confessed to not even knowing that a retired basketball star was on holiday in Florida that week.

As I have already explained, my reasons for joining the *New Yorker* were not wholly serious. I was feeling that I wanted an adventure of some kind (although, since I was nearly fifty-three and timid by nature, not too gruelling a one); I was badly overdrawn at the bank and welcomed the money that Tina was offering me; I loved what I knew of New York and wanted to get to know it better; and I was flattered by Tina's belief that I was suitable for the job. I should perhaps have thought more deeply about whether I was suitable or not; but I must have really wanted to come, for Tina had little difficulty in persuading me. I also felt reasonably confident, for I had spent many years writing or editing diaries for magazines in London, and that was what I was being asked to do in New York.

However, having agreed to come, I soon felt a slight sense of alarm. This started with the press announcement of my appointment which Tina faxed to me in London. It included the following statement by her: ' "Talk of the Town" is the only job in the world that would have lured such a celebrated editor and writer to give up his own magazine and cross the Atlantic. Alexander has perfect pitch. When he was Editor of the *Spectator*, nobody in London could go out anywhere without first having read his notebook. The range of his American contacts, his authority and his wit make him a *New Yorker* natural. I am delighted that he is coming aboard.'

It wasn't the hyperbole, embarrassing though it was, which alarmed me, despite the mockery it predictably provoked among my friends in Fleet Street ('Oh, so *nobody* in London could go out *anywhere* without reading your *Spectator* notebook? I never knew *that*! Ha, ha, ha!'). What alarmed me was the loud trumpeting of my appointment in New York, when I had hoped to steal furtively into the place.

It was, of course, absurd of me to have ever imagined I could do so. As the headline writers kept unimaginatively repeating, Tina was quite literally 'the talk of the town'. Her appointment to the *New Yorker* was a subject of continuous discussion and speculation. On my very first night in New York, when I went out to dinner with Susanna in a little restaurant on the Upper East Side, two women at the next table spent most of the evening arguing about the effect she would have on this mythical institution. I began to realise something I hadn't completely grasped before—that Tina was a fully fledged celebrity in the United States, far more famous than any editor in Britain could ever be. There was interest in everything she did, even in the recruitment of someone like myself.

Still, it would have been nice, at the beginning, to have received a little less attention than I did, for it wasn't the kind of attention I would have sought. I am told by Christopher Hitchens that it was partly my fault. He recalls that when I was on a reconnaissance visit to New York, shortly before starting work there, I turned up for lunch at the Royalton on West 44th Street, where media people eat, very publicly clutching a copy of the *Blue Guide to New York* to my chest. He says that from that moment on, he knew I wasn't going to have an easy ride.

Actually, the *Blue Guide to New York* is a very good book, written by a talented woman with the intriguing name of Carol von Pressentin Wright, and anyone should be proud to carry it; but apparently, in my case, it didn't enhance the image of authority, wit, urbanity and so on which Tina had tried to create for me. On the contrary, it was the beginning of a new image—that of a dopy provincial booby, at sea among the sophisticates of New York.

It was reported in the *New York Observer* that 'a remark made by a magazine editor who knows Mr Chancellor is making the rounds: "Chancellor wouldn't know 57th Street if you pointed it out to him." ' That didn't annoy me because it was such a silly remark. You obviously know anything which has been pointed out to you: and anyway, the names of New York streets are very clearly marked. Later I read somewhere—and I assume it to be true—that my nickname in the *New Yorker* office was 'Stockdale'. This was a reference to Admiral James Stockdale, the 1992 vice-presidential running mate of Ross Perot, the impish multibillionaire from Texas who challenged the two-party system by founding his own populist movement, 'United We Stand, America'.

This previously unknown admiral had become a national figure—a figure of fun, that is—because of a televised election debate with the other vice-presidential candidates in which his opening words were: 'Who am I? What am I doing here?' Somebody must have thought that this captured my own air of bemusement. I actually liked the idea of being called Stockdale. It seemed an amiable joke.

There was, however, one story chosen to symbolise my naivety which did succeed in irritating me. This was the story of the Christmas tree at Rockefeller Center. It appeared in the press and even ended up between hard covers in a leaden biography of Si Newhouse by a journalist called Thomas Maier. In an account of my 'less-than-auspicious beginning' at the *New Yorker*, Maier wrote: 'There were a few embarrassing moments, such as when Chancellor tried to run an item about the arrival of a large Christmas tree at Rockefeller Center—a familiar Yuletide ritual to most New Yorkers but touted as news by the unfamiliar [sic] Brit. (Fortunately, he was persuaded otherwise and that item didn't appear.)'

You would have to be remarkably stupid to regard the appearance of a Christmas tree at Christmas time anywhere in Christendom as 'news', and I will offer no further defence on that point. I will, however, attempt to explain the origins of this calumny. I have always admired the Christmas tree at Rockefeller Center and compared it favourably in my mind to the one in Trafalgar Square in London. The Trafalgar Square tree is an annual gift to London by the people of Norway in gratitude for the sacrifices made by the British on their behalf in the Second World War; and sometimes I have berated the Norwegians in print for sending us such a small one. Maybe it just looks small because of its proximity to Nelson's Column, but the Rockefeller Plaza tree always manages to look magnificent, despite the fact that it stands immediately in front of the towering RCA Building.

In November 1992, soon after my arrival at the *New Yorker*, I received a press release informing me of the day and the time when the tree was to be put in place; and since I always passed Rockefeller Plaza on my twenty-block walk down Fifth Avenue from home to the office, I thought I might stop by and take a look. As the ceremony took place at 7.30 a.m., I doubted if many New Yorkers had ever actually seen it; and it occurred to me that it might just make a 'Talk of the Town' item if I could find a way of describing it amusingly. As it turned out, I couldn't. I enjoyed the spectacle of the great tree arriving on a colossal trailer and being lifted delicately up by cranes to its fourteen-storey height, but the piece I subsequently wrote struck me as rather boring, and I decided not to use it.

Then, as she often did during my first few weeks at the *New Yorker*, Tina read the completed 'Talk of the Town' section just before deadline and decided, infuriatingly, to reject a couple of items. Her decision created gaps which needed to be filled immediately. I riffled through my bottom drawer for possible substitutes and pulled out, among other unpublished items, my Christmas-tree piece. I showed it to Charles ('Chip') McGrath, Tina's deputy editor, who agreed that it wasn't quite right. But I don't believe he thought there was anything inherently inappropriate about its subject matter. In fact, it was exactly the kind of thing that *New Yorker* writers of the past had often chosen to write about in a breezy, laconic sort of way. But Chip and I both knew that Tina wouldn't have liked it in any event, precisely because it wasn't 'news'. She would have found it 'wet' or 'pathetic'—two of her favourite terms of disparagement. She had talked of reviving the spirit of Ross, who had died more than forty years earlier, but she didn't evince much enthusiasm for the kind of cheerfully inconsequential item that he had liked. What she really wanted were news and gossip about the movers and shakers of New York, and she wasn't getting them. I remember her once, on a grey after-noon, gazing dejectedly out of her office window and say-ing, 'It's all happening out there, but we just don't seem to know about it.'

My wife says that at around that time I told her in a trans-atlantic call that things were going badly at 'The Talk of the Town' because I couldn't do the kind of column Tina wanted, and she didn't want me to do the kind of column I could do. Whether or not that was exactly the case—I now think that I may, in self-justification, have been unfair on Tina—it was clear that 'Talk' (as everyone at the *New Yorker* called the section) badly needed more reporting manpower. On the recommendation of David Remnick, Rick Hertzberg and others, I hired a young man called Jef-frey Toobin, a qualified lawyer who had served in the legal team of Lawrence Walsh, the special prosecutor in the Iran-Contra affair, and had subsequently written a book about the experience. Jeffrey proved an assiduous and effective investigative reporter who rapidly moved on to become the magazine's chief writer on legal matters. His big break came with the O. J. Simpson trial, on which he made himself not only the *New Yorker*'s resident expert but also one of the country's experts, appearing frequently on television and later writing a best-selling book on the case which was pub-lished for Random House by Harry Evans.

Next, I hired Adam Platt, who, although he got on well with Jeffrey, was his opposite in every way. Jeffrey was as-sertive, Adam self-effacing; Jeffrey direct, Adam oblique; Jeffrey determined, Adam fatalistic. When I got in touch with Adam, he was freelancing in Washington for glossy magazines, still recovering from his traumatic collaboration with the dying Joe Alsop on his memoirs. He agreed to join the *New Yorker*, but without great enthusiasm. He possibly suspected that he wouldn't be Tina's cup of tea, and that I wouldn't be his. He had a certain idea of the *New Yorker*, as most Americans of his upper-class background did, and this was unlikely to have encompassed an Englishman as editor of 'The Talk of the Town'. I suspect that, in his pessimistic way, he assumed that all of us were doomed, but decided to come to the magazine all the same because the *New Yorker*, although currently in the hands of barbarians, was still the *New Yorker*. If he didn't feel that, I know the others did. I once said to Chip McGrath that the *New Yorker*'s old guard reminded me a bit of the Italians—for ever being overrun and subjugated, but always confident in the ultimate triumph of their own cultural values—and he gave me a surreptitious smile.

Adam was a subtle and funny writer, and I looked to him to do what Brendan Gill, in 'Here at the New Yorker', had said, somewhat preciously, that 'Talk' writers were required to do—cram paragraphs full of facts and give them 'a weight and shape no greater than that of a cloud of blue butterflies'. He turned out to be good at this, and initially he went down well with editorial barons, especially with Chip who may have recognised him as a natural old *New Yorker* type. Tina seemed to like him too at first; but slowly he fell from grace, and his contract was not renewed. I felt indignant about this on his behalf, but Adam didn't appear to be surprised and he accepted his fate philosophically.

Adam was very tall—about six foot four inches—but he was joined at 'The Talk of the Town' by a young writer who was even taller. Tom Beller was not my own recruit, but was handed down to me by Tina who had hired him in a fit of excitement without having worked out exactly what to do with him. Before long he was established, raring to go, in one of the cubicles outside my office. One of Tom's salient qualities was enthusiasm—enthusiasm for everything, but especially for his own literary output. This wasn't unreasonable, for he wrote very well. But it earned him the opprobrium of the *New Yorker*'s old guard against whose standards of modesty and decorum he was seen to offend.

It was the old guard who brought Tom Beller on to the magazine, and it was they who in due course had him ejected from it. Roger Angell had appointed himself Tom's patron and mentor after eagerly accepting one of his excellent short stories for publication. But it was also Roger who felt the greatest outrage when Tom broke the unwritten rules of *New Yorker* behaviour by lobbying too brazenly on behalf of an article he had written about the Oscars. This described his and his mother's disappointment when she failed to win an Academy award for a television documentary she had made about the German resistance to Hitler. Everyone liked the article, but Tom's insubordination earned him a bruising dressing-down by Roger from which he never completely recovered.

Like Adam, Tom left the *New Yorker* when I did. So did Helen Thorpe. The one survivor from my time at 'The Talk of the Town' was Jeffrey Toobin. When Tina renewed his contract, she told him that hiring him had been the most important thing I had done at the *New Yorker*—my one enduring legacy.

CHAPTER 10

The Principle of Lunch

On 2 November 1992, the eve of the presidential election, Tina and Harry gave a dinner party in their apartment on East 57th Street to welcome me to the *New Yorker*. Susanna, who had come with me to New York to help me settle in, was there as well. Over drinks beforehand, I met Tina's parents for the first and only time. They were an engaging couple—he an easy-going old boy with a genial manner, and she of gypsy-dancer appearance with jet-black hair swept tightly back into a bun. Every now and then she would put on a mischievous expression and say, 'I'm the *original* Tina Brown, you know.' She would then explain that she had been christened Bettina and her daughter Christina, so both of them had come to have the same nickname. Tina, the daughter, had established her parents in a flat just across the corridor from hers, which meant that her two young children, George and Isabel, could dash backwards and forwards between them.

Although twenty-five years older than his wife, Harry was exceptionally sprightly, so animated and so eager to please that I couldn't resist reminding him of the opinion he had once expressed to Rupert Murdoch about me, that I represented 'part of the effete old tired England'. But he was only fleetingly disconcerted. He apologised graciously for his old-fashioned class consciousness, claiming now to have put this trait behind him, and then quickly recovered his puppydog energy and enthusiasm.

There were about thirty guests at dinner, culled from the senior staff of the *New Yorker* and from the upper echelons of publishing and the media. At the end there was the traditional ping with a spoon on the side of a glass. Tina spoke with brisk fluency about my journalistic career in Britain and claimed, implausibly, that it had uniquely qualified me to edit 'The Talk of the Town'. It then fell to me to say something. Perhaps an amusing speech was expected, but I couldn't get out more than a single sentence, expressing humility and gratitude for the honour bestowed upon me. I think this made an unfavourable impression on everyone except my wife, who thanked me from the bottom of her heart for having said so little. Susanna was about to go back to England in a day or two, never to return to New York except on a couple of brief visits, and Tina put a hand on her arm as we left and said, 'Don't worry. We'll take good care of him.'

To begin with, I thought it was Tina more than me who needed taking care of. She seemed to feel permanently got at and put upon. Despite Si Newhouse's obvious admiration for her, she never behaved as if she felt secure in her job. Newhouse treated his editors well. He gave them large limousines with chauffeurs; he bought them apartments. But he also fired them capriciously, and would then take their cars and apartments back again. It was a sign of Tina's modesty and practicality that she never took her position for granted. She and Harry had bought their Manhattan apartment with their own money.

Although, at nearly forty, Tina had changed a lot from when she was young, she was still very attractive, even as a short-haired, square-shouldered, slimmed-down New York executive. She also hadn't lost the ability to arouse a man's protective instincts. But sometimes I wondered if she wasn't a little paranoid. She seemed to fear that the people around her were conspiring to make her fail in her great task—some even by the cunning device of writing bad articles. She was convinced that half New York was out to get her, and perhaps she was right.

Once I put it to a *New Yorker* colleague that Tina didn't

actually seem to like America very much at all. 'Not surprising,' he replied. 'She's never been there.' And up to a point I could see what he meant. When Newhouse brought her to America, he put her straight into a limousine. From there she had learnt all that there was to be known about how to be a New York media success, but this had made her dislike the city more and more. She had also had very little contact, by way of mitigation, with the gentler aspects of America, such as the decency and modesty and thoughtfulness of so many of its unsung citizens in regions like the Midwest. Even in New York, I doubt if she had often—if ever—done many of the ordinary things that people do, like ride on a bus or on the subway.

Her attitude to Britain was hard to fathom. She had been longing to escape its stifling atmosphere when she left London in the eighties, but had afterwards developed an apparent nostalgia for it. Almost a decade later at the *New Yorker*, she was still going on about how much she missed England. Whenever I got back from one of my *New Yorker*-subsidised trips to London, she would make me sit down in her office and tell her all about it. And then, before I was through, she would start musing aloud about cowslips and buttercups and long grass and picnics beside the River Thames.

'I think Harry and I should take a holiday in London this year,' she concluded after one of these conversations. 'Why London?' I asked. 'Why not rent a nice house in the English countryside?' 'We did that last year,' she said. 'Oh, where?' I asked. 'It was an old mill in Oxfordshire,' she replied. 'What was it like?' I asked. 'Well, we didn't actually go there in the end. We went to Montana instead. But it looked idyllic in the photographs.' She was even nostalgic for the much-despised British journalist, with his gift for churning out a serviceable article on almost any subject within a couple of hours.

By contrast, she regarded most American journalists, whatever their other merits, as self-important, self-righteous and slow. Slowness had never before been a handicap on the *New Yorker*: it had usually been equated with thoroughness. When a huge terrorist bomb—almost a ton of explosives—went off in a garage in the foundation of the World Trade Center in March 1993, causing several deaths and many injuries, Philip Hamburger dropped by my office to tell me that nobody in the world knew more about the foundation of the stricken skyscraper than his former wife, Edith Iglauer.

And that was true, for Ms Iglauer had spent seven years—*seven* years—gathering material for an article which was published in the *New Yorker* in November 1972 under the headline 'The Biggest Foundation' (for that is what it was at the time: the biggest foundation ever built, ten storeys deep and occupying eight acres beneath the ground). Ms Iglauer regularly visited the site from 1965 to 1972, because that was how long the foundation took to build; and William Shawn was quite content to wait that long for the piece she eventually wrote. Twenty-one years later she reported for 'The Talk of the Town' that the foundation walls and tunnels had withstood the enormous blast, although other structural damage to the building had been immense.

No blame can be attached to Tina for wanting to speed things up a bit. She had been made Editor to jerk the *New Yorker* out of its complacency, to make it talked about again, to find it a new audience, and to attract new advertisers. And, although the financial cost was reportedly enormous, with the magazine's loss running into many millions of dollars a year, she was certainly beginning to achieve what she had set out to do. But the strain on the great editorial apparatus of the *New Yorker* was severe.

In her pursuit of excitement, topicality and the perfect 'mix' (a word from the world of glossy magazines), she would perpetually rejig the contents of the magazine right up to its publishing deadline, pulling out articles and replacing them with others, but getting furious if there were any detectable lapses from the *New Yorker*'s exemplary standards of editing and fact-checking. Although editors and fact-checkers tried hard to appear calm and unruffled in the genteel tradition of the magazine, I could sense that many of them were secretly distraught, especially as errors kept creeping in. Unusually for an American office, a lot of people were smoking heavily; and some of them, I suspected, had never smoked before.

I too was trying to conceal deep inner anxiety as a large chunk of 'The Talk of the Town' was binned each week by Tina, sometimes only a few hours before deadline. And I too had taken up smoking again after five years of abstinence. It was a ludicrous thing to have done, and it even landed me in trouble with the charming Ruth Diem, the head of 'human resources', who had received a formal complaint from a member of the editorial staff that I had been seen smoking in the corridor on my way to the coffee machine when smoking was only permitted inside offices. I wasn't convinced that Tina's conduct at this time was compatible with her promise to my wife that she would 'take good care' of me. But just as I was beginning to feel fed up and to wonder whether I shouldn't perhaps pack the job in immediately and go straight home to London, a curious thing happened.

It was late one night, as I was waiting to pass the final page proofs of 'The Talk of the Town' section, that I dropped into Rick Hertzberg's office for a chat. 'You realise,' he said suddenly, 'that you have the most stressful job on the magazine?' 'Do I really?' I said, delighted at the idea that I might have plausible grounds for a nervous breakdown if one should happen to come along. 'Oh, yes,' said Rick. 'In fact, I think I will have a word with Tina. I will tell you what she is doing. She is giving you responsibility without authority. That is an impossible situation for you.' I begged him not to say anything to Tina, since I had decided from the outset that I would be a good trooper and never complain about anything, and he said OK, he wouldn't. 'Remember, it's only a magazine,' he whispered, as I got up to leave. 'It's only a magazine,' I whispered back.

But a couple of days later Tina called me from a car phone out at Quogue on Long Island, where she and Harry had a seaside house. 'I've just been thinking about things,' she said, 'and I think I've been giving you a hard time. What I've been doing, I think, is giving you responsibility without authority. I am very sorry about that, and I promise to stop doing it from now on.' And she *did* stop doing it for quite a while, which made me very grateful to Rick for breaking his promise. She continued, quite properly, to make sharp comments about 'The Talk of the Town', but she stopped creating unfillable gaps in it. My mood improved, and so did hers. She was friendlier and altogether less fretful. An old colleague of hers from *Vanity Fair* days explained to me that Tina often seemed oblivious to the personal problems of her staff until somebody drew them to her attention, at which point she would be tremendously concerned and do everything she could to resolve them. She was, in other words, insensitive, but not at all uncaring.

When I returned to England for Christmas with my family, I found waiting for me at home in Hammersmith a case of excellent red wine from Harrods and an affectionate note from Tina thanking me for my efforts and congratulating me on my stoicism. After a fraught initiation to the *New Yorker*, I returned to my job there in January feeling almost American in my energy and optimism.

The easing of some of the tension at the *New Yorker* put me in a better frame of mind for enjoying New York. I had brought with me from London a firm commitment to the principle of lunch; and, unlike most people at the *New Yorker*, the question I faced each day wasn't *whether* to have lunch, but *where*. When I left the *Independent Magazine* in October 1992, its staff presented me as a farewell gift with two spoof columns, each purporting to be written by me but both written in fact by a gifted colleague, Mark

Lawson. One was a parody of 'Up and Down the City Road', a column I had been writing in the magazine since it started under the pseudonym 'The Weasel'; and the other was a parody of 'The Talk of the Town' as Lawson imagined me writing it. Both of them had lunch as their principal topic.

Here's how the 'City Road' spoof began:

I have been reflecting on differing British and American attitudes to lunch. In this country it is still, as far as I have been able to ascertain, considered normal for a senior executive to spend three or even three-and-a-half hours over lunch with a colleague or friend. If the restaurant should be some distance from his office, he might even be absent for as much as four or five hours in the middle of the day. And yet his absence from his desk is scarcely noticed, his colleagues make no comment whatsoever.

However, in the United States of America, attitudes are apparently very different. Lunch is no more than a functional nutritional interlude, lasting perhaps as little as forty-five minutes. Even the swishest eateries look as if botulism has been reported there after two in the afternoon. A friend who recently visited Tina Brown, the dynamic new Editor of the *New Yorker*, was thrilled to receive an invitation to lunch with the great lady. Imagine his surprise when the meal turned out to consist of chicken salad and Diet Coke eaten on paper plates across her desk.

This seems to me another of the unfortunate neuroses of our American friends. It is well known that weasels are slow eaters, and I will be sticking to my five-hour digestion routine. As for the American habits, I simply give thanks that I will never have to make my living in a nation with such barbaric midday practices.

And here's the start of the 'Talk of the Town' parody:

Therapeutic Methods

Dining Eastside Sunday evening, we heard of a new diet-and-relaxation craze, apparently imported—in a reverse, we're big enough to note, of the general culture trend—from our former colonist, Britain.

The sexy regimen—name: The Alexander Technique—involves minimum exercise and maximum relaxation. Motto: Did you ever meet an old jogger? Ideally, the disciple rises late, consumes a full English breakfast, and drives to the office after the worst of the morning traffic. After a couple of hours of light work on the telephone—dialling transatlantic numbers is good for the circulation in the fingers—a taxi is taken to an expensive restaurant. Here, it is important not to hurry consumption. Liquid—particularly fruit-based—aids digestion. Subsequently, the morning and lunchtime routines should be repeated in the afternoon and the evening, etc., etc. . . .

Few writers about New York have ever found it a leisurely city, but one distinguished Irish one did. Claud Cockburn, who went there in 1929 as a correspondent of the London *Times*, claimed to find the tempo of New York on a day of business like the tempo of Brighton, the English seaside town, on a day of holiday. I don't think he would find it so now, but his comments on the practices of New York businessmen between the wars have an element of timelessness about them:

European visitors to the United States often imagine that because an American businessman tells them that the only time he can make an appointment is at ten-thirty in the evening this must indicate the immense busyness and hustle of the man's life. Every so often it does, but quite equally often it simply means that the man, in his nervous, high-strung, time-squandering, lavish American way, has spent most of the day not getting on with the things that he theoretically should be getting on with, and therefore finds himself at about six in the evening with the whole day's work to do. Or at least he has to jam into the afternoon the work which he could, theoretically, have tackled in the morning, had he not spent a great deal of the morning thinking—as no Englishman would in office hours—of the meaning of life, sex problems, what would happen if there were a war, and (in this case more along English lines) what is going to happen in the ball game on Saturday?

Cockburn made no mention of the American businessman's lunching habits, but he described other ways by which he would try to relax the recurring tension in his mind—'by little walks about the room to get glasses of ice-water, and every so often by trips in the elevator down to the ground floor—to get one's shoes shined, or pick out a cigar, or possibly buy the latest edition of the midday papers. In extreme cases,' he added, 'it becomes necessary to go round the corner and have a little drink or even play a little snooker.' Cockburn noted that since the trip in the elevator took place inside the building, it wasn't really a departure from work; 'but since also the trip is apt to be as lengthy as a short suburban journey—what with waiting for the elevator and then riding down in it at sixty miles an hour and jostling one's way across the lobby, all this to be repeated again on the return journey—these little excursions can take up a great deal of time.'

In addition to my daily luncheon outing, I quite often found myself being driven by the same urges as Cockburn's businessman and making trips in the elevator from the sixteenth to the ground floor to buy cigarettes or magazines from the Pakistani newsagent in the lobby. Sometimes too there were 'extreme cases' in which I needed to go round the corner and have a little drink. But what did the proper executives at the *New Yorker* do when they felt an aversion to the job in hand? They had several strategically located coffee machines to huddle around, and a gloomy common room on the seventeenth floor where they could sit about and get soft drinks and snacks out of machines. But mostly, when nervous tension got the better of them, they would repair to each other's offices and talk about Tina. Talking about Tina always had a calming effect.

One work replacement therapy device that wasn't available in Cockburn's day was the desktop computer. Nobody spent longer in the office than my clever and charming friend Rick Hertzberg, a man of many accomplishments, irresistible to women, and blessed with the secret of eternal youth. But not even he could account satisfactorily for how all his time there was spent. He had important editorial duties to perform, some of which were doubtless very taxing, but they hardly seemed taxing enough to keep him at his desk until 2 a.m., which was often the time when he finally dragged himself away. I did once ask him to explain in detail how he occupied his working day, but the task defeated him.

Slowly it dawned on me that much of his time in the office was spent in private communion with his Macintosh desktop computer. Sometimes he was writing on it—he would write elegant editorials in support of liberal causes—and sometimes he was editing other people's articles on it. But much of the time he was searching out its secrets, just for their own sake. He liked to discover all the little tricks it could perform. He liked using it to exchange e-mail messages and to ramble around the Web. The computer was a great solace to Rick, but not the only one. He would also make a point of watching all the main news bulletins on all the major television networks, of which there were a great many and to which he was periodically alerted by loud beeps emanating from his wrist-watch; and he had a powerful telescope set up in his window through which he could peer across the roof of the Public Library into the rooms in the skyscrapers beyond.

Some years earlier he had even published a book comprising one million dots, his idea being to demonstrate what one million looked like, and while I was at the *New Yorker*, he spent some time editing the proofs of a new edition of this intriguing work. This had been spiced up a bit by the periodic insertion of facts relating to different numbers. For example, when you got to, say, 50,000 dots, there might be a note pointing out that this was also the number of political prisoners in Turkey. (That is an invented example: I have no idea how many political prisoners there may be in Turkey.) I suggested to Rick that his next book should show what Si Newhouse's fortune would look like if displayed as one-dollar bills. Mr Newhouse was rumoured to be worth many billions of dollars, so the new book would have comprised many volumes. I thought these could all be beautifully bound in leather and kept in an air-conditioned shrine somewhere in Manhattan to which New Yorkers could go in their lunch breaks for quiet contemplation and spiritual refreshment.

Rick was too busy to go out to lunch very often, but on my second day at the *New Yorker*, he took me to lunch at his club, the Harvard Club, which was founded in 1865 as a home-from-home for Harvard University graduates living in New York. At the turn of the century it was given an imposing new building on West 44th Street, with huge rooms inside. The biggest of them, Harvard Hall, was three storeys high and had on its walls not only some vast Flemish tapestries but also a stuffed elephant's head. Rick drew my attention to a plaque, commemorating the club's Second World War dead, which controversially included the name Franklin Delano Roosevelt, one of three American presidents who had been members (the others being Theodore Roosevelt and John F. Kennedy). President Roosevelt did indeed die before the war ended, but he was a war victim only in the sense that it might have hastened his death from a brain haemorrhage by giving him too much stressful work to do.

There were various gentlemen's clubs in the vicinity of the *New Yorker*, and I, by virtue of my membership of the

Garrick Club in London, was entitled to use the grandest of these—the Century Association at 7 West 43rd Street. The Century was just up the road from the *New Yorker*, no more than a couple of minutes' walk, and therefore extremely convenient from a lunching point of view. To begin with, I was a little bit shy about going there with my Garrick Club introduction; but then, on the initiative of a charming man with the lovely name of Ormonde DeKay, whose son Tom (nicknamed 'Tooth Decay') was a *New Yorker* fact-checker, I was made a temporary member in my own right at the same time as the Tanzanian Ambassador to the United Nations. We were both elected in the 'distinguished visitor' category.

Ormonde, whom I met through mutual friends from England—George and Mary Christie, owners of the Glyndebourne Opera House—was one of those incredibly well-mannered, gentle, kind, self-effacing American gentlemen whose praises cannot be too warmly sung. In Britain, such people have almost ceased to exist. A committed clubman, Ormonde was busily engaged on writing the official history of the Harvard Club of which he was also a member. Being in retirement, he hadn't got a great deal else to do and had already written many tens of thousands more words than requested without being even in sight of the end. In 1994, shortly after I had left New York, the 118 members of the staff of the Harvard Club were to begin a lengthy strike which so embarrassed the club's management that they forbade Ormonde to mention it in his book, though it was quite probably the most interesting thing to have happened at the club in all its 130-year history. Ormonde died in 1998 after the book had been published.

The strike was a public relations disaster for the management. The picture that reached the public was of low-paid servants—mostly Hispanic immigrants of whom quite a few had worked at the club for thirty years or more—being rewarded for their loyalty with singularly heartless treatment by a bunch of rich, self-important toffs. It also

vividly illustrated how old-fashioned many American institutions are. Among the reasons why a proposed new Harvard Club labour contract was rejected by the Hotel,
Restaurant and Club Employees and Bartenders Union was
a management decision to do away with some of the club's
traditional staff bonuses—fifteen dollars, for example, for
shovelling snow; and ten dollars for cleaning up any vomit
or excrement that might be found in a member's bedroom
after a lively evening.

The staff also fiercely objected to proposed changes in the
restrictive hierarchical arrangements within which they
worked. At the Harvard Club, only the 'oysterman' might
shuck an oyster; only the 'silverman' might clean silver; only
the 'sushiman' might make sushi; only the 'potwasher'
might wash pots. The management had planned to abolish
all such titles and lump them together in a category called
'utility worker'. The staff, being proud of their specialities,
were deeply affronted at the thought of being mere 'utility
workers'. During a brief return visit to New York while the
strike was going on, I chatted on the picket line with two
Dominican 'busboys'. They were particularly objecting to a
demand that in the future, when they cleared the tables,
they should deposit the dirty cutlery in one container and
the dirty crockery in another. This would have made their
hands dirty, they said: and it would also have done the
'silver separator' out of a job.

If the staff of the Century had grievances, as they surely
must have had, they never let them show. They were polite
and attentive, and the doorman welcomed me by name
from my first visit onwards. (Remembering names is one of
the great American achievements: I still don't know how
Americans do it, or, indeed, why.) The Century was like a
London club in most respects—the old leather chairs, the
feeling of tradition, and so on—but, being American, it had
an air of efficiency and good management about it. Even
when Americans are trying to be old-fashioned in a British
sort of way, they draw the line at British-style dilapidation.

The Century was well-maintained, and the silver beautifully polished by, presumably, the 'silverman'.

The Century was founded in 1846 as 'an association of artists, writers, musicians and amateurs of the arts and letters devoted to companionship and conversation' (I quote from the pamphlet 'Century Customs: the Spirit and the Letter' which I was given when I became a member). The Garrick, founded only fifteen years earlier, in 1831, had been intended for a similarly Bohemian crowd, but in fact, being in England, included one duke, five marquesses, six earls, and twelve barons among its early members. In recent times, both clubs had fallen largely under the sway of lawyers and media people who would probably take over every club in the world if they got the chance. The Garrick and the Century had also, in the eighties, been targets of emotional public campaigns to get them to admit women as members. Although riven by controversy on the issue, the Century had eventually let women in, while the Garrick had continued to stand firm against them.

I was totally converted to the principle of women joining gentlemen's clubs when I paid my first visit to the Century's tiny members-only bar. The only person standing at the bar when I came in was an elegant woman in her fifties who immediately asked me if she could buy me a drink. It was only while she was ordering me a dry martini, straight up with a twist of lemon, that I noticed she was wearing a clerical collar. It turned out that she was the Vicar of a fashionable Episcopalian church on the Upper East Side. In the words with which Cindy Adams liked to end her daily gossip column in the *New York Daily News*, 'Only in New York, folks, only in New York.'

Tina Brown was also a member of the Century Association, but I don't think I ever saw her there. When she wasn't lunching on chicken salad and Diet Coke at a table in her office, she was doing so at the Forty-Four Restaurant in the Royalton Hotel, which was also less than five minutes' walk from the *New Yorker*. The Royalton was where Si Newhouse and his top editors regularly took guests to lunch. Along one wall was a row of luxurious banquettes on which, on a good day, you could see the lot of them—Tina Brown of the *New Yorker*, Anna Wintour of *Vogue*, Graydon Carter of *Vanity Fair*, and Newhouse himself. They never appeared at all embarrassed at being thus lined up for public display.

Although it was a kind of canteen for tense media personalities, and although its waiters were indecently young and handsome and recited the 'specials of the day' at you in baggy linen suits, the Forty-Four was actually a good restaurant. It was friendly and comfortable, and its dishes were much better and simpler than the pretentious descriptions on the menu made them sound. Its guiding spirit was its cheerful ex-cockney British owner, Brian McNally, who managed to keep up an air of mild ironic detachment however obsequious he needed to be.

In addition to the Century and the Royalton, I had a third regular lunching place in New York—the Oyster Bar beneath Grand Central Station which was also only a few minutes' walk away from the office. It was an enormous tiled and vaulted cellar serving fish, crab, lobster, and up to a dozen varieties of oyster, either on stools at a bar or at tables cheerfully adorned with red-and-white-check tablecloths and attended by friendly, efficient, no-nonsense waiters. In the nineteenth century, when the city was surrounded by rich oyster beds, oyster bars were common in New York. In the eighteen-fifties, according to *The Encyclopaedia of New York City*, about six million dollars' worth of oysters were consumed by New Yorkers each year, and the merits of the different varieties were hotly debated. But the city's oyster beds had vanished long ago, and with them its oyster bars, so that the huge one still flourishing at Grand Central Station was a unique establishment.

When I wasn't lunching with anyone else, I would sometimes go to an Indian restaurant on West 44th Street near Fifth Avenue to indulge my nostalgia for London (London being, gastronomically speaking, an Indian city) or, on the other side of the same street, to a little Irish pub—there were many such in New York—where the customers were generally rather fat and slightly tipsy and smoked cigarettes without shame or embarrassment. They were also quite eager to converse, and it was here that a man on a bar stool once told me a story that seemed too neat but worth repeating about his planned prostate operation.

His doctor had given him two choices, he said. For a few hundred dollars, he could have the basic operation which would leave him impotent. Or, for an extra thousand dollars, he could have additional surgery that would restore his manhood. 'Well,' he said, 'I went home that evening and told my wife about the two operations and what they cost, and I said, "Sweetheart, which one do you think I should have?" And do you know what she said? She said, "Bill, don't bother with the expensive one. Frankly, I'd rather have a holiday in Florida." '

CHAPTER 11

The Democratic Dawn

My year in New York almost synchronised with Bill Clinton's first year as President of the United States. He was elected on Tuesday 3 November 1992, in my second week as editor of 'The Talk of the Town'. Among the liberal journalists at the *New Yorker* there was much excitement about Clinton's victory, but I was not so pleased about it because I didn't like his simpering expression and his habit of jogging in public, forcing his large white thighs upon the attention of the world.

Although jogging's greatest advocate, Jim Fixx, had died in 1984 at the young age of fifty-two, it was by then too late to halt the craze he had started. His 1977 best-seller, *The Complete Book of Running*, had been so influential that nobody dared attribute his death seven years later of 'an undiagnosed coronary-artery blockage' to his ferocious exercise regime, or to the fact that he had run the Boston Marathon eight times. Fixx's son John, announcing that he, too, would run the Boston Marathon when he was thirty-four, pointed out that his grandfather had died even younger than his father had, at the age of forty-three. 'Just as my father, through exercise, was a part of our lives longer than his father was able to be for his children,' he said, 'so too would I like to be around for my children considerably longer than my father.' There is an awful poignancy in this crazy logic.

In the year of his election Clinton was about halfway between the ages of father Fixx and grandfather Fixx at the time of their deaths, but he went on jogging regardless of the dangers, just as Jimmy Carter, the last Democrat in the White House, had done before him. An acquaintance of mine, one of President Carter's speechwriters while he was in office, once described to me how Carter had made him jog with him round the Rose Garden while they discussed the text of a speech. This young man had done everything he could to wriggle out of it. He had said he had no jogging shoes, but the President had opened a closet crammed with shoes of every size. He had pleaded exhaustion, but the President had said that a run would do him good. And so this poor hard-drinking, heavy-smoking fellow had his life put at risk by the leader of his nation who should have had the welfare of all its citizens at heart.

In 1982, a year after Jimmy Carter had been dispatched from the White House by Ronald Reagan, who was much too dignified to jog and therefore looked set to live for ever, I happened to be visiting Jerusalem while Carter was there on one of his Middle Eastern peace missions. The fifty-eight-year-old Carter was still jogging regularly (even though as President he had once collapsed while doing it), and I learned one morning that he had just jogged round the wall of Jerusalem seven times. Pondering this curious piece of intelligence, I recalled that this was exactly the same number of times that Joshua, following God's instructions, had jogged round the wall of Jericho a few thousand years earlier—with the result 'that the wall fell down flat' and Joshua's soldiers 'utterly destroyed all that was in the city, both man and woman, young and old, and ox, and sheep, and ass, with the edge of the sword'. And looking out of my borrowed apartment straight on to the wall of Jerusalem, I feared that a similar disaster might now befall this other ancient circle of masonry, and all the people and oxen and sheep and asses within it, because of the ill-considered behaviour of one foolish old jogger.

Still, an old jogger is easier to understand than a young jogger. In New York there were still young men and women, perfect in health and physique, struggling through their daily ordeal as if their lives depended on it. Some of them had weights attached to their wrists and ankles. None of them ever paused for a rest. If forced to stop by a red light at a street corner, they would continue jogging on the spot until the lights turned green. When Susanna and I had whippets years ago in London, I would sometimes take them to Hyde Park and let them off their leads to exercise. If they saw joggers, they would dash joyfully after them, assuming that they wanted to play. But that, of course, is the last thing any jogger ever wants to do. It is pain, not fun, that the jogger yearns for. And I would chortle at the jogger's distress as my dogs gambolled alongside him, pulling playfully at his running shorts; for he, being ruled by his stopwatch, could not even find the time to shoo a troublesome dog away. I had no dogs in America to set on Clinton's heels, but he deserved such treatment for publicly boasting that he typically jogged one mile in eight and a half minutes each day.

Tina Brown had decreed that 'The Talk of the Town' that week should be about the presidential election and nothing else. I watched the results at the home of William Buckley Jr., whose house in the east Seventies was furnished with all the heavy opulence of an Edwardian brothel. Buckley, with his craggy face and monogrammed shirts and strange patrician accent, was an idealised English aristocrat of a kind only America could invent. He had his own television talk show and his own conservative magazine, the *National Review*, which was then edited—like almost everything else in New York—by an Englishman. Its editor was John O'Sullivan, who in London had been a star journalist on the *Daily Telegraph* and a speechwriter for Margaret Thatcher.

My friend Taki Theodoracopulos was my link to this extravagantly right-wing world, and it was he who took me along to the Buckleys' that night. I had somehow expected them all to sink into despondency as early results showed the jogging, pot-smoking, draft-dodging Arkansan coasting towards the White House; but they all seemed relaxed, be-nevolent and detached. Bill Buckley himself just sat in his shirtsleeves in front of the television set, mechanically flicking from channel to channel with the remote control.

Eventually Clinton appeared on the screen to acknowledge victory and call for 'a new beginning'. Down in Little Rock, Arkansas, his home town, twenty of Clinton's top advisers—including James Carville and George Stephanopoulos—were watching television in the Camelot Hotel when the result from Ohio guaranteed Clinton his victory. As it was reported in 'The Talk of the Town', they let out ear-splitting screams and 'In the manner of a victorious football team, piled on top of one another to form a writhing, ululating heap. Thus began the new Democratic dawn.'

The new Democratic dawn had to wait, in fact, for a couple of months until the Presidential Inauguration on 20 January the following year, when Clinton took the oath of office and George and Barbara Bush flew once round the Capitol in a helicopter before heading off sadly into enforced retirement. Two weeks after the election, George Bush's mother, Dorothy, died of a stroke, aged ninety-one; and Christopher Buckley, Bill Buckley's son and a close friend of the Bush family, interviewed the President by telephone for 'The Talk of the Town'. Dorothy Bush, described by Buckley as 'a matriarchal American aristocrat', had far greater influence on her son than his father, Senator Prescott Bush, ever had—'ten times' as much, according to Barbara Bush. And some people thought that her influence might ultimately have cost George the presidency.

Dorothy Bush excelled at competitive sports and games. She was, as her daughter Nancy Ellis put it to Buckley, 'an enormous athlete . . . a beautiful shot and a good horsewoman and a fabulous swimmer—and tennis, and golf, and paddle tennis. And a fantastic game player. Bridge, Scrabble, anagrams, backgammon, Peggoty, gin rummy, Sir Hinkam Funny-Duster—marvellous card game, Mother was a champ at it. Russian bank, tiddly-winks.' Thus did the American upper classes while away their leisure hours. But Mrs Bush was also a devout Episcopalian who abhorred boastfulness, and she would get very cross with her children if they showed greater interest in their own sporting performances than in the collective achievements of their teams.

And when her son was making his first attempt at the presidency in 1979, she rang him after watching him on television to say, 'George, you're talking about yourself too much.' An old friend of the Bush family, Alixe Glen, told Buckley: 'Mrs Bush hammering that into him—"I don't care how many home runs you made, it's how the team did"—for *so* many years, even as an adult, is what made him unable to brag about himself as President, which many people, myself very much included, feel was part of his demise.'

The period between the election and the Inauguration was one of crisis for the British royal family, whose everyday standards of conduct were vastly inferior to those of old-fashioned American families like the Bushes. Already, in what the Queen was to call her 'annus horribilis', there had been not only the marriage break-up of her second son, the Duke of York, but a series of embarrassing exposures of royal hedonism and self-indulgence—ranging from the topless, toe-sucking activities of 'Fergie', the Duchess of York, and her Texan 'financial adviser', John Bryan, in the South of France, to the Princess of Wales's hysterical illnesses and adulterous romances, allegedly brought on by her husband the Prince's renewed involvement with his former mistress, Camilla Parker-Bowles. Then in December 1992 came a prime ministerial announcement to the House of Commons: the Prince and Princess were to be formally separated.

Tina rang me early in the morning in the Barbizon Hotel to tell me the news and to urge me to follow it up energetically in 'The Talk of the Town', pointing out that, being British, we were better placed than any American journalist to spill whatever beans there were to spill. We didn't manage to spill any, as it turned out, but we did cause some offence by giving the subject the attention that we did. Some *New Yorker* readers reproached me quite severely for giving over 'The Talk of the Town' to so much tittle-tattle about British royalty, and I felt that they had a point. It was the talk of the wrong town.

But in this early phase of Tina's editorship, there was such strong prejudice against her among some of the old *New Yorker* loyalists that hardly anything she did, however harmless, was spared criticism. One day I was in the New York Public Library making an enquiry at the information desk. When I mentioned my connection with the *New Yorker*, one of the two elderly women behind the desk, who both had glasses hanging from their necks on chains, wagged her finger at me and said, 'You go back to the *New Yorker*, and you tell that Miss Brown that we're not stupid. You go tell her that we don't need to have it explained to us what's in the magazine.' All Tina had done was to expand the content's page to include little summaries of what the articles were about. It was a perfectly sensible thing to do, and one that could not rationally be taken as any threat to the magazine's integrity. But to the two stern ladies of the Public Library, it was a clear case of 'dumbing down'.

On another occasion, I was at dinner with Drue Heinz, the lovable ketchup heiress and patron of literature, whose guest of honour was James Laughlin, one of America's most celebrated men of letters. Laughlin, who, like Mrs Heinz, had inherited a Pittsburgh fortune (though his was in steel rather than ketchup), had used his money to found, in 1936, his own publishing house, New Directions. A poet in his own right, though derided as such by his friend Ezra Pound, under whom he studied, Laughlin had published many of the greatest writers of the twentieth century including Pound himself, Vladimir Nabokov, Tennessee Williams, Henry Miller, F. Scott Fitzgerald, Pablo Neruda, Boris Pasternak, and so on and so on.

When he died at eighty-three in November 1997, his contemporary Brendan Gill, who was himself suddenly to die the following month, said, 'He was the greatest publisher America ever had. Look at his backlist: there's nothing comparable.' Well, I had no sooner been introduced to this revered and gentle man than he launched into a strong attack on the manner in which Tina's magazine had taken to publishing poetry. The poems in the *New Yorker*, he protested, had suddenly become enclosed by rules. 'You can't box a poem in,' he said indignantly. 'A poem has to breathe.'

These examples illustrate the irrationality of many of the criticisms with which Tina had to contend. But there seemed to me to be some justice in the frequently made charge that the *New Yorker* under her had acquired a bias towards British themes. I believed this was to some extent so; and I was puzzled by it because Tina knew better than anyone else that enemies would try to pin this accusation on her. I would have expected her to react, if at all, by giving Britain a wide berth in the pages of the magazine. Its public relations machine did not encourage much airing of reader discontent, but early on I met a woman in the elevator who said she had the job of answering letters of complaint. So far, she claimed, she had replied to at least three thousand of them.

Halfway through January, 'The Talk of the Town' decamped to Washington to produce a Clinton Inauguration special. I stayed a few nights with Evangeline Bruce in her Georgetown house, but then moved on Inauguration day itself into the Hay Adams Hotel, establishing my headquarters in an enormous upstairs room exactly opposite the front of the White House, one that a presidential assassin might choose. I accompanied Evangeline to several parties, even including a 'Welcome to America' supper given for me by my friend Michael Kinsley, who had invited a number of writers and journalists along.

I brought with me to Kinsley's house the most talked-about document of the moment, a transcript of the so-called 'Camillagate' tape. The secret recording of a telephone conversation between the Prince of Wales and Camilla Parker-Bowles, made by an unscrupulous private citizen who sold it to the Press, had raised the royal soap opera to new heights of surrealism. In it, the Prince of Wales and Camilla Parker-Bowles professed their love for each other in bizarre imagery, with Charles even expressing a wish to be reborn as a tampon. It followed hot on the heels of the so-called 'Squidgy' tape in which the Princess of Wales was affectionately addressed as 'Squidgy' by one of her male admirers.

After dinner I produced the 'Camillagate' transcript from my pocket and suggested a public reading. This proposal was later to bring me some grief, but at the time it was enthusiastically welcomed by the assembled company. I took the part of Prince Charles, employing a strangled English upper-class accent, while the wife of a well-known American historian gave an uncompromisingly American-accented reading of Camilla. The transcript was then grabbed by Meg Greenfield, editor of the *Washington Post*'s editorials and opinion columns, whose rendition of Camilla seemed especially exotic because of her uncanny physical resemblance to the Queen of England.

As I was to write later that week in the London *Times*, I was slightly shocked by how heartless these Americans were. They showed not the slightest sympathy for either the Prince or his mistress. They did not care that a telephone conversation of such intimacy had been bugged and exposed to public mockery around the world. Their reaction was simply one of glee, mingled with contempt.

Yet there was something touching, as well as comic, about the 'Camillagate' tape. The couple were clearly in love, and, as the interminable goodnight sequence showed, neither could face the idea of being the first to put the telephone down—'Night,' 'Night,' 'Night,' 'Love you for ever,' 'Night,' 'G'bye,' 'Bye, my darling,' and so on, and so on. If the protagonists had been different, the audience might have shed a tear or two. But no American would ever shed a tear for the Prince of Wales.

The presidency has its monarchical aspect too, of course, and this is reflected in the panoply surrounding an Inauguration. The basic ceremony for the transference of power from one president to another is a brief and rather moving one. But it is hardly enough to satisfy an entire nation glued to the television in hope of patriotic uplift, let alone the many thousands of people who flood into Washington, hoping to be entertained. So pageants and diversions have to be invented, several days of parties arranged, and Hollywood brought in to assist. At the Clinton Inauguration, the main attractions to which people were clamouring for tickets were dominated not by politicians but by the stars. As 'The Talk of the Town' put it, 'For a few days, Washington was a convention center for the entertainment industry. For ever status-conscious, producers, actors, agents, and their various clients and acolytes jostled frantically for the best hotel rooms, the best seats, and invitations to the best parties.'

The night before the Inauguration, Evangeline took me along to a party given for Bill Clinton's mother, Virginia Kelley, by Yolande Fox, a former Miss America and the widow of the Holywood producer Matthew Fox, in her Georgetown mansion. This was a large house immediately across N Street from the even larger one of Ben Bradlee, the former Editor of the *Washington Post*, and it had been lived in for a while by Jacqueline Kennedy after President Kennedy was assassinated. Mrs Fox had gone to great lengths to make her home feel as cosy and welcoming as possible to the new First Mom from Arkansas. She had provided Southern food, an old-time piano player, and, among the guests, an assortment of show business legends, such as Mickey Rooney, Lauren Bacall, Shelley Winters, and Harry Belafonte. The seventy-seven-year-old musical-comedy writer Adolph Green ('On the Town', 'Wonderful Town') and the sixty-six-year-old cabaret singer Barbara Cook were the principal vocalists.

Mrs Kelley, a former nurse, was a short, rotund, ebullient woman in a trouser suit and lots of heavy jewellery. Despite her background, she was perfectly at ease among George-town's millionaires, and she dealt skilfully with the hoopla about her son. 'He's going to do us proud,' she told every-body, repeating time and again that ever since he had been a child, he had always made his own decisions (including the decision to change his surname from Blythe to Clinton). Hadn't he been a bit of a bookworm? someone asked. Well, he had studied a lot, she replied. 'But he also liked sports and girls. He wasn't a nerd.'

Meeting Mrs Kelley for the first time, I could understand why Bill Clinton seemed to have such difficulty in keeping his hands off people. His mother was a compulsive hugger. She hugged me when I was introduced to her and she hugged me several more times thereafter, often when I was least expecting it. My moment of greatest intimacy with the First Mom came when she told me sorrowfully she had asked the pianist to play her favourite song, Billy Joel's 'Just the Way You Are', but that he had said he didn't know it. Being by then a little drunk, I thought it preposterous that the President's mother should be denied such a modest re-quest on the eve of her son's Inauguration and decided, un-bidden, to see what could be done about it. Adolph Green, when I approached him, said he didn't know the song ei-ther, and perhaps this was because it was too modern, having been written only fifteen years earlier.

Eventually I approached Mickey Rooney, who didn't seem at all pleased. 'Do you know the song "Just the Way You Are"?' I asked him. 'Of course I do,' he replied crossly. 'Well, would you terribly mind singing it?' 'Of course I would,' he said. 'Oh, but it's Mrs Kelley's favourite song, and she is longing for someone to sing it, but nobody seems to know it. It would be doing her the most tremendous favour, and her son is going to be made President tomorrow.' He still looked doubtful, so I ran and grabbed Mrs Kelley and told her that Mickey Rooney knew the song, and that if she were to ask him herself to sing it, he could hardly turn her down.

She did as I suggested, and Mickey Rooney approached the piano, promising to oblige. But perhaps he didn't know the song as well as he'd said he did; for after throwing his hat (he was wearing a hat) on to the top of the piano, he limited himself to plucking the inside of his mouth with a finger and making funny faces while somebody played the tune. The following night, Mrs Kelley slept for the first time in the White House and then, being a keen racegoer, visited the Laurel Race Course near Washington before returning to Arkansas, where soon afterwards she died.

The weather was glorious on Inauguration Day, and Evangeline took me to watch the ceremony from the East Wing of the National Gallery of Art, the massive marble building designed in the seventies by the architect I. M. Pei to house the Gallery's collection of twentieth-century art. From an upstairs terrace on its east side, we had an uninterrupted view across The Mall to the front of the Capitol Building where Clinton's swearing-in was to be held in the open air. The presidential motorcade up Pennsylvania Avenue to the Capitol steps was preceded by a parade of bands, floats, tumblers, and jugglers. There was a huge, festive crowd cheering them on, and I took lots of photographs from my privileged vantage point.

From inside the National Gallery, two images remain in my memory: Mr and Mrs I. M. Pei sitting grave, motionless and inscrutable for hours on end in front of a television set, and the smooth, tranquil, smiling face of Pamela Churchill Harriman. In any great hubbub, it is stillness that stands out; and Mrs Harriman created around her a little island of calm amid the turmoil. *New York* magazine had just billed her on its cover as 'The Queen Mother of the Clinton Court', and, despite her rackety past, there did now seem to be something regal about her. That evening, while the dinner-jacketed multitudes stormed ballroom after ballroom to catch glimpses of Bill and Hillary on their triumphal progress around town, Mrs Harriman stayed quietly at home in her handsome Georgetown house with her Picasso, her Renoir and her Van Gogh. There, in majestic style, she entertained almost everybody else of importance in the Democratic Party, including all the senior members of Mr Clinton's new cabinet.

Evangeline did not allow her hatred of Pamela to keep her away from what was clearly going to be the party of the night, and she asked me to accompany her there. In the Cadillac on the way, she discussed our hostess with icy disdain, but greeted her on arrival with a terrific show of warmth. That is what life at Court—any court—has always been like. Earlier, at lunchtime, Mrs Harriman had slipped away from the National Gallery and reappeared shortly afterwards, not in the flesh but on the television screen. She had gone to some studio to be interviewed about her friend Mr Clinton. He reminded her, she said, of her former father-in-law, Winston Churchill. Bill and Winston were just the same: resolute and resilient. She said this without hint of affectation or irony, and it was as if all the events in her tumultuous life had suddenly come together in a happy synthesis.

'The Talk of the Town's' Inauguration special, produced in a rush verging on panic in the Hay Adams Hotel, was generally well received, but generated another of those acrimonious disputes which were coming to seem a routine feature of my job. The aggrieved individual this time was the American Poet Laureate, Mona van Duyn. A new Poet Laureate is appointed each year by the Librarian of Congress, so the position doesn't have anything like the prestige of its British equivalent. Its holder isn't even expected to write poems for state occasions, as the British Poet Laureate is; but Ms Van Duyn had felt inspired nevertheless to celebrate Bill Clinton's election victory with a poem which had been published earlier that January in the *Washington Post*.

This act of homage went unappreciated by the new President, who commissioned not Ms Van Duyn but the very much more famous Maya Angelou to write an official poem for his Inauguration. Ms Angelou was black. She had been raped by her mother's boyfriend when she was eight years old and struck dumb for five years as a result. After giving birth to a son at sixteen, she had started out on a varied career as a nightclub singer, dancer, actress and writer. She had published several volumes of autobiography and several of verse.

In the sixties she had been active in the black civil rights movement. For some years she had lived in Ghana, editing the *African Review*. And from 1981 onwards she had been the Reynolds Professor of American Studies at Wake Forest University in North Carolina. If these were not qualifications enough to be chosen as the presidential troubadour, there was the clinching fact that Maya Angelou had spent much of her childhood in the care of her grandmother in the town of Stamps in Arkansas, Bill Clinton's home state.

Her Inauguration poem was called 'On the Pulse of the Morning', and she read it with great passion from the Capitol steps. Personally, I couldn't make much sense of it, and I responded enthusiastically to someone's troublemaking proposal that we should contact the slighted Poet Laureate for her opinion. Maybe the suggestion came from Emma Gilbey, who was by nature troublemaking and who was in Washington for the Inauguration as my helper. Emma, whom I had originally known as a London party girl and friend of Taki, had soon revealed an earnest and ambitious side, deriving perhaps from the fact that her late mother had been American and had bequeathed her an American passport. After a spell as a schoolteacher in New York, she had broken into journalism in the eighties as a reporter for a Congressional gossip sheet called *Roll Call*.

Whether it was Emma's idea or not, it was she who tracked down Mona van Duyn by telephone to St Louis, Missouri, and interviewed her about Ms Angelou's poem.

'She achieved brilliantly what she intended to do—that is, to speak to all parts of the diversity of this country,' Ms Van Duyn said. But the compliment was then qualified in a way which made it sound a little sour. 'It is extremely dangerous to write a poem of that kind for so gigantic an audience, and Ms Angelou certainly knows, as I do, that to do so one must give up some of the strategies and resources of poetry that might be very effective.' What kind of strategies and resources? asked Emma. 'A certain density of imagery and a tightness in the poem—any kind of complicated imagery.'

When this was published, Mona Van Duyn was greatly embarrassed and denied having said any of it. She furiously demanded a correction. It turned out she was a contributor of poems to the *New Yorker*, and our poetry editor, a great admirer of her work, was desperate for us to make our peace with her. I think peace was eventually made. The only work of Ms Van Duyn that I ever read was a verse we published in that same edition of 'The Talk of the Town'. She had revealed to Emma Gilbey that Clinton's victory had inspired her to write another, so far unpublished poem, which she had entitled: 'On Seeing a TV Shot of Mrs Bush, Her Arm Around the Younger Woman's Waist, Leading Mrs Clinton into the White House.' Its first verse read:

> What form of government shall
>   we choose for the self?
> Maps and histories are no help
>   in this.
> We cannot change regimes, nor
>   alter borders,
> Nor create new laws, new policies,
>   new orders.

I cannot say that I liked this much either.

As I mentioned earlier, my public reading of the 'Camillagate' transcript was to bring me grief—or rather my account of it in *The Times* was to do so. There had, I was later told, been many angry letters of protest to the newspaper about this, but nobody told me about them at the time. All I had received by way of reaction was a warm letter of congratulation from the Editor, Peter Stothard. 'Thank you for two wonderful opening columns,' he wrote. 'The mugging caused some worry for your friends (at least in our house), but the Camillagate piece brought pleasure undiluted. We have had an excellent anecdotal response of the sort that editors like so much, and there is a lot more to come, I am sure.' I was, of course, delighted by this letter.

But then a couple of other letters arrived. One was from an elderly aunt whose husband, my mother's brother, had recently died. 'I feel I must write to you after reading your beastly article in the *Times*,' she wrote. 'I feel so shocked and sad that you could behave like you said you did.' She went on to say that she was glad her late husband wasn't alive to read it and that she felt so sorry for my mother. Sorry for my mother about what, exactly? About having such a monster for a son? I noticed when I returned to England a year later that the 'Camillagate' article was among the *Times* columns of mine which my mother, then over ninety, had touchingly pasted into a scrapbook.

One month later I received a much longer letter from a devoutly royalist cousin of mine with whom, over dinner a few weeks earlier, I had wholeheartedly agreed that the publication in the British tabloids of a bugged telephone conversation between the Prince and Camilla was an unpardonable invasion of their privacy. In his letter, he recalled that I had taken this position and said this had made him doubly appalled by the behaviour to which I had confessed in Washington. My article in the *Times*, he wrote, had 'caused much unhappiness and a feeling of distaste', and it had been 'incredible and unworthy' of me 'to become part of that very indifferent group of people who are seeking to profit from what most people regard as an intrusion into a private conversation'.

I continue to think that the publication in the British press of the 'Camillagate' tape was disgusting. But, once it *had* been published, it had become public property and an irresistible topic of light-hearted discussion, especially among journalists. But the emotional reactions to my article did undermine my confidence in my own judgement. Why, I asked myself, had I failed to anticipate the outrage it would cause? I expect some people were upset at the idea of an Englishman behaving as I did among strangers in a foreign land. Others may have resented the fact that the article appeared in the *Times*, a newspaper from which many still expected propriety and restraint.

In any event, this unhappy episode seems to me to have been indicative of the crisis of the monarchy which was to reach its ghoulish climax some years later with the death of Diana, Princess of Wales. Already by then, there had ceased to be any national consensus about how the royal family should be regarded, treated, or discussed.

CHAPTER 12

The Merry Widows

On 15 January 1993, I was invited to dinner by Jayne Wrightsman. Mrs Wrightsman was my close neighbour. She lived just around the corner from me at 820 Fifth Avenue, a First World War limestone palace overlooking Central Park, and one of the grandest addresses in New York. All I had to do to get to Mrs Wrightsman's apartment was to turn left out of my front door on the south side of East 63rd Street, stroll past the imposing façade of the New York Academy of Sciences (a building constructed in 1920 as home for the President of the Royal Baking Powder Company), cross the road at the corner of Fifth Avenue, and persuade one of the group of superior-looking doormen guarding the lobby of No. 820 to accompany me in the elevator up to the fourth floor. The whole business took less than five minutes.

However, this was the first time I had ever done it because until that evening I had not met Mrs Wrightsman, nor even heard of her, despite the fact that she was famously rich and spent a considerable part of every year in London where she had a flat in St James's, overlooking Green Park. I was invited that evening because she was giving a dinner party for an old friend of mine from England, Tessa Keswick. Tessa, the wife of my former benefactor and even older friend Henry Keswick, was in New York on her way to Washington for Bill Clinton's Inauguration and had asked Mrs Wrightsman to include me among her guests.

This was the first of more than a dozen such invitations from Mrs Wrightsman during the course of my year in New

York. She seemed to have picked on me immediately as a potential spare man, someone with whom to fill an empty seat at a dinner table. This was a role I had already performed in Washington for Evangeline Bruce, and I used to wonder why I was considered suitable for it. Perhaps others were less aware than I was of my social deficiencies—like the fact that I generally drank too much, and that this would often begin to show by the end of an evening when my natural timidity could suddenly turn to embarrassing familiarity.

I also smoked continuously and found it very difficult to stop, even during meals. On all the occasions at which I was Mrs Wrightsman's guest, I think I only ever met one other person who smoked heavily, and she was a rich, grand lady from Washington who could do as she wished. Yet my smoking was tolerated. ('It is only for *you* that I mind,' Mrs Wrightsman would say kindly, as she ordered a servant to bring me an ashtray.)

I can only guess at the reasons for my being favoured with so many dinner invitations. Being temporarily single in New York, but nevertheless married for thirty years, and with a grandchild on the way, I may have seemed to offer respectability as well as availability. As editor of 'The Talk of the Town', I had a job that didn't need explaining or justifying. Furthermore, I was a foreigner who would be going home in due course. If I turned out to be a liability, I would not, at least, be a permanent one.

I don't think it helped much that I was English. It is widely assumed in Britain that it is an advantage to be English in New York since Americans are supposed to be in awe of people who talk in refined accents. But one shouldn't underestimate the amount of visceral hostility which, for sound historical reasons, many Americans feel towards the British; and one shouldn't forget that the posh British accent is associated in some American minds less with charm, wit, and sophistication than with deviousness, exploitation, and snobbery.

Anyway, the invitations dribbled in, and I always accepted them if I possibly could. I liked Jayne Wrightsman very much. She was always so cheerful and enthusiastic. Everything and everybody was 'divine', and her account of any outing would include the intelligence that everyone had drunk 'lots and lots of champagne'. She didn't, in fact, eat or drink lots of anything, for she had an exceedingly slim figure to maintain. But I have never eaten or drunk better in my life than I have in her apartment. She had a French chef of prodigious talent who made me understand, for the first time, the attractions of French *haute cuisine*. It was the sheer cleverness of it that beguiled me.

At my first dinner, the dessert looked like an ordinary slice of water-melon; but it then turned out that the pink flesh had been removed and transformed into a sorbet, its pips replaced by chips of chocolate, and the resulting mixture restored to the water-melon's rind in a form indistinguishable from that of a freshly cut slice. On another occasion, an hors-d'oeuvre was produced which looked like a dish of shiny black plums. In fact, the 'plums' were little balls of pt de foie gras covered by a thin skin of glazed black truffle. I can't imagine how this was achieved. When one comes across a black truffle in the middle of a slab of foie gras, where it is most commonly found, it is a rather hard and rubbery thing, not looking in the least as if it could be moulded into a soft and shiny skin.

The elevator opened straight into Mrs Wrightsman's front hall in which hung four of the finest Canalettos in the world. 'I want to show you a picture of your Queen,' she said within seconds of welcoming me there for the first time. 'Oh Lord,' I thought. 'Not that!' But 'my Queen' turned out to be Henrietta Maria, the wife of King Charles I, magnificently painted by Sir Anthony Van Dyck. However, most of the art and furnishings in the apartment were French—paintings by Ingres and David and many splendid examples of decorative French furniture. On the floor of the drawing room lay one of her first major acquisitions—an enormous

Savonnerie carpet commissioned for Versailles by Louis XIV.

These were just the remnants of the Wrightsman collection, most of which had been presented to the Metropolitan Museum of Art in 1969 and accommodated in a suite of rooms rechristened 'The Wrightsman Galleries'. They contain much the best assemblage of eighteenth-century French furniture and *objets d'art* in America. But Mrs Wrightsman and her late husband, Charles, an oil tycoon, also gave the museum a number of old-master paintings, including works by Rubens, El Greco, Vermeer, Tiepolo, La Tour, and David. They were a very generous couple.

Mrs Wrightsman was a discreet woman who avoided publicity, but in 1991 the now defunct American magazine *Connoisseur* published a long profile of her, tracing her life's journey from the grimy industrial Midwest, where she was born with the name of Jane Larkin, in 1920 (or thereabouts), to her eventual vast wealth and social eminence in Palm Beach, New York and London. In Flint, Michigan, the town of her birth, her father had died when she was very young, and her widowed mother had tried to make ends meet by opening a nightclub for workers at the local Buick factory. But in the middle of the thirties, when Hollywood was the focus of all aspirations, she moved to Los Angeles where she hoped to carve out a better future for her two daughters.

Jayne (who added the 'y' to her name at Beverly Hills High School) was said by *Connoisseur* to have evolved by then 'into an attractive if not altogether stunning young woman'. And the magazine's description of her at that time still seemed perfectly applicable almost sixty years later:

Her wide-set eyes glimmered under the high arches of her brows. She always wore her dark hair up and brushed back, exposing an expansive forehead. Her nose, delicately hooked, was underlined by a pair of thin lips . . . Her long limbs complemented a narrow frame, which would one day set new standards for high fashion slimness.

Although, said the magazine, she wasn't the stuff of a southern Californian goddess, she was set apart by a poise and a gracefulness which had fortunately replaced the shyness and insecurity she had felt as a child.

After graduating from high school, Jayne Larkin got a job as a sales clerk in a Los Angeles department store, and it was there at the perfume counter that she is reputed to have met her future husband, Charles Bierer Wrightsman. Wrightsman had been born at the turn of the century in Pawnee, Oklahoma, and had inherited an expanding oil fortune. He had then tried to launch himself into smart society by taking up polo. According to legend, he wanted to buy a bottle of scent for one of his girlfriends, and Jayne sprayed a sample on to the back of his hand with such a firm grip on his fingers and such a bold stare into his eyes that he asked her out to dinner there and then.

Charlie Wrightsman had discarded his first wife, Irene Stafford, by whom he had two daughters, a couple of years earlier, and was now amusing himself with large numbers of young women. But in 1943 he contracted lip cancer and, deciding that his days were numbered, started to focus almost exclusively on Jayne, whom he married in 1944 and took with him to live in Palm Beach, then the seaside resort of choice for the American social élite. He was forty-eight years old, roughly double her age. The marriage, which lasted until his death at the age of ninety in 1986, would have been unbearable to many women, but Jayne had sufficient resilience to survive it.

According to the *Connoisseur* article, Charlie Wrightsman was a tyrant. Embarrassed by his wife's working-class origins, he organised tutors to teach her French, the arts, etiquette, and refined English, but still ordered her to sit still and say nothing even at their own parties in case she should make a fool of herself. He would tell her to 'shut up' or 'sit down' in front of guests, forbid her to receive either her mother or her sister at home (reportedly agreeing to support them on condition that they stayed away from Palm Beach), and keep the tightest control over her movements.

The way in which he had treated his first wife, Irene, and their daughters, Irene and Charlene, didn't bode well for Jayne. By trying to control every detail of their lives, he had driven all three of them to drink and drugs. In March 1963, Irene Stafford Wrightsman was found dead in her New York apartment after a heart attack caused by sleeping pills and alcohol. A month later, Charlene died from an overdose of sleeping pills at the age of thirty-eight. Two years after that, her sister Irene died at forty-four. According to *Connoisseur*, 'drugs were also a factor in Irene's death'.

Jayne's way of trying to loosen her husband's grip on her was to become an expert in French furniture. Both to impress him and to earn wider respect for herself, she threw herself into the redecoration of their grand Palm Beach home, carefully emulating the taste of leading society women such as Martha Baird Rockefeller and the Chrysler heiress, Thelma Foy. These women were the leaders of Palm Beach fashion who, according to *Connoisseur*, 'chose to abandon the Waspy dowdiness of English furniture for the lushness of the French decorative arts'.

At around that time, two very grand European adventurers, Baroness Rene de Becker and her distant cousin Baron Eric von Goldschmidt-Rothschild, established themselves at 820 Fifth Avenue in the apartment which the Wrightsmans would eventually occupy. Lacking the wealth that their name implied, they intended to sell their own collection of eighteenth-century French furniture—then commanding much lower prices than equivalent English furniture—to the American *nouveaux riches*. Baroness de Becker transformed their apartment into a showcase for the French aristocratic way of life. It was a slick marketing operation, and it worked. Her guests were dazzled by her title, her elegance, her white-gloved servants, and her foie gras and caviare luncheons, and they were soon competing to buy French furniture from her at prices far higher than those in the auction houses.

Jayne Wrightsman was one of Baroness de Becker's contented customers, and through her she met a smart Parisian decorator called Stephane Boudin, a great authority on her kind of furniture, whom she was to retain as her mentor for some fifteen years. The late Sir Francis Watson, a former director of the Wallace Collection in London, which claimed to have the best collection of eighteenth-century French furniture outside France, was another of her close advisers. But Mrs Wrightsman was determined to be her own expert.

She kept piles of furniture books beside her bed and would study them into the early hours after her husband had gone to bed. She would order sales catalogues from all over the world and make frequent museum tours of Europe in the company of experts. When Sir Francis Watson visited her in New York in 1959, seven years after she started collecting, he showed her 240 transparencies of pieces from the Wallace Collection, and she was able to identify the dates, makers, and provenance of each item correctly. She had become an expert in her own right, just as she had planned.

By now 'FFF'—gossip columnists' shorthand for Fine French Furniture—employed stylistic supremacy among the richest people in America, and the Wrightsmans had more and better examples of it than anybody else. This was very good for Mrs Wrightsman's social standing and for her morale. She became a friend of Jacqueline Kennedy, who considered her to be highly cultured and appointed her to a White House art-selection committee. In 1961, with Mrs Kennedy and Evangeline Bruce (among others), she was named by the New York Couture Group as one of the best-dressed women in the world.

And, according to *Connoisseur*, she grew in bravery towards her husband: 'In dealing with Charlie, she displayed noticeably more confidence, developing a highly effective silent and icy gaze to thwart his frequent rudeness. Though still the servile wife, she had learned to circumvent some of Charlie's restrictions.' (For example, when they were in Palm Beach together and he told her she couldn't go to Paris for the Givenchy show, she left for New York saying she would work on their collection instead—but, on arriving there, immediately changed planes and flew to Paris.)

Having bought the Fifth Avenue apartment in 1955 from the Rothschild pair, who returned to Europe loaded with money, Mrs Wrightsman proceeded to live in it rather as they had, with French furniture, uniformed servants, foie gras and caviare, and regular lunch and dinner parties for rich and important people. I imagine that her way of life was much the same in the fifties as it was when I visited there forty years later.

By the nineties, Mrs Wrightsman's social position was so long established, her life's purpose so fully and perfectly accomplished, that no one would have wished any longer to deny her the status of aristocrat. Explaining her reticence about her past, Sir Francis Watson had once said, 'The problem is, regardless of how much one has achieved or succeeded, when one traverses from rags to riches, people are always going to be fixated on the rags.' I'm not sure that in America that is true. I think that Mrs Wrightsman's rags had been well and truly forgotten.

I, at any rate, had no wish to contemplate them. As far as I was concerned, she was as aristocratic as any English aristocrat I had met, and more stylish, better mannered, and a lot more generous than most of them. She had some curious little affectations. One was to spell 'honour' in the British manner with the 'u' in it. Her dinners were usually 'in honour of' somebody or other, and she would write out her own invitation cards. Before sending you the card, she would telephone to see if you were available for the evening in question, and then she would tell you whether it was 'dressed' or 'undressed'—her way of saying whether or not you should wear a dinner jacket. I had never heard anyone use the word 'undressed' in this context before, and I am sure she meant it as a joke.

At her dinners there was a hard core of regular guests from the moneyed and cultural establishments of New York. Some of them even lived in the same legendary apartment building—for example, Michel David-Weill, the chairman of Lazard Frès, and John Gutfreund, the former chairman of Salamon Brothers who had fallen foul of the financial regulators. Other people I would often meet there included Robert Silvers, the Editor of the *New York Review of Books*, and his companion Grace, Countess of Dudley (a lively Croatian who had been married to Prince Stanislas Radziwill before she became, in 1961, the third wife of the third Earl of Dudley, who died in 1969); Barbara Walters, the celebrated television interviewer; Oscar and Annette de la Renta, the Dominican fashion designer and his American heiress wife; and, among others, Brooke Astor.

I will stop at Brooke Astor. When I met her, she was more than ninety years old and still the unchallenged 'Queen of New York', despite the claims of vulgar pretenders like Leona Helmsley. She was famous for her wealth, her good works, her charm, and her energy. In a *New Yorker* interview with Brendan Gill to mark her ninety fifth birthday in 1997, she said, 'Sometimes I wonder why, at my age, I like to go out every night, but I do.' If there really were such a thing as an American aristocrat, Brooke Astor would be it, though her own family background was respectable rather than grand. Her father, John Russell, was an officer in the Marines and her mother, according to Gill, 'of Southern stock—a flirtatious social butterfly'.

The family lived at first in Washington DC but, because of her father's job, Brooke spent part of her childhood in China. At sixteen, she dropped out of school and at seventeen married her first husband, John Dryden Kuser, who, according to Gill again, was 'the alcoholic son of a very rich family, given to physically abusing Brooke and to incessant womanising'. Divorced after eight years with a solid financial settlement, she was still only in her mid-twenties when she moved to New York 'to make a place for herself in Scott Fitzgerald's Jazz Age'. She was of literary bent and was writing book reviews for *Vogue* when, in 1932, she married a stockbroker, Charles Henry Marshall, whom she afterwards described as the great love of her life. During twenty happy years of marriage she worked as an editor at *House & Garden*, but then Mr Marshall died suddenly of a heart attack in her arms, and she was on her own once more.

Within a year, she was married again, this time to an enormous fortune. Her third husband, Viscount Astor, was the great-great-grandson of John Jacob Astor, the German-born financier who founded the Astor dynasty in the first half of the nineteenth century, and the son of John Jacob Astor IV, one of two feuding Astor cousins who in the eighteen-nineties built hotels side by side on the sites of their parents' Fifth Avenue mansions and subsequently united the two establishments as the Waldorf-Astoria hotel. (The original Waldorf-Astoria was demolished in 1929 to make way for the Empire State Building. The present one, which occupies the entire block between Park and Lexington and 49th and 50th Streets, opened in 1931.)

Vincent Astor came into his fortune when his father John Jacob IV went down with the *Titanic* in 1912. He was already in his sixties, and Brooke in her fifties, when he fell hopelessly in love with her and stormed her with letters and telephone calls, promising to divorce his wife. Although, according to Gill, his face 'wore an inscrutable, often sour expression' and he had a 'reputation for being truculent and often deliberately rude', Brooke did not resist him for long. In marriage, she appears to have found him no more than 'an interesting companion'. They had about eight years together before he died in 1959, leaving $67 million to her and the same amount to the Vincent Astor Foundation of which Brooke immediately became president. The Foundation had been created with 'the alleviation of human misery' as its declared purpose, but Brooke decided that all its money should be spent within New York City where most of the Astor fortune had been made. (This, in the parlance of the American rich, is called 'giving something back'. The politician's equivalent piety is 'making a difference'.)

When, as she approached ninety-five, Mrs Astor decided to put an end to the Foundation's philanthropic activities, it had spent a total of $195 million on thousands of youth and housing projects, parks and playgrounds, and historic buildings. That is a large amount of money; but the United States is a country without historical parallel in the munificence of its private citizens. On 17 December 1993, the day I left New York permanently for England, I marvelled to read in the *New York Times* that Walter Annenberg, the former US Ambassador to London, was giving away $500 million in educational grants. A few years later, Ted Turner, the television mogul who married Jane Fonda, pledged $1 billion of his own money to the United Nations. But they have all been outclassed by Bill Gates of Microsoft, of whom it was revealed in 1999 that he had by then given $15 billion to his two charitable foundations.

If there is any single conclusion to be drawn from the lives of Brooke Astor and Jayne Wrightsman, it is that widow power is rarely achieved without struggle and sacrifice. It isn't easy to steer a listing multimillionaire safely into port, so it's no wonder America's richest widows are often exceptional women. Usually, they have had to put up with years of brutish or neurotic behaviour and to train long and hard for their future roles as philanthropists, society hostesses, or art connoisseurs. In short, they have earned their mountain of money with just as much toil and sweat as the men from whom they have inherited it.

On 21 October 1993, I was bidden to celebrate Mrs Wrightsman's birthday—nobody, of course, mentioned which birthday it was—at a dinner in the splendid upstairs room at La Grenouille, the grand French restaurant on East

52nd Street between Fifth and Madison. The invitation came from a certain Mr and Mrs William McCormick Blair Jr. of Washington DC, whom I had never met. I felt flattered by the seating arrangements. I had been placed, at one of the half-dozen tables, between Barbara Walters and Mrs Astor.

I talked mainly to Mrs Astor, because I had never had the chance to do so properly before. She said she wasn't feeling well, but seemed quite animated to me. Had I noticed, she asked me at one point, that we were the only people laughing in the room? English people laughed more than Americans did, and she liked that, she said. Then she started to talk somewhat competitively about her English contemporary, the ninety-two-year-old novelist Dame Barbara Cartland. Was I aware, she asked, that Barbara Cartland claimed still to have milk in her breasts? I looked appropriately appalled, but the thought of this seemed suddenly to make her feel rather worse, and she started talking across me to Barbara Walters about whether or not she should go to South Carolina in the morning to launch a ship. Ms Walters was urging her strongly not to go. 'Are they sending a plane for you?' she asked. 'No, they're not,' said Mrs Astor. 'In which case, it's out of the question,' said Ms Walters.

Mrs Astor was still reluctant to cancel her journey because the ship she was due to launch was named after an Astor, possibly her late husband. She said she would go home early and make her decision in the morning. So when the first opportunity arose, she stood up, made an elegant little speech of congratulation to Mrs Wrightsman on her birthday, and then slipped out of the room. When she had gone, I turned to Barbara Walters and said, 'She *will* launch that ship, won't she?' 'I don't think so,' she replied. 'Want a bet?' I said. 'Sure.' 'Five dollars?' 'Sure.' And we shook hands.

I had never felt more confident of winning anything. It would not have been in character for Mrs Astor to fail to launch a ship merely because she wasn't feeling well. Her sense of duty, her American grit, would ensure that she didn't let the people in South Carolina down. Anyway, launching ships was what Mrs Astor was all about. If she stopped launching ships, then she might as well pack everything in. About a week later, I found her sitting on a sofa at a reception in Mrs Wrightsman's apartment and asked her how the ship-launching had gone. 'I didn't go,' she said. I was furious. Next time I saw Barbara Walters, which was at a 'Literary Lions' dinner in the New York Public Library, I paid her the five dollars.

An important person in Mrs Wrightsman's life was Philippe de Montebello, the director of the Metropolitan Museum of Art. As one of the museum's biggest benefactors, she was entitled to his deference, and he gave it to her in great Gallic dollops. Although smooth and preposterously French for someone who had lived in America since he was fourteen, he enjoyed a very high reputation as a curator and administrator. It was better to be French than English in New York, I had decided. France had not only been on the right side in the War for Independence but had never made the mistake of oppressing the Irish. It was also a more polished thing to be, and it went better with Mrs Wrightsman's furniture. Of the regular guests at her dinner table, one of the ones who charmed her most was the amiable French Consul-General in New York (and later Ambassador to Prague), Benoit d'Aboville.

It is odd how many Frenchmen with aristocratic names go abroad to represent a republic which was founded on severed aristocratic heads. Perhaps some of them aren't aristocratic at all, but Philippe de Montebello certainly was. I read about him in an article in the *New Yorker*:

It might be said that élitism came naturally to Guy-Philippe Lannes de Montebello, who was born in Paris in 1936, and grew up in a family that was descended on his mother's side from the Marquis de Sade and on his father's side from Marshal Jean Lannes, one of Napoleon's generals, whom Napoleon named Duc de Montebello after his victory in the battle of Montebello [wrote Calvin Tomkins]. Philippe's great-grandmother, the Comtesse Laure de Chevigne, was one of the models for Proust's Duchesse de Guermantes. His aunt, Marie-Laure de Noailles, was a famous and somewhat scandalous patron of avant-garde art and letters in Paris between the wars.

Right-minded Americans oughtn't to take any interest in such comic-opera genealogy, but I'm afraid it is probably swoony stuff for the widows. Anyway, in April 1993, before I had met or even heard of Mr de Montebello, a fax arrived for me from Mrs Wrightsman, written in her own hand and saying, 'If you are free on Thursday the 13th of May, will you come to a small dinner that Annette [Mrs de la Renta] and I are giving for Philippe de Montebello's birthday. It is meant to be a surprise, so we have said that we are having dinner here at eight—informal. After a drink, the surprise—we shall leap into cars and go to the private dining room at La Grenouille' (a restaurant of which the Zagat Survey ludicrously says, 'It is worth mortgaging the house for a sneak preview of heaven').

The surprise happened as planned. We 'leapt' into a fleet of cars and drove eleven blocks down the road to La Grenouille where waiters were lining the staircase up to the private room. We took our places at the usual small group of round tables, surrounded by flower arrangements large enough for a society wedding. Being an outsider on this occasion was embarrassing, for when the speeches came, one speaker after another singled me out for special acknowledgement as the one person there whom they were still yearning to know. Even Mr de Montebello did so in an emotional speech otherwise devoted to his immeasurable joy at finding himself surrounded that night by all his very dearest friends.

Mrs Wrightsman was a patron of music as well as of art—in particular, of the Metropolitan Opera House—and she would also occasionally invite me to concerts. The most memorable of these was a concert given by Luciano Pavarotti in aid of the Metropolitan Opera Pension Fund. It took place on a Sunday evening in May 1993, and I had gone to her apartment beforehand to fortify myself with a few of her excellent home-made potato chips. It seemed curious to me that the great tenor, notorious at that time for cancelling important engagements all over the place, should have agreed to cross the Atlantic to sing unpaid for something as unglamorous as a pension fund. But I think that the Met's music director, James Levine, had some kind of hold over him. When I interviewed Pavarotti in Italy a few years later, he said that Levine was the conductor he most liked to work with. Levine, it seemed, treated him kindly and made allowance for the fears and phobias of a megastar approaching the end of his career.

At that time, there was a passionate debate ranging around the world about whether or not Pavarotti, at fifty-seven, was finished as a singer. He had been given a couple of nasty jolts the previous year when he had been booed during a performance of *Don Carlos* at La Scala for cracking on a climactic high note, and booed again for the same thing at a concert in Düsseldorf. But when I heard him at Lincoln Center that May night, where he was partnered on stage by the soprano Aprile Millo, I wondered what all the doubts were about. The programme of Puccini and Verdi arias may have been designed not to stretch him too far, but he sang almost flawlessly. Whatever his voice might have been like before (and this was the first time I had heard him live, except for once from a great distance and in pouring rain in Hyde Park), it was still beautiful and thrilling.

I also noted at the time that he ought to be cherished for his value as a unique type of megastar. With his vast bulk and his elaborate courtly gestures, he was like a great Edwardian showman. He looked about a hundred years out of date, and yet he was as big a star in the United States of the nineties as any pop singer or Hollywood actor could hope to be. The wonderful thing about him was that he had achieved this status merely by being himself. One couldn't imagine him espousing fashionable causes, wearing the Aids ribbon on his lapel, promoting multiculturalism, or hanging around the Clinton White House in the hope of being taken seriously. And one certainly couldn't imagine him ever having worked out in a gym. What other star would tolerate his weight being freely discussed in public like that of a prize pig? Pavarotti didn't seem to mind a bit.

(But that was then. During my interview with him in Italy in 1997, he said that he always dealt with questions about his weight by singing a couple of lines from 'Nessun dorma'—the song from Puccini's opera Turandot in which Calaf, Turandot's suitor, ponders the grim possibility of execution at dawn if the cruel Chinese princess finds out his name. 'Il mio mistero è chiuso in me / Il nome mio nessuno saprà.' ['My mystery is sealed inside me / Nobody will know my name.'] And then he sang those two lines just for me, changing the word 'nome' ['name'] to 'peso' ['weight'].)

The opera box to which Jayne Wrightsman had brought me turned out to be discreetly filled with celebrities. Nancy Reagan was there. So were Henry and Nancy Kissinger, Barbara Walters, Beverly Sills, and Oscar and Annette de la Renta, who turned out to be footing the bill. After the concert, the Met's leading benefactors assembled for a gala dinner in the upstairs foyer of the opera house, and I was at Mr de la Renta's table with the other members of his party. After a while, Pavarotti appeared before us, seized the fragile Mrs Reagan and crushed her to his vast bosom. Then he threw his arms around Henry Kissinger and held him for a long time in a painful, bear-like embrace. These formalities over, Pavarotti plodded off to a long table full of opera-house workers, stuffed a napkin into his collar, and started tucking in to an enormous place of pasta.

My last farewells to the world of widows were blighted

by illness. On 14 December, three days before I was due to leave New York, I had been invited to a dinner Mrs Wrightsman was giving for Lord and Lady Weidenfeld, the British publisher and his new wife. But she had been rushed into hospital beforehand with a surprisingly well-publicised intestinal blockage, which prompted some crude New Yorkers to suggest that she must, possibly for the first time in her life, have eaten something. And on the very eve of my departure, 16 December, Mrs Astor had caught the flu and so had to cancel a dinner to which she had invited me. Fortunately, both these admirable women were to be restored to perfect health, but only after I was back in London and no longer available to enjoy their hospitality.

Mrs Wrightsman's dinner party was transferred to the de la Rentas' Park Avenue apartment, which boasted an enormous Edward Lear landscape in the hall. The familiar group of guests was augmented on this occasion by Jacqueline Kennedy Onassis, with whom I didn't exchange a word. At the end of dinner, after toasts to the Weidenfelds and to the absent Jayne Wrightsman, Barbara Walters raised her glass to me and asked the company to share in her regret at my imminent departure and to wish me well. Thus did Jackie Kennedy express her sense of loss over the departure of a person she had never met.

CHAPTER 13

Passing the Time

One of my friends in New York was the hat-check girl at Brio, a small Italian family restaurant on Lexington Avenue between 61st and 62nd Streets. I used to go there often for dinner because the food was good and it was only ten minutes' walk from my apartment. Also, I thought it prudent to go regularly to the same restaurant. You got to know the waiters, and they would do their very best to find you a table at short notice. Brio was particularly good at this. It was a very small restaurant, but even when full it could always somehow conjure up a table for any number of people.

The hat-check girl was a pale-skinned black girl whom I will call Rachelle. She was attractive, but big—well over six feet tall. This made her ill-qualified for her job. Hat-check girls should be small, for they normally have to crouch in tiny cubicles stuffed with coats and hats. At Brio, there was no such cubicle, which was fortunate, as Rachelle wouldn't have fitted inside it. Even so, she seemed to take up too much space as she sashayed up and down the aisle between the tables, taking coats from people arriving at the front and delivering them to some place behind a door at the back where they would stay until the customers were ready to leave.

Rachelle became eager to get to know me better when she somehow discovered—maybe I boasted of it—that my daughter Cecilia was a model. It turned out, of course, that she wanted to be a model too. All waiters, waitresses and hat-check girls in New York wanted to be either actors or models. Rachelle quickly became an expert on Cecilia's modelling activities, telling me what magazines and catalogues I would be able to find her picture in. She was hungry for any information about Cecilia's career that might help her fulfil her own modelling ambitions.

Rachelle seemed to me at the time to symbolise the optimism felt by many Americans even in the face of apparently hopeless odds. It never occurred to her that, because of her height, she might not eventually succeed in her ambition. There was a Japanese freelance photographer who had taken pictures of her on beaches in bathing costumes and who she believed might launch her on a modelling career, but that sounded more creepy than encouraging to me. In the meantime, I discovered that being a hat-check girl was not a secure job. When the spring of 1993 came, Rachelle suddenly disappeared from the restaurant. Only then did I realise that hat-check girls are as seasonal as the swallow or the cuckoo, with the difference that their season is the winter. When customers dispense with their coats and hats, restaurants dispense with their hat-check girls.

One day Rachelle mentioned that she had always longed to go to the Metropolitan Opera House, so I said I would take her there. I got tickets to Zeffirelli's sumptuous production of *La Bohème*, mainly because I thought she would like it but also because I was reminded of the film *Moonstruck*, a sentimental comedy about Italian immigrants in Brooklyn which was released in 1987. *Moonstruck* ends with its brooding, working-class hero, Nicolas Cage, introducing his great passion, Cher, to his even greater passion, grand opera, by taking her to *La Bohème* at the Met. Rachelle took the occasion so seriously that she practically missed it. She was so long getting dressed at home in the Bronx that she arrived at Lincoln Center just as the curtain was about to go up, rushing across the deserted piazza in a borrowed black velvet cloak to meet me by the floodlit fountain where Cage and Cher had also met.

She was wildly enthusiastic about the opera, which was

gratifying, and equally enthusiastic about the expensive restaurant I took her to afterwards where she pocketed a dozen books of matches as souvenirs. I asked her about her life. She had spent her childhood in Connecticut, where her father had been in the military and her mother a model, she said. But her parents had separated, and her mother now lived in Hawaii, while she, their daughter, had been reduced to sharing an apartment in the Bronx with her aunt and her grandmother who did nothing, according to her, but nag and exploit her. At college she had studied 'videography', but had been 'bored to death' by it because she had always wanted to be in front of the camera rather than behind it. And now she was a hat-check girl.

As I have just been trying not so subtly to imply, I did not spend all my time in New York in the company of rich widows. I had other friends as well, mostly journalists, several of whom I have mentioned already. At the *New Yorker*, two of my best friends were Alison Rose and Katrina Heron. Alison, a loyal contributor during my difficult early days on 'The Talk of the Town', lived alone with a cat ('Toast') and a lap dog ('Puppy Jane') in a tiny apartment a few blocks away from me on the Upper East Side. She had the aura of a woman with a colourful past who had deliberately chosen to remain single. I didn't know how old she was, and wouldn't have dreamt of asking, but she had on the wall of her little office a large photograph of herself in a Clinique advertisement which was clearly intended to remind visitors—who would not have needed reminding— that she had been a considerable beauty.

She was of slight, almost sylph-like, appearance, and practically always wore black, the colour of her eyes and hair. She was a product of the old *New Yorker*, which she had joined long ago in some insignificant administrative capacity and then, under the tutelage of Harold Brodkey, Garrison Keillor, George Trow and other idols of hers, transformed herself into a writer for the magazine. Her room contained various sentimental relics of the *ancien ré-*

gime, such as half-consumed bottles of vodka and Noilly Prat left over from the days when she and George Trow would give miniature cocktail parties in the office. On the walls there were bulletin boards covered with ancient notes and messages from members of the old gang. She had even preserved a dime given her by Harold Brodkey in payment for a letter she had written him, it having been the practice of her mentors to pay her to write them letters. And while she affected displeasure with almost every change that was made under Tina, she remained materially and emotionally dependent on the *New Yorker*, which she always referred to as 'school'.

Tina, with her dislike of whimsy, might have been expected to take against Alison, but in fact the opposite occurred. Alison's celebrity interviews, in which she would figure almost as prominently as the interviewee, were intimate and revealing in just the way that Tina wanted. (She wrote a particularly good one of the film director James L. Brooks, who became her friend and later rewarded her with a brief appearance as a psychiatric patient in his 1997 Jack Nicholson comedy, *As Good as it Gets*.) And an account Alison later wrote for the *New Yorker* of her own romantic history, giving no quarter to her ex-boyfriends, was received with great enthusiasm by Tina.

But this triumph came after I had left New York. While I was there, Alison contributed frequently to 'The Talk of the Town' and would sit for long periods in my office gossiping about the *New Yorker* or listening to my grievances. While I was blathering away during one of these sessions, Alison's eyes became fixed on the front of my white shirt where a spot of blood had appeared and was rapidly expanding into a large red patch. There being no ready explanation for the bleeding, she decided I must be acquiring the stigmata and called in colleagues to bear witness to this miracle. I was so alarmed that I stripped off my shirt in front of everybody and rushed off to wash the mysterious wound before going home to change. I still don't know what the problem was, but it never occurred again.

Alison would often stop by at my apartment for a drink after work, and sometimes we would go out to dinner after that—usually at Le Relais, my nearest restaurant, at the corner of 63rd Street and Madison Avenue. This was a typical Upper-East-Side French bistro, frequented mainly by elderly Europeans and described in the Zagat Restaurant Guide as 'best for watching the latest advances in plastic surgery'. It had a thin, stooping, sallow-faced *maître d'hôtel* with the French accent and the surliness which are crucial to the success of such establishments. I liked Le Relais nevertheless, and it seemed a good place to take Alison, who was generally out of sympathy with contemporary America and every day would bitterly mourn the vanished elegance of Fifth Avenue.

Katrina Heron was a tall, handsome woman in her thirties who had been one of Tina's editors at *Vanity Fair* before going with her to the *New Yorker*. I liked to imagine that she and I became close because we were both seen as aliens on West 43rd Street—she because she came from the meretricious world of glossy magazines, and I because I came from England. I don't know which provenance was considered worse. As well as being very supportive of me at work, Katrina was eager to show me New York and to ensure that my experience of it wasn't restricted to rich ladies' dinner tables and bourgeois restaurants on the Upper East Side.

Katrina was as modern as Alison was old-fashioned. She made it her mission to acquaint me with the trendy bars and restaurants of downtown Manhattan where she lived. Katrina loved Tina and said she would be eternally grateful to her for having rescued her from the gloom and drabness of the *New York Times Magazine* and brought her to the exciting world of *Vanity Fair*; but she was no happier at the *New Yorker* than she had been at the *Times*. After a while, she married a man whose first name was Winter and moved with him to California. I think this was a sad moment for Tina, who valued her greatly as a friend and as an editor. It would have been a sad moment for me too, if I hadn't already left New York before it happened.

Tina would sometimes invite me to the charity dinners at which the *New Yorker* would buy tables for eight or more people at five hundred to one thousand dollars a plate. One of these, held on 1 February 1993 (which I could tell from my diary was the day on which pheasant and partridge shooting ended in England), was a huge affair for the American fashion-industry awards. It took place in the New York State Theater at Lincoln Center, and sitting one place away from me at dinner was a photographer, David Seidner, who began to complain bitterly about the way in which every American celebrity, from tycoon to teenage model, would wear the red Aids awareness loop on such occasions. He was suffering from Aids, he said, and it made him sick.

As it turned out, this loop of red ribbon was honoured at this very event as the fashion accessory of the year. A Special Award was given for it to Visual Aids, a design group 'devoted to increasing awareness and promoting action to end the social and health crisis, Aids'. Seidner was so angry about this that I asked him if he would like to express his feelings in a piece for 'The Talk of the Town'. In this he wrote of his 'rage at the trivialisation of this catastrophe into a Special Award at a glittering event full of red ribbons and gleaming white teeth'. The loop had been beneficial in one respect, he admitted. Designer versions of it in rhinestones or garnets or solid gold—and even one in diamond-*pavé*—had been sold at auctions to raise money for Aids care and research. But the ribbon's main function, he said, was 'to make people feel comfortable without having to do anything'.

Another way of spending the evening was to go to a private film screening in a Manhattan cinema. All film screenings appeared to be controlled by a powerful public relations woman called Peggy Segal who sent out press invitations with long lists, as bait, of celebrities who had promised to attend. Although most of the celebrities usually didn't turn up, lots of photographers always did, giving even the dullest event some of the trappings of a great occasion. I would occasionally go to screenings, but usually preferred to watch films on television. I became a great devotee of the cable channel American Movie Classics. I was seldom happier than alone at night on my enormous bed, watching Ginger Rogers and Fred Astaire on my gigantic television set.

Rogers, then eighty-one years old, had belatedly received one of the annual Kennedy Center Honors in Washington DC. The ceremony was broadcast on television at the end of December 1992, but it was a sadly inadequate affair because it included no film clips or still photographs of Ginger and Fred together. Robyn Astaire, Fred's widow, had refused to give the Kennedy Center permission to use them. Jealousy seems to have been the motive, although Fred had been dead for quite a while and the last of the ten movies he made with Ginger had been released almost half a century earlier. 'The Talk of the Town' rose to Ginger's defence and informed Mrs Astaire that her decision 'would discredit her husband's memory and sour the spirit of the Kennedy Center Honors' which Astaire himself had been among the first to receive.

One day my television set went blank, and I called the cable company. An engineer discovered that the cable terminal on the roof didn't have enough sockets to accommodate the cables from all the sets in the building, and that another tenant had unplugged my cable from its socket and replaced it with his own. There followed an exhausting battle of wills between myself and this unidentified person as we took it in turns to climb up a ladder on to the roof to change the cables around. The contest continued until the terminal was replaced with a new one, and the problem resolved.

In New York I went to many more films and plays and concerts than I had ever done in London because the wonderful compactness of Manhattan made it so easy getting to them. Thanks to the *New Yorker*'s generosity with expenses, I also went to many more restaurants. With my beautiful friend Lynn Wagenknecht, however, I was never allowed to pay. She was the owner of two fashionable bistros—the Odéon in TriBeCa and the Café Luxembourg on the Upper West Side, close to Lincoln Center—and when we went out in the evenings together, we would nearly always go to one of them.

As a young woman, Lynn had left the Midwest, as Midwesterners do, to come to New York, where she had found a job as a waitress in a restaurant employing two young fortune-seekers from London, Brian McNally and his older brother Keith. The three of them had become friends and, as I imagine it, one of them had said to the others in true Hollywood-movie style, 'I know, I've had a *great* idea. Why don't we start our *own* restaurant?' In any case, they not only started the Odéon, but Lynn and Keith fell in love, got married, and had three children. Later, they started the Café Luxembourg and, with their Australian friend Nell Campbell, a nightclub called Nell's down on West 14th Street.

Nell's was a very fashionable nightclub in the eighties, and I was taken there a few times by Taki long before I met Lynn in 1993 at a dinner in his house in New York. By then, Nell's had ceased to be so fashionable, but was doing good business all the same. Well-intentioned efforts by Lynn and her colleagues to attract blacks to the place had been so successful that blacks had replaced whites as the large majority of its customers.

In the meantime, Lynn and Keith had separated, and she had dropped the surname McNally in favour of Wagenknecht, her unpronounceable maiden name. Alone at forty, Lynn was managing the restaurant and nightclub business and bringing up three children at the same time. Some people said she was tougher than she looked; and I expect they

were right, because she didn't look tough at all. To me she
came to represent a model of a certain kind of admirable
American woman—capable, independent, and self-
disciplined, but also modest, unassuming, and kind.

Julia Reed, whom I had got to know in Washington DC in
the eighties, had remained a good friend ever since. She had
a habit of storming in and out of my life at unexpected
moments and lying doggo for great stretches in between. In
fact, my relations with several American friends have been
of this nature. They often don't return telephone calls or e-
mail messages, but I try not to be offended by this. I hope
it is a sign of their confidence in the strength of their friendships that they are willing to leave them untended for long
periods of time.

American effusiveness on first acquaintance can be another source of misunderstanding. At a party given by Drue
Heinz, I was befriended with great enthusiasm by the writer
George Plimpton, a charming and cultivated man, who
spent most of the evening talking only to me. He was full
of warm solicitude for my welfare and bubbled with ideas
for 'The Talk of the Town'. I was greatly flattered and
thought I had made an important social conquest. I could
even imagine us becoming regular lunching partners at the
Century club. But then the moment of departure came, and
Plimpton took his leave of me with the words: 'I hope our
paths may cross again one day.' I was mortified.

In Washington, Julia Reed had been working as a reporter for the *US News and World Report* at the start of a
brilliant journalistic career. At that time, she was only in
her mid-twenties, but was renting a very grown-up apartment in Georgetown with silver candlesticks and family
portraits in it. Julia is a Southerner from Greenville, Mis-
sissippi, with a well-established Republican family and pronounced conservative views. But she also has a strong
anarchic streak, which may explain why she once nearly
married a divorced, middle-aged Australian socialist with a

beard. I could not, however, have asked for a more loyal, clever and entertaining friend. I am crazy about her and always will be.

Julia was, in effect, the leader of a gang of Southern belles, including fellow ex-students of the Madeira School for Girls. Madeira, a private boarding-school near Washington in the Virginia countryside, was founded in 1906 by a high-minded schoolteacher called Lucy Madeira. Julia's headmistress there was Jean Harris, who in 1980 shot dead her lover, Dr Herman Tarnower, after he left her for a younger woman. Jean Harris's trial aroused huge world-wide interest, mainly because the victim of the murder, Dr Tarnower, was the author of *The Scarsdale Diet*, a best-selling slimming guide which Susanna and I once attempted to follow. It also earned Julia her first by-line, in *Newsweek*.

By the time I came to work in New York, Julia was a staff feature writer for American *Vogue* and living mainly in New Orleans, where she was working on a book about the South. But she also had a flat on the Upper East Side and was frequently popping in and out of New York, where I would often dine with her at Elaine's and listen to her torrents of politically incorrect talk on the matters of the moment. One of her obsessions in 1993 was the hounding of Senator Bob Packwood of Oregon by a large group of women who claimed to have been kissed, touched or otherwise sexually harassed by him over the previous couple of decades. They had improbably ganged together as 'the Packwood Twenty-six' and organised banquets in Washington to raise money for their legal expenses. Julia was withering in her contempt for them and warm in her sympathy for the poor Republican Senator, who generally supported women's issues and had never tried to force himself on any woman who had rejected his advances. Packwood defended himself as best he could, but would be forced in the end to resign his Senate seat.

Another of Julia's hate figures was Bill Clinton, who early in his first term had already run into all kinds of trouble—

over charges of adultery to ones of financial impropriety; over his pledge to let homosexuals into the armed forces; over the habits of his Cabinet nominees of employing illegal immigrants as servants. His friend and White House legal adviser, Vincent Foster, had also gone and shot himself in a Washington park. Julia's fury with Mr Clinton was exacerbated by her despairing conviction that whatever he did wrong, he would be bound to get away with it. How right she proved to be!

Julia Reed saw it as one of her functions to provide me with authentic American experiences. One summer, she persuaded me to fly down to Nashville, Tennessee, for the annual Swan Ball, the city's most important social event for which white tie and tails were the obligatory male uniform. Her mother's family were from Nashville, and the Reeds were therefore recognised by Nashville society, which was why she was permitted to bring guests to this exclusive affair. Four years later, in 1997, Julia was to invite me to the Swan Ball again, and I went for the second and probably the last time—for an account of it I wrote for the *Guardian* in London was reported to have given considerable offence:

You probably think that the most important people in Nashville, Tennessee, are country music people . . . But you are wrong. The most important people in Nashville are the people who live in the grand mansions of Belle Meade, a leafy paradise which would be called an 'exclusive suburb' if it didn't happen to be eccentrically situated right in the heart of the city. The people in Belle Meade are very rich. Most of them are much richer than any of the country music millionaires. And their money is old money, so old that some of them cannot even remember where it came from. This is known as being 'rich for ever'.

One Nashville woman who is 'rich for ever' recently bought herself a colossal stretch limousine. A horrified friend asked her why she had done such a tasteless thing. 'Well,' she replied, 'I'm a big girl, and big girls should have big cars. And anyway, it's much more fun being *nouveau* than being rich for ever.' But most members of Nashville high society associate stretch limos with country music stars and therefore wouldn't be seen dead in them.

Their two main preoccupations are spending money and being exclusive. Their houses contain large quantities of excellent china and silver, most of which is kept on display. The women possess jewellery so spectacular that it wouldn't look out of place in the Tower of London. They travel a great deal, sometimes on shopping trips to New York or London, sometimes on exotic holidays. Britain is a favourite destination, and within Britain, the Cotswolds. I suspect they have a visceral feeling that dear little Britain is somehow in itself as exclusive as the Belle Meade Country Club. This is probably because Britain— the way they experience it, at any rate—is fantastically expensive, even if it doesn't quite cost half a million dollars to join, as the Country Club does.

Their yearning for exclusivity climaxes each year in the Swan Ball, the most lavish and most revered social event of the South. This is a charity ball started in 1963 to raise money for the art collection and botanical garden of a Belle Meade mansion called Cheekwood, which was donated to the city by its former owners, the Cheeks. But the importance of Cheekwood and its uninspiring art collection is massively overshadowed by the importance of the ball itself, of which the *New York Times* accurately wrote this week: 'It is hard to overstate what the Swan Ball means to Nashville society.'

Every year one Nashville woman is selected to be chairman of the ball. This is usually the most important moment in her life, after which she will be able to die happy and fulfilled. If she messed it up, she would presumably have to leave town or kill herself, but nobody has ever messed it up. This year's chairman was a nice and enthusiastic lady called Carol Sergent who, despite the different spelling of her name, claims a family connection to the painter, John Singer Sargent. Every Swan Ball chairman does her best to leave her mark on Nashville social history, but none has ever succeeded as well as Mrs Sergent has. For she took a momentous decision which will remain the talk of Nashville for years to come: she invited a substantial number of blacks.

There is some disagreement about how historic this decision was. Mrs Sergent herself claims that blacks have never been excluded from the Swan Ball, but nobody can remember more than one or two token blacks ever attending it in the past. Last Saturday, by contrast, there were about thirty blacks among the 900 guests—a small but visible presence. It was sufficient to attract the attention of the mighty *New York Times*, which sent a reporter to the ball and published his account of it under the headline 'Diversity Makes a Debut at High-Society Party'.

Nashville is whiter than many Southern cities, with blacks forming only 23 per cent of its population. But they include some of its most prominent citizens, among them doctors, professors and college presidents. According to Mrs Sergent, black community leaders have been invited to the Swan Ball in the past but have usually declined. This time the invitations were followed up by telephone calls begging them to attend, and quite a few did.

It was good of them to come, for attendance at the Swan Ball is no light undertaking. It costs $500 per person, and male guests have to get themselves kitted out in white tie and tails. Given that the vast majority of the Swan Ball guests are rich whites who have little regular contact with blacks except as servants, one wouldn't expect blacks to feel particularly comfortable there. But they received a lot of polite attention and seemed to be pleased about that.

Some white guests were privately questioning the wisdom of this calculated integration, but only one went on the record. This was the husband of the ball's founder, a ninety-year-old former American ambassador whose face has been so devastated by cosmetic surgery that it somehow resembles that of the burnt Ralph Fiennes in the film *The English Patient*. 'I'm not exactly sold on it,' he told the *New York Times* reporter. 'I'm not against it, but I just don't see any particular point in it. With only a few of them [blacks] here, I would think they would feel they're at the wrong place. I'd feel at the wrong place at their parties.'

Nevertheless, the reporter concluded in his article that the presence of a handful of blacks at this year's Swan Ball represented 'another halting step on the road to a new South'. He might have found it harder to arrive at that meaningless conclusion if he had attended one or two of the other social events which took place in Nashville during the run-up to the Swan Ball. The night before the ball there was a black-tie 'dinner dance'—a pre-ball ball, in effect—in honour of the chairman, at which all the guests were white and all the waiters black.

This racial pattern was repeated next day at 'The Swan Ball Luncheon', with the small difference that one of the waiters was white and came from Bury in Lancashire. This dainty luncheon (*la soupe de carottes et noix en croûte, artichauts avec salade de crevettes, charlotte russe au citron*) was held alfresco at Hunters Hill, a neo-Gothic baronial castle belonging to the extremely 'for ever rich' Mr Harold Henry Stream III, known to his friends as Spook Stream because he was born on Hallowe'en.

Present there, as everywhere else, were a reporter and female photographer from the society magazine *Town and Country* who spookily reminded me of Frank Sinatra and Celeste Holm in those roles in the film *High Society*—the main difference being that the *Town and Country* reporter was treated with ridiculous deference by the

Nashville toffs and looked, unlike Frank Sinatra, as if he would have no objection to being a millionaire. I thought no journalist could ever have been so fawned over until I witnessed the treatment meted out to the *New York Times* reporter, who was almost subjected to sexual abuse by some of the Nashville women. It is strange how people can pursue both exclusivity and publicity with equal fervour.

It was a swell party all right, and—in the self-congratulatory words of the Swan Ball programme—'a magical time' for everyone (except, that is, for some hundreds of rich white Tennesseeans bristling at home with indignation that blacks had been invited and they had not). Also missing were any of the aristocrats listed as members of the ball's International Committee, such as the Duchess of Marlborough and the Countess of Wilton (not to mention HRH Princess Maria Pia de Savoie and HH The Rajmata of Jaipur).

A lot of money must have been raised for Cheekwood from the proceeds of an auction which was held after the sit-down dinner for 900 people in a vast marquee on the lawn. I thought of bidding for a private aeroplane which seemed very reasonably priced at $22,000, but this then turned out to be the price not of the plane itself but of a single flight in it. Well, did you evah?

An amusing diversion towards the end of my time in New York was a visit there in November 1993 by Terry Major-Ball, the elder brother of John Major, the then British Prime Minister. Terry, a sixty-year-old former electrical-goods salesman from Croydon, south London, then unemployed, had captured the imagination of the British Press as the archetypal English suburban man. The narrowness of his horizons—he had never left the country except to go to Germany on military service and he had never flown in an airplane—reinforced the image of 'greyness' which journalists and cartoonists had attached to his younger brother

John. Yet, in reality, their family background was the opposite of grey.

Their grandfather, Abraham Ball, had emigrated to the United States from the English Midlands in the eighteen-eighties and found a job building blast furnaces for the Andrew Carnegie Steel Works in Pittsburgh, Pennsylvania. His son, their father, Tom Major-Ball, was a circus clown and trapeze artist in America before returning with his parents to England in the eighteen-nineties and embarking on a career in music hall (Major was his stage name, which he eventually combined with Ball). Then, in the thirties, having retired from show business, he settled down in south London and set up a little company manufacturing garden ornaments, especially gnomes. But after the Second World War the gnome business failed, and the family was reduced to living in poverty in two rented rooms in Brixton.

When it emerged in 1993 that Terry had never been in an aeroplane (nor even visited an 'aerodrome', as he quaintly put it), the London *Evening Standard* offered to fly him to America where his father had grown up. But since there were no records in Pittsburgh to show where the Major family had lived or, indeed, that they had lived there at all, it was decided it would be more fun—and a better newspaper story—to take this blinkered English suburban man to the ultimate cosmopolitan metropolis, New York. The joke was that the journalist accompanying him there from London, James Hughes-Onslow, an old friend of mine, had never been to New York either; and he telephoned ahead to ask if I could help show him and Terry around. So we arranged to meet at the Westbury Hotel on Madison Avenue the morning after their arrival.

When I saw Terry for the first time at the Westbury the next morning (after a flight on which he had noted that 'the inside of the first-class compartment looked remarkably like the InterCity trains I have seen at Victoria Station, spacious and comfortable-looking, not that I have ever been on an

InterCity train—yet') he could have been a distinguished Wall Street banker in his dark suit and tie, but his conversation was entirely about his electric razor which had failed to work on American current because he had brought with him a faulty adaptor. The problem had baffled a hotel engineer, but he had subsequently managed to repair the adaptor himself with a nail file, he announced proudly.

An *Evening Standard* photographer accompanied us into Central Park to take pictures of Terry pretending to read the *New York Times* while seated on a slab of Manhattan schist with the towers of Central Park South in the background. There followed a walk down Fifth Avenue during which he said that he had so far noticed only one difference between New York and London, and this was the instruction 'Walk' or 'Don't Walk' at street crossings. 'We don't have that in London,' he explained. If James had been hoping, for the purposes of his article, that Terry would be awed by New York, he was out of luck, for the man was fearless. When Terry started to address a couple of heavily armed policemen in front of Grand Central Station, I moved away out of embarrassment. But I could see that the policemen were smiling happily as this extraordinary alien chatted away with them and opened up their jackets without their permission to look at their hidden radios and batons. When I enquired afterwards how the conversation had gone, Terry said he had asked them whether New York police stations were as messy as they appeared in films on British television. Remarkably, they had taken the question seriously and debated between themselves which New York precinct had the tidiest station. On another occasion, when I wasn't with him, Terry had put his head down a manhole to discuss with some electricians his favourite subject. 'They were very interested to know how the underground electrical system works in Croydon,' he reported.

On their first evening in New York, I took James and Terry to *Guys and Dolls* at the Martin Beck Theater—a production I saw five times before leaving New York—and afterwards to supper at Joe Allen on West 46th Street, where Liza Minnelli, with a couple of male companions, arrived soon afterwards and sat down at the table next to us. James saw this as a perfect photo opportunity, but I forced him to put his camera back in his pocket, for by now my embarrassment had become ingrained. But he sidled up to her all the same and asked her if she would be willing to have a few words with the British Prime Minister's brother as she left the restaurant. When that moment arrived, Liza Minnelli came over to our table and, while Terry rose to his feet, grasped his right hand with both of hers and gave him one of those all-embracing superstar smiles. But the smile faded just a little as Terry said to her, 'I thought you would like to know that I have always been a great admirer of your mother.'

Terry's experiences in New York confirmed my long-held belief that New Yorkers, contrary to their reputation, are generally very polite to strangers. The only bit of rudeness he encountered—though I don't believe it was intended to be rude—came from the British Editor of the *New Yorker*. After a visit to the New York Public Library, where staff showed astonishing patience as Terry told them the full, unabridged history of his family, we went across the road to the magazine after I had alerted Chip McGrath, now book review editor of the *New York Times*, that we were on our way. Chip greeted us in the public area known as the 'piazza' around which the top editorial executives had their offices, and was gradually joined by other passing editors who sensed that something unusual was going on. Terry had finished describing a helicopter ride he had taken around Manhattan and was back on to the subject of his father when a brisk clicking noise in the corridor heralded the arrival of Tina Brown.

Tina was on her way past us to her office when I beckoned her over, saying, 'Tina, we have the Prime Minister's brother here,' and she quickly changed direction and put on a special smile. But when Terry started to address her, she showed signs of unease. Then suddenly she detached herself and said out loud—though to nobody in particular and as if she were talking to herself—'You never know what you're going to bump into in the office these days.' 'I hope that's not supposed to be a disparaging remark, young lady,' Terry exclaimed, as she vanished through the door of her office.

I was later told that this incident had created more happiness at the *New Yorker* than anything for a very long time. Chip McGrath was said to have been so affected by it that he collapsed to the floor and had to crawl back to his desk.

CHAPTER 14

The Fourth Estate

There was a letter waiting for me at the *New Yorker* when I first arrived from London. It was from the Graduate School of Journalism of Columbia University inviting me to take part in a public forum there. This was an annual event named 'The Delacorte Forum' after its financial sponsor, and its theme this year was to be 'The British Are Coming'—this having been Paul Revere's warning on his midnight ride through Massachusetts in 1775, but used here to denote the contemporary occupation by British journalists of many top American magazine and newspaper jobs. A panel of four British editors working on American publications were to discuss the causes and implications of this phenomenon with an audience of American journalists and journalism students. As well as myself, the panel was to include the British Editors of two leading American political weeklies, John O'Sullivan of the *National Review* and Andrew Sullivan of the *New Republic*, and the Editor of the mass circulation *TV Guide*, Anthea Disney (subsequently to be the supremo of HarperCollins, Rupert Murdoch's publishing company).

The forum was to take place on 24 February 1993, almost four months away, and I decided I would attend it. I didn't know whether Humbert Wolfe's famous pre-war couplet about the British journalist was familiar to Americans, but I thought it probably represented their current sentiments quite well:

SOME TIMES IN AMERICA

You cannot hope
to bribe or twist,
thank God! the
British journalist.
But, seeing what
the man will do
unbribed, there's
no occasion to.

I imagined it could be fun to make American flesh creep with tales of dark journalistic practices on the other side of the Atlantic. So I replied to the Columbia School of Journalism, accepting its invitation.

At the time, it did not occur to me to consult anybody about this, since I assumed it to be nobody's business but my own. And after mailing my acceptance, I forgot all about the forum until well into February when suddenly I noticed in my diary that it was due to take place in a couple of weeks' time. This rang an alarm bell in my brain, for I had come to realise by then that one of the *New Yorker*'s greatest preoccupations was its own media image; and I feared that Tina might regard my participation with some concern. The *New York Times* had still to give its anxiously awaited verdict on her editorship. Maurie Perl, her PR adviser, was on permanent red alert. And I, over the previous few months, had been involved in some distressing episodes.

I have already discussed the Honecker episode, but there had been lesser embarrassments too, such as one in which I was strongly criticised for defending the novelist Salman Rushdie against the magazine *Esquire*, after it had published a derogatory article about him. But here I will only discuss my rash provocation of Michael Kramer, the chief political correspondent of *Time* magazine. I had drawn attention in 'The Talk of the Town' to a little case of suspected plagiarism involving Mr Kramer. In a column on the eve of the presidential election, in which he had urged people not to abuse the two-party system by voting for the populist third candidate, Ross Perot, Mr Kramer had concluded: 'Remember that in a democratic republic, a citizen discharges his duty not by making a vindictive gesture but by voting as if the outcome depended on his vote alone. It's just that simple.'

A couple of weeks earlier, the *Los Angeles Times* had published an article with the same message, jointly written by two Harvard Law School professors—Alan Dershowitz, a Clinton supporter, and Charles Fried, a supporter of Bush. This had been the last sentence of *their* article: 'Remember, a voter discharges his or her duty as a participant in a democratic republic not by making a vindictive gesture or hoping to effect some far-fetched strategy, but by voting as if the outcome depended on his or her vote alone.' It was just that simple.

Professor Fried, who had once been in a Ronald Reagan administration as Solicitor-General, demanded that *Time* apologise publicly for stealing his rather ponderous sentence, but he received only a personal letter from Mr Kramer declaring himself 'devastated' and 'profoundly embarrassed' by what had happened, but denying plagiarism. 'Your felicitous phrase clearly stuck in my mind,' he wrote. 'I should have realised when I "wrote" it that it was too well put to have sprung from me unassisted.' I think it was the Uriah Heep-ish tone of this last sentence that made me want to get at Mr Kramer.

But I would have been wiser to have ignored the whole thing, for someone was bound to try to get at me in return. The counter-attack came eventually from *New York* magazine, which suggested that I was a plagiarist too, because, it claimed, a piece I had written in 1986 for the first issue of the *Independent*, when I was starting out as its Washington correspondent, had been lifted straight out of the *New York Times*. The piece in question told the touching story of an unemployed twenty-two-year-old called Bob Redman who had built himself a series of thirteen elaborate tree-houses in Central Park and camouflaged them so well that whenever the Parks Enforcement Patrol found one of them, he had already moved into another. When they finally did catch him and dismantled his last five-room, tree-top penthouse, they were so impressed by his tree-climbing ability that he was given a job as a professional pruner by the Central Park Conservancy.

An anxious Maurice Perl pressed me to produce evidence that would clear my name of this charge of plagiarism, but I told her that, since I had been heavily reliant on the American Press at the beginning of my time in Washington, when the *Independent* didn't yet even have an office, I probably *had* lifted the story from the *New York Times*. Still, I asked the *Independent* to fax me from London a copy of this ancient article and found somewhat to my surprise that I had in fact honourably credited the *New York Times* as my source.

New York magazine had been less honourable. Its item accusing me of plagiarism had been lifted without attribution from the British satirical magazine *Private Eye*, which in turn had reprinted without attribution to itself a story it had first run seven years earlier. The source of that original story had inadvertently been me, for I had modestly deflected compliments about my tree-house article by saying that all the credit for it, if credit were due, belonged to the *New York Times*. It was just a typical case of journalists running round in circles, snapping at each other's behinds.

Reflecting on the general delicacy of the situation, I decided to trot along to Maurie Perl's office and tell her about my plan to attend the forum at Columbia University. When I did so, she stiffened, went white, and said, 'Please, go back to your desk. Don't move from there. I am going to see Tina.' A few minutes later the telephone rang. It was Tina in sergeant-major mode on the other end of the line. 'Will you come up to my office immediately,' she said. When I got to her office, she was on her feet, pacing about. 'Alexander,' she said, '*you* don't need this, the *New Yorker* doesn't need this, *I* don't need this. You really shouldn't do it. They'll make mincemeat of you.'

I said I was sorry she felt that way, because I was rather looking forward to the forum. I had had what I considered to be some rather unjust and patronising things written about me since I came to New York, and I would have welcomed an opportunity to refute them. I didn't believe anyone would make mincemeat of me. I even thought it possible that I might acquit myself with dignity. I should emphasise that Tina never went so far as to order me not to take part in the forum, but she was unshakeable in her conviction that my doing so would be a public relations catastrophe.

Soon she was discussing what I might do to pull out of it at this late stage without causing offence to the Columbia Journalism School. I was more worried that, if I did pull out, everyone would suspect me of cowardice. Tina proposed that I should pretend to be ill, but I told her I couldn't possibly do that. Lots of people at the *New Yorker* would know that I wasn't really ill, and some of them would be certain to disseminate this knowledge widely. To use illness as an excuse, I said, would be to court humiliation.

Then Tina had a brainwave. 'I know what!' she said. 'I could send you to London for a day or two. You like London, don't you?' I said, 'Yes, I like London. But this would not be the ideal moment for me to go there. My wife and daughter and son-in-law are arriving in New York to visit me on the day that the forum is being held, and I think they would be surprised to discover that I was in London instead of here.' 'Oh, I see. What about Washington, then? I could send you to Washington.' 'I think they would be fairly surprised by that as well.' I left her saying that I would think hard about what she had said and report back later.

I still thought that I should disregard her opinion and attend the forum; but when I consulted one or two of my friends and allies on the *New Yorker*, they tended, rather to my surprise, to support her point of view. They did so, it seemed, for the best of motives, for they wanted to spare me embarrassment; but I still felt a little hurt that nobody seemed to believe I was capable of standing up for myself. After a bit, I gave in. With all the tension in the air, the forum was beginning to seem less and less like fun. Then I was suddenly given plausible grounds for backing out. I was told that the deadline for 'The Talk of the Town' was to be brought forward by a day, which would, in truth, have made my participation difficult (though not impossible).

I told Tina I was willing to use the new deadline as an excuse for not taking part, and she was delighted. Then she said that, before calling the organisers, I ought to find someone to take my place on the panel. 'Believe me, they never mind you cancelling, so long as you have found someone to replace you,' she explained. I immediately thought of the British journalist Christopher Hitchens in Washington. He appeared often on television and had columns in both *Vanity Fair* and the left-wing political weekly the *Nation*. He was also a most clever and entertaining man and, unlike me, an excellent debater. The Delacorte Forum would not know its luck.

Christopher immediately agreed to come in my place, provided that the *New Yorker* paid his return fare from Washington and put him up in a hotel. I told him this would not be a problem. Then I telephoned Osborn Elliott, a former editor of *Newsweek* who was Professor of Magazine Journalism at the School, to say I would not, alas, be able to attend. He sounded quite frosty at first, but, as Tina had predicted, began to melt when I told him that I had already lined up a substitute. He asked for biographical details of Mr Hitchens. I told him what I could, but forgot to say that Christopher was especially well qualified for this particular debate because he had written a book about the Anglo-American relationship, *Blood, Class, and Nostalgia*. This is an interesting book which suggests, in an analysis of the 'special relationship', that the United States in the twentieth century turned to Britain, its former colonial master, to provide the 'class' and the 'tone' with which to dignify its own imperial ambitions, thus also permitting the British in their much reduced circumstances to fantasise that they too still enjoyed an imperial role.

On the day before the forum, Harold Evans telephoned me to say that he was going to be on the panel too, and that he looked forward to seeing me there. Harry had been called in to replace Andrew Sullivan of the *New Republic*, who had pleaded flu; but he clearly had no idea that I had pulled out as well. It seemed curious to me that his wife, Tina, had not mentioned this to him after all the fuss that had gone on beforehand, unless (though this would have been hardly less curious) he had failed to mention to her that he was going to join the panel.

The report of the forum which appeared subsequently in the *New York Times* contained a sceptical reference to my absence, clearly implying that my deadline excuse was phoney. But I couldn't complain about that, for phoney was what it had been. Later the Columbia Journalism School sent me a full transcript of the debate, which turned out to have been a rather lame and muddled affair.

The scene was set by Suzanne Levine, editor of the *Columbia Journalism Review*, who pointed out that the *New Yorker*, *Vogue*, *Harper's Bazaar*, the *New Republic*, *TV Guide*, and the *National Review* were all now edited by Britons. Ms Levine (who had spent seventeen years editing *Ms* magazine before coming to Columbia) began by implying that British journalists owed most of their success in America to their accents. 'There is something about the British accent that we all feel is associated with class, and style, and elegance, and historic value,' she said. 'I think that is what generally comes up whenever people try and figure out what is the appeal of the British editors in the journalistic community.' It would be hard to think of anything more insulting to say to the British panelists—or, for that matter, to their American employers—than that they owed their positions in American journalism to their accents. But Ms Levine was effectively presenting the case for the prosecution.

'Along with class,' she went on, 'they have been accused

of bringing trash: a kind of journalism that is characterised by an intense newsstand imperative, as opposed to American publications—magazines which are subscription-supported. They are obsessed with celebrities, scandal, glitz, and gossip.' (On reading that, I thought how fortunate it was for Tina that Harry had been on the panel. It was against Tina that this charge was usually made, but she was unlikely to be abused while her husband was present.)

'They also bring a certain energy,' continued Ms Levine. 'Some say recklessness. Maybe this is because they are so exhilarated by a lot of the freedoms they find here that were not available to the Press in Britain.' If those words, despite the charge of 'recklessness', for a moment sounded almost complimentary, she quickly made up for it as follows: 'But the British group has also been accused of bringing with it a virus from British journalism, which is called "Fleet Street Ethics". These are the phrases given to me by a critic who will remain nameless: sucking up to advertisers, carrying water for friends, and taking revenge on enemies. John le Carré has called it English standards of malice and English standards of inaccuracy.'

Perhaps out of good manners, or just inhibition, the panelists did not choose to deal head-on with this analysis of British journalism, made all the more surprising in its superficiality and ignorance by the fact that its author was the Editor of a celebrated journalism review. I felt quite sorry for Harry Evans when Ms Levine introduced him to the audience as a man whose principal claim to fame was that he had 'created a whole new kind of travel journalism' when he founded the *Condé Nast Traveler*, but credited him, wrongly, with having been merely 'chairman' of the London *Sunday Times*. In fact, that newspaper under his fourteen-year editorship had been acclaimed, not only in Britain but also in America, as possibly the finest investigative paper in the world.

Harry Evans opened the forum by comparing the blandness and uniformity of the American Press with the far greater diversity of the British. 'The British Press ranges from the worst examples you could possibly imagine in the world of the printed word being abused, to relatively high degrees of sainthood,' he said. Rather surprisingly, he even suggested that British journalists were generally speaking more truthful than American ones. He said that America's lack of an effective libel law had 'allowed very sloppy journalism'. 'There's a great deal of malice in American journalism, where facts are printed which are not even remotely within a million miles of the truth,' he added. 'So I think that the tough law of libel under which we laboured in England makes the British journalist arriving here much more willing to work hard to get the facts.' Harry said, nevertheless, that the United States was 'the ideal place in which to practise journalism' because the openness of American society made access to information much easier than in Britain.

Three years later, when under attack in the American newspapers for importing 'Fleet Street ethics' into American publishing by giving a multi-million-dollar advance to the former White House election strategist, Dick Morris, who had shared presidential confidences with a prostitute, Harry lashed out at American 'sanctimoniousness' and said in a British newspaper interview, 'England and France are much freer in this regard.' ('More tolerant' is perhaps what he meant.)

And a year after that, when he announced at the age of sixty-nine that he was leaving publishing to return to journalism as editorial supremo of Mort Zuckerman's press empire, which included *US News and World Report* and the *New York Daily News*, he lashed out once again at the American Press for its untruthfulness, particularly insofar as it had suggested that his departure from Random House after eight years as its president might not have been wholly voluntary. I sometimes wondered whether Tina's constant burnishing of her own public image and sharp reaction to criticism could have been attributes that she had picked up from her husband.

When the panelists at the Delacorte Forum were asked to comment on Tina's new *New Yorker*, Harry, of course, refused to do so, but the others praised its liveliness and topicality. None of them accused her of lowering its standards, glitzing it up, or recruiting it to the cult of celebrity. And I was pleased to note that none of the controversies affecting 'The Talk of the Town', which had loomed so large on 43rd Street and had caused Tina to predict I would be reduced to mincemeat, were mentioned at all during the debate.

After a discussion of various possible explanations for British pre-eminence in New York journalism—the unique skills of the British tabloid journalist, the natural drift from a cultural province like Britain to the cultural metropolis of the Anglo-Saxon world, or (the explanation put forward by John O'Sullivan and to me the most plausible) mere coincidence—the subject of 'class' made its final grand appearance. A *New York Times* journalist called Mike Kaufman asked the panel to comment on his theory that American publishers chose British editors to improve the demographic profiles of their magazines.

'I love the metaphor of the butler,' Mr Kaufman said. 'At a time when magazines are shaping their audiences, where we don't want mass circulation but we want quality circulation, where we want thirty-three-year-olds with five buttons on their sleeves to read our magazines, is it possible that publishers understand that who better can lure a particular kind of readership than people who were raised in a culture where you can identify those who are let in . . . Is there not a market factor involved here that would explain, to some extent, how publishers could think to themselves— and act upon their thoughts—that Brits, better than us, know how to keep people out? And that may be the role of publishing these days: to keep the wrong kind of people from reading your publication so that you can tell the advertisers that only the right kind of people do.'

The proposition was obviously too far-fetched to be taken seriously, but it gave Christopher Hitchens the chance to confirm 'that subliminally class [in America] means Englishness, and it's been market-tested and road-tested and found to work'. He also made the point that 'you can be proudly a Greek-American, Polish-American, Italian-American, and now an African-American, but there's no such thing as an English-American'. That is quite true. The British are the only people in the whole world who can never be accepted as Americans. They may, like Anna Wintour or Anthea Disney, have American citizenship, but they will always be regarded as British. Even Alistair Cooke, after sixty years in the United States, is still valued there for his Englishness and remembered mainly as the authority on English manners and customs who for twenty-two years introduced BBC costume dramas on *Masterpiece Theatre*, the cult television programme.

It was on the day before the Delacorte Forum that the Public Boadcasting Service announced that Alistair Cooke was finally standing down as the host of *Masterpiece Theatre* and would be replaced by Russell Baker, the celebrated writer of humorous columns in the *New York Times*. Mr Baker, then aged sixty-seven, held a news conference at the Helmsley Palace Hotel which I covered for 'The Talk of the Town'. When a reporter suggested that his newspaper column revealed him as 'quintessentially American', and therefore perhaps ill-suited to step into Mr Cooke's shoes, Mr Baker replied, 'I demur from the suggestion that I'm a quintessential American—a quintessential WASP, perhaps.'

In a *New York Times* column a few weeks earlier, mocking the jargon of the age, he had defined himself in greater detail as 'a genderly enlightened, Celt-sensitive, politically unpredictable, comparatively financially disadvantaged, square, married, heterosexual, comb-carrying, hearing-impaired,

Depression-generation, male European-American'. Of his fitness to replace Mr Cooke, this is what I wrote in 'The Talk of the Town':

> Mr Baker's hair is not smooth and silky, like Mr Cooke's, but it is almost as silvery and, in its unruliness, certainly more British-looking. As an interpreter of British culture to an American audience, Mr Baker can also claim the qualification of having lived in Britain more recently than his predecessor, for Mr Cooke, although he is of British birth, has lived in the United States since the thirties, whereas Mr Baker was the London correspondent of the *Baltimore Sun* in the early fifties, when he covered the Coronation of Queen Elizabeth II and wrote a weekly feature for his American readers called 'Window on Fleet Street'.

In other words, there isn't anything to choose between the 'stage Englishman' (as Mr Baker called Mr Cooke) and 'the quintessential WASP'. To most Americans they are the same thing: the lucky possessors of that indefinable asset called 'class'. As Christopher Hitchens pointed out in the debate, 'class' is the key to it all and explains why someone like Bill Buckley, an Irish Roman Catholic, would be unhesitatingly categorised as a WASP, whereas the late Governor George Wallace of Alabama, than whom 'you couldn't have anyone more white, more Anglo-Saxon, or more Protestant', would definitely not be, because he was a gross Southern redneck.

To the mass of the people, WASPs and Englishmen all seem alien, as Mr Baker implicitly recognised when he rejected the appellation 'quintessential American'. When asked why, after forty-five years of confinement to the printed page, he had agreed to become a television host, he replied, 'In America, if you're not on television, somehow you're not an American. And, like all Americans, I want to be on television.'

I am suddenly reminded of an incident which well illustrates the strangeness of being British in the United States. Soon after Susanna arrived to join me in Washington in 1986, she telephoned a pizza parlour to ask for two pizzas to be delivered to our house in Georgetown. She said our address as clearly as she could, but the man at the other end of the line just couldn't understand her. After she had repeated it several times, he suddenly lost patience and slammed down the telephone with the words: 'Why can ya notta speeka da Eengleesh, for Chrissakes!' We had to go out for dinner.

In 1993, the New York tabloid press was going through one of its crises. Since none of the city's tabloid newspapers seemed capable of making money in any circumstance, these crises would happen every year or so; but this one was of rare entertainment value. The city's largest circulation tabloid, the *New York Daily News*, which had once been ostentatiously 'saved' by Robert Maxwell, had been 'saved' again in January 1993 by Mort Zuckerman. It had been left bankrupt by Maxwell the year before when, overwhelmed by debt, he fell or jumped off his yacht into the Mediterranean and drowned. Meanwhile, the *New York Post*, which had once been 'saved' by Rupert Murdoch, was yet again on the brink of closure and in desperate need of another saviour. Into the breach stepped Steven Hoffenburg, a man of whom practically nobody had ever heard.

Though his reign as a press baron lasted only a couple of months, Hoffenburg made his mark as one of the great deflaters of American journalistic pretension. Not even the most fatalistic of the *Post*'s disillusioned journalists could have envisaged a more spectacularly undesirable proprietor. Hoffenburg, then aged forty-eight, had made his fortune out of debt-collecting. His company, Towers Financial Corporation, settled companies' outstanding bills at discounts and then collected the money in full from their debtors. This was not a gentle or compassionate business, and it brought Hoffenburg a deluge of lawsuits and involved him in many brushes with the regulatory authorities. But Hoffenburg was proud of his debt-collecting company and let it be known that he intended to use the *Post*—that caring, people's newspaper—to promote it. 'We think that getting an intelligent voice makes sense for Towers,' he said to the *New York Times*. 'We think our company has made a great contribution. We're worth knowing about.'

Immediately after acquiring the *Post*, Hoffenburg cut its journalists' salaries by 20 per cent and then called them together to explain his future plans. Asked why he had wanted to own America's oldest newspaper (the *Post* was founded in 1801 by Alexander Hamilton), Hoffenburg replied, 'You know why men or women buy newspapers? I gotta tell ya, if they tell you they do it for any other reason but glory, they're not telling you the truth.' He made an even more startlingly frank reply to a question about his business reputation. 'My reputation is terrible,' he said, 'but let's be honest. The *Post*'s isn't so great either. It seems we're a perfect marriage.' To emphasise the point that he didn't take American journalists at their own high estimation, Hoffenburg revealed that he intended to write a column for the *Post* himself.

When he arrived at the paper, Hoffenburg's first meeting was not with its Editor but with its sales manager, to whom he not only confided that advertisement sales, rather than journalism, were the key to the paper's salvation but proposed an extraordinary scheme by which advertisers would be allowed to pay for space not with money but with unsold goods, which would then be sold off by the *Post* to remainder outlets. Asked what kind of goods he had in mind for this barter scheme, he mentioned jeans. One could imagine the paper's South Street offices gradually filling up with jeans until they clogged up every corridor, covered every desk, and finally suffocated every member of the staff. But Hoffenburg was thrilled with his idea. 'This is a street company, we are street people, and we're making it into a street newspaper,' he explained. Maybe he would dress the staff in jeans.

The journalists were also eager to hear his plans for the circulation war that was about to begin between the *Post* and Mort Zuckerman's *Daily News*. 'Fuck Zuckerman!' Hoffenburg replied. 'He's a blue-blooded wannabe. I ain't aristocracy. I don't want to know from aristocracy. I'm a Brooklyn guy. I eat guys like Zuckerman for lunch.' Here was another example of American class attitudes as described by Christopher Hitchens in his book about the Anglo-American relationship. Zuckerman was far from being 'aristocracy'. His father had sold candy in Montreal. His grandfather had been a rabbi in the Steppes. Zuckerman was a self-made man. But on the way up he had acquired some of the airs and graces of the WASP ascendancy and had therefore become, in Hoffenburg's eyes, a class enemy.

The journalists didn't immediately write Hoffenburg off, for they hoped that, against the odds, he would turn out all right. And some of them really liked his astonishing frankness. Two days after he appeared at the *Post*, it ran a piece about him by its columnist Mike McAlary under the headline 'Shady? Yeah! But I kinda like him—for now'—not a great welcome, but certainly not a rejection. He 'may be a bum, but he's my bum', McAlary wrote. And when I had lunch with McAlary shortly afterwards, he confessed that he had been attracted by Hoffenburg's reckless way with words. 'He works without a net,' he said. 'He says whatever comes into his head.' But the charm wore off for McAlary when his weekly pay cheques bounced twice in succession, and he began to suspect that Hoffenburg's secret purpose in buying the newspaper had been all along to close it down and sell off its assets.

Hoffenburg's tense little honeymoon with his journalists lasted exactly five days, after which McAlary and three of the *Post*'s other top journalists, including its Editor, Lou

Colasuonno, decided to defect to the *Daily News*. McAlary claimed to have told Hoffenburg during a farewell meeting, 'I can't work for you. You're a bad guy. How can I cover bad guys for the paper when I walk past your office every day?' To which Hoffenburg, urging him to change his mind and stay at the *Post*, had replied, 'You can fill up the paper with bad things about *me*.' McAlary resisted this generous invitation and went to join Zuckerman, of whom he had written only a month earlier that he was 'a filthy little dictator'. ('Nobody plays fair in a street fight,' Zuckerman said, forgiving him.)

Shortly afterwards, Hoffenburg was forced to divest himself of the *Post* after the Securities and Exchange Commission charged that he and his debt-collection company had used false financial statements to sell more than four hundred million dollars' worth of securities. The company and five of its subsidiaries then declared themselves bankrupt. The last I ever heard of Hoffenburg was in September 1993 when he announced that he was still 'bitten by the newspaper bug' and was about to launch a daily tabloid for women called *Her New York*, with Lisa Sliwa, of Guardian Angels fame, as one of its columnists. This clearly wasn't a very good idea.

The remarkable sequel to the Hoffenburg episode was that his successor as would-be owner of the *Post* was an even greater disaster. When Abraham Hirschfeld showed up at South Street in March, the journalists broke into open rebellion and devoted the whole front page of the paper to a portrait of its founder, Alexander Hamilton, with a single tear falling from his right eye. 'Who Is This Nut?' asked a headline inside. Abe Hirschfeld, then aged seventy-three, was described by Adam Platt in 'The Talk of the Town' as having 'the face of a dazed old comedian' and skin that looked as if it had been 'soaked in water, then dried out, away from the sun'. Born in a Polish village called Tarnow, Hirschfeld came young to America and made his fortune out of multi-storey car-parks. He was famous for various eccentricities, such as spitting in public at people who displeased him and having once held a New York city official hostage in her office because she had refused him a clean-air permit for one of his car-parks.

When Adam Platt visited him in South Street for 'The Talk of the Town', Hirschfeld proudly held up the 'Who Is This Nut?' edition of the *Post*, which contained nothing but insults to him, and called it 'historic'. 'The Press!' he cried. 'I love 'em! I love 'em!' And in explanation of why the *Post* would be safe in his hands, he announced in his heavy Polish accent, 'I am an American. I tell you this off the cuff.' If successful Americans sometimes seem odd, this is because a great number of them really *are* odd. Hirschfeld soon left the *Post*, and Rupert Murdoch resumed control of the paper which he had earlier been forced to offload under rules restricting media ownership. On 13 July 1993, a portrait of Alexander Hamilton was back on the *Post*'s front page, smiling this time and showing a thumbs-up. 'Here To Stay', said the cover line.

One big difference between the New York and the London tabloids is that the former are local newspapers committed to glorifying and romanticising the city of New York, while the latter are British national newspapers without metropolitan pride or loyalty. The *Post* and the *Daily News* think of themselves as old-time city institutions like Macy's, or Radio City Music Hall. When the *Post* appeared doomed in 1993, its veteran gossip columnist, Cindy Adams, wrote in its anti-Hirschfeld edition that losing the *Post* was 'just another symbol of the death around us'. After listing all the great department stores, movie palaces, and daily newspapers that had vanished from New York over the years, she sank deeper into nostalgia, lamenting 'the death of the corner candy store, the neighborhood shoe-repair man, the kindly general practitioner who'd make house calls and care about you'. There were things she could do without, Cindy Adams went on, 'but do without respect for parents, teachers, cops, my flag? Do without the freedom to stroll my street safely? Do without a rare thick sirloin that I'm now guaranteed will stuff up my arteries? A steaming cup of breakfast caffeine? The delicious *New York Post*? . . . Oh, Alex,' she concluded, addressing Alexander Hamilton. 'What's happened to us all?'

There is an old-fashioned atmosphere about the New York tabloids which the British ones—much slicker and trashier—don't have at all. The wordier *Post* and *Daily News* publish syndicated columns by political pundits and quite long, serious editorials which would be unthinkable in the British *Sun* or *Daily Mirror*. Every now and then a British editor of the Murdoch school is imported to try to popularise them, but this never seems to work. They are too attached to their traditions and too inhibited by ideas of responsible journalism to embrace the shameless gimickry of their modern British equivalents.

It is, for example, extraordinary that a tabloid like the *Post*, engaged in a life-or-death struggle for readers among the New York working class, should have decided a few years ago to publish a regular column devoted only to exposing the liberal, politically correct agenda of the *New York Times*. Written by Hilton Kramer, a former art critic of the *Times*, the column was provocative and frequently perspicacious and had the gratifying effect of causing much irritation to the journalistic priesthood on West 43rd Street. But who in his right mind could have imagined that this would help the *Post* in its battle with the *Daily News*, few of whose readers ever see the *Times*? In fact, the column was the idea of the proprietor himself, Rupert Murdoch, which suggests that the great businessman has a rather less commercial attitude towards his struggling New York tabloid than he has towards his two British money-spinners, the *Sun* and the *News of the World*.

In Britain, the *Sun*, despite its calculated smuttiness and stupidity, is considered the most powerful newspaper because of its enormous circulation. In America, no newspaper compares in power with the self-consciously high-minded *New York Times*. The power of the *Sun* resides in the belief of politicians that it can win or lose them elections. The power of the *Times* is not so much political as cultural. The old sixties advertising slogan of the London *Times*—'Top People Read the *Times*'—could be applied perfectly truthfully to the *New York Times*. It stands unchallenged as the paper of the élite and of all those who aspire to join it. There are people not only in New York but throughout America who would be rudderless without it. They rely on it to tell them what to think, what to talk about, what books to buy, what plays to go to, what restaurants to eat at. 'The *Times* is like a public utility, like the gas or the electricity,' Rick Hertzberg once explained to me. 'You just can't do without it.'

In 1994 I went back to New York to research a piece about the *New York Times* for the London *Sunday Telegraph*, which hoped that I would pull that great institution down a peg or two. The foreign editor of the *Sunday Telegraph*, being typically resentful of the contempt felt by American journalists for their British colleagues, had persuaded himself that the *Times* was both turgid and hypocritical and hoped I would corroborate Hilton Kramer's summary of its faults—'the remorseless reign of Political Correctness, the slanted and shrunken character of hard-news reporting, the "sensitivity" policies that result in distorted coverage of certain minorities and the virtual collapse of all cultural news that isn't directly concerned with mass entertainment and pop culture'.

These criticisms were greatly overstated, but then readers of the *New York Times*, like readers of the *New Yorker*, are extraordinarily sensitive to change of any kind. Shortly before I arrived in New York in September 1994, the *Times* had enlarged the size of its type and the spacing between the lines. This made the paper easier to read. But to many people in New York it was taken as a sign that the *Times* was trying to appeal to a larger and stupider readership. The bigger type meant a loss of about ten thousand words a day from a previous daily average of 254,000 words (625,000 words on Sunday). Given that large tracts of the newspaper were exhausting to read, one might have expected a rousing welcome for this modest reduction in verbosity. But many people saw it as a sad sign of declining standards.

Once at a dinner in the country in upstate New York an English friend of mine, a fellow journalist, suddenly launched into an attack on *The New York Times*—how boring it was, how priggish, and so on. An American woman at the table took enormous offence. She was a liberal and broad-minded person, but she was deeply shocked to hear a foreigner treat America's greatest newspaper with so little respect. She reacted as if the attack were on the President or the flag. I tried unavailingly to explain that in Britain it would have been perfectly acceptable for foreigners to criticise any of our newspapers. We mightn't like it if they were to attack the Queen, or our parliamentary system, or even the BBC. But newspapers were just newspapers, not patriotic totems of any kind.

'We have too much power,' said Warren Hoge, the editor then in charge of the *Times*'s cultural coverage. 'I wish we didn't have that power. It puts too much pressure on our critics.' (Warren Hoge later became head of the *Times*'s London bureau which Rick Hertzberg described to me as 'the finishing school for *Times* editors, where they go to learn what fork to use'.) All this power is backed by a formidable if old-fashioned machine, churning out an average of 1.2 million copies on weekdays and 1.8 million on Sundays.

The New York Times employs more than a thousand staff journalists (as against about two hundred and seventy at the *Times* of London) and thousands more people on the company's business side. But is it, as a result, what its employees and most Americans believe it to be: the world's greatest newspaper? It certainly has some great virtues. It has hundreds of assiduous reporters. When a big story breaks, it will be covered exhaustively, with an impressive wealth of detail. The paper also strives to be meticulously accurate and publishes daily corrections on page two, some of which are agreeably absurd, like this 1994 example: 'A picture caption yesterday with an article about Barbara Bush's memoirs misidentified the needlework she displayed in the 1975 photograph. It was needlepoint, not knitting.'

But in recent years the paper seems to have suffered an identity crisis caused by a conflict between its old values and the search for a broader and younger readership launched by its publisher, Arthur Ochs Sulzberger Jr., when he took over from his father, Arthur Snr., in 1992. The old values were defined to me by Howell Raines, editor of the editorial pages, as 'the American journalistic equivalent of what Matthew Arnold called "high seriousness" '. But then you look at the *Times*'s front page, and you wonder. The front page has always been regarded as a sacred thing, the highest expression of the collective wisdom of a priesthood meeting in endless conclave on West 43rd Street.

It sets the nation's agenda for the day and was described to me by Rick Hertzberg as 'an exquisite calibration of the relative importance of the previous day's news'. But that really isn't so any more. As well as the highlights of yesterday's news, it regularly contains 'soft' features on subjects like obesity, and 'human interest' stories about society's 'victims', such as drug addicts and Aids sufferers. And sometimes it offers joky, opinionated pieces by one of its licensed star writers which are run side by side, without differentiation, with straight news reports written in the paper's normal formulaic journalese.

A famous example was a front-page report by Maureen Dowd, later to become a much-admired *Times* columnist, about Bill Clinton's return as President to Oxford University, where he had once studied as a Rhodes scholar. 'President Clinton returned today for a sentimental journey to the university where he didn't inhale, didn't get drafted, and didn't get a degree,' the report began. The foreign desk was appalled by this sentence, which it saw as wholly lacking in 'high seriousness'. Frantic attempts were made to contact Maureen Dowd in England, but she was already on the plane home. So there followed a long and angst-ridden internal debate which ended close to deadline when the editor finally decided to let the piece run as it stood.

The traditionalists on the *Times* regard April 1994 as a pivotal moment when the suicide of Kurt Cobain, a twenty-seven-year-old 'grunge' rock singer, was reported on its front page, an act of obeisance towards popular culture which would never have taken place before. (Interestingly, the death of Cobain was also a turning-point for the British broadsheet newspapers, whose male, middle-aged editors had never previously heard of him and were amazed to find their teenage daughters weeping inconsolably on their beds.

The New York Times now regularly reviews rock music and other forms of pop culture as part of its efforts to broaden its appeal. But it still espouses high seriousness in one particularly irritating way. This is to be wary of news stories which cannot be shown to illustrate some broad problem or trend. The O. J. Simpson murder trial was an example. The *Times* focused on what it considered to be the most serious issues involved—race, the cult of celebrity, the corruption of money, and so on. It was as if, without these, it wouldn't have felt justified in covering the case, even though the entire world was gripped by it.

The *Times*'s slogan is 'All the News That's Fit to Print', but its distaste for straightforward events and its obsession with analysis and interpretation can give its news reporting an oddly dead and unreal feel. Its other annoying tendency, which it shares with the rest of the American Press, is the obverse of this—to believe that no one will be interested in a story about, let us say, a crisis in the automobile industry unless it starts with a description of the particular circumstances of one Detroit automobile worker and his family. The generally held journalistic assumption that every story, on whatever subject, must have a thick coating of 'human interest' to make it palatable is a thoroughly misguided one. Often it just makes the reader want to scream, 'Get to the point!'

Of all Hilton Kramer's charges against the *New York Times*, the charge that hit home the hardest was that of Political Correctness. When I interviewed the paper's Editor, Joseph Lelyveld, in 1994, he angrily described this accusation as 'just pathetic'. It related principally to the paper's 'diversity programme' which had been set up to ensure that more women and more members of racial and other minority groups were hired or promoted to senior editorial positions. This policy had disturbed even some of the most liberal journalists on the *Times*. One of these, a senior editor himself, told me he found it 'vaguely corrupting' that 'merit is no longer the sole criterion for promotion'. But Lelyveld said that critics of diversity were implicitly 'racist'.

I never got to see Arthur Sulzberger Jr., the fifth member of his family to run the newspaper since it was purchased by one of his forebears in 1896. But I heard that he was an enthusiast for self-discovery by climbing rocks and conquering wildernesses and that he had already begun imposing his own 'touchy-feely' philosophy on the *Times*. One of the paper's business managers was quoted in *Vanity Fair* as saying, 'There's a lot of hugging at the *New York Times* now. I've been hugged by people I don't want to shake hands with.' Young Arthur had reportedly organised seminars which were meant to generate love between journalists and managers, but which had produced nothing but tension and even deeper loathing. It was he who had invented 'diversity' and who was behind the drive to make the paper appeal to the young. Matthew Arnold, at any rate, would not have approved.

By the time I left New York, I had acquired a much greater appreciation than before of the diversity (in the usual sense of the word) of the British Press. In New York, if you discount the two surviving tabloids and the somewhat specialised *Wall Street Journal*, print journalism is effectively controlled by two great publishing empires, the New York Times Company and Condé Nast. The New York Times is in its way a benevolent organisation, well-intentioned and decent to its employees who, if they behave themselves, are assured of jobs for life. But it is a bureaucratic monolith which crushes many a free spirit, whether it wants to or not.

Condé Nast treats its top editors and writers with such generosity that they often become hopelessly dependent on their enormous perks and expenses. But the company would not lay claim to benevolence. It exists to increase the wealth and nurture the ego of one strange, capricious man, S. I. Newhouse, whose shyness and personal modesty lend him a certain charm but do not mitigate the cold commercial ruthlessness with which he operates. In London, I have worked at different times for four different broadsheet newspapers, all with separate ownerships. In New York, such a possibility does not exist. If a journalist were to fall foul of both Condé Nast and the New York Times, he would be in serious professional difficulty.

It often occurred to me when I was in New York that Condé Nast, with its vast power and the secretiveness with which—as a private family business—it was able to conduct its affairs, was an obvious subject for scrutiny by the *New York Times*. But never once did that newspaper give it a hard time. For example, when Newhouse closed down *House & Garden* in 1993, the *Times* published a bland article accepting at face value both his reasons for doing so and his promises about the redeployment of its staff, and so on. There was no criticism of him for failing to keep alive a venerable New York publication (founded in 1904) which had once been so successful and so admired that it had spawned magazines with the same title all over the world. There was no questioning, nor any subsequent monitoring, of his statement that he would find other jobs for most of *House & Garden*'s staff.

House & Garden was subsequently to be resurrected by Newhouse, but that is not the point. The point is that the *New York Times* wouldn't want to cross Newhouse any more than he would want to cross them. This is not a very healthy state of affairs.

CHAPTER 15

Out in the Country

New York is perhaps at its best in the snow. Certainly many New Yorkers love it then. They pour into Central Park with their toboggans, and some of them even try to ski in the streets. A snowstorm is a summons to fun and frolics. The city is disrupted, of course. Many of its streets become impassable, and the taxis brave enough to keep working slither gently from side to side along the avenues. But a wonderful quiet falls over Manhattan with the snow, making any inconvenience worthwhile. The beauty of the city is never more evident, especially in the run-up to Christmas when the trees are festooned not only with snow but with hundreds of thousands of little white lights.

Christmas is the time of the year in which the contrast between London and New York is never greater and never more decisively in New York's favour. The belief encouraged by the British that the Americans are vulgar and ostentatious by comparison with us is sometimes the opposite of the truth. They are often more tasteful and restrained. And this trait is most evident at Christmas when New York glitters and glistens with whiteness, while the dark wet shopping streets of London are illuminated by crude colour decorations bearing the names of their commercial sponsors.

The snow also brings out the best in New Yorkers, who pride themselves on their ability to overcome obstacles. When I was visiting London in April 1993, I found the town deserted on a Friday because of a transport strike. Such a response would have been unimaginable in New York where people will not be prevented by anything from getting to work. A month earlier, there had been a tremendous snow blizzard in New York, and although this happened on a Saturday, a large proportion of the shops in Manhattan stayed open; and when I dropped into Bloomingdale's to buy one of its woolly hats to warm my ears, it had already sold out of them. The clearing of the snow was carried out with extraordinary speed and efficiency. Thousands of labourers appeared as if by magic to shovel the snow into huge ten-foot-high mounds on street corners. Then it was removed bit by bit by garbage trucks which postponed all their normal rubbish-collecting activities until the job was done.

The great American commitment to work, to the accomplishment of tasks, and to the achievement of goals makes everyday life in New York easier than it is in London. You can order anything by telephone and get it quickly delivered, even in the middle of the night; and almost every couple of blocks there is a Korean deli open twenty-four hours a day and selling all basic necessities (and many less basic ones such as flowers, for which New Yorkers have a passion).

But because one grows accustomed to things working with great efficiency, it can be devastating when they don't work. In the summer of my year in the city, I went away for a few days and returned to find that my flat had been visited in my absence by an evil spirit. Nearly everything that mattered was broken: the refrigerator, the television set, the word-processor, and the air-conditioner. They had all failed simultaneously, but each in its own special way. There was no discernible pattern to this multiple disaster.

The refrigerator's motor was boiling hot; the television emitted only blurred pictures and a crackling sound; the word-processor displayed nothing but one flashing red light; and the air-conditioner roared away as noisily as usual, but had ceased to produce any cold air. One can live quite happily without a television set, and even without a word-processor, but living in New York in the summer without any means of getting cool is another matter—especially in the record-breaking heatwave of July 1993 in which temperatures regularly exceeded 100 degrees. Finding oneself without air-conditioning in such circumstances is to be transported into a different social milieu. If you move only in prosperous circles, you get the impression that all New York homes are air-conditioned. But, of course, many thousands of them are not. These are the homes in which the poor people live.

While middle-class Americans create their own private climates around them in their houses, their offices, and their cars, the poor have to put up with what the weather provides. The prosperous sleep comfortably in their beds at night, the poor toss and turn and wake up early, drenched in sweat; and this was what was now happening to me. But even the poor tend to have working refrigerators. To be without one is to be reduced to the lowest possible social level. How do people survive in hot climates without refrigerators? How do they manage without ice and cold drinks? How do they keep their milk from curdling and their chocolate from melting? One of the great gulfs between America and the rest of the world is that the vast majority of Americans do not know the answers to these questions.

Naturally, when I found all my essential machines broken, I made haste to try to get them mended, using the Yellow Pages as my guide. I called a twenty-four-hour-a-day refrigerator-repair service, and a man came round to the apartment within an hour. But he declared the machine beyond fixing, told me to buy a new one, and charged me seventy dollars for this advice. I then looked up the address of the nearest refrigerator store, which was a few blocks away, and walked there through the oppressive heat. I eventually chose a refrigerator for which I had to write out a cheque for nearly a thousand dollars. Less than three-quarters of this sum was the cost of the machine itself. On top of that, there was first the tax to consider, then the delivery charge. I told the salesman that I lived up two flights of stairs in a building without a lift. That added another thirty-five dollars. I told him that the doors of the refrigerator opened on the wrong side for my kitchen and would have to be turned round. That added another twenty dollars. And so it went on.

The shop also happened to sell air-conditioners, and I was tempted to solve my other big problem by buying a new air-conditioner on the spot. I noticed a free-standing one that did not require elaborate installation in a wall or a window, and I asked how much it cost. But the salesman, whose fetish was to discourage customers from purchasing whatever it was they happened to want, said it was 'a personal cooler' and would be of no use to me unless I spent all of my time sitting immediately in front of it. He was a black man, and he asked, 'Why can't you do without an air-conditioner, like the rest of us?' But not all blacks in New York were of his resigned disposition. I had lately seen photographs in the newspapers of blacks queuing forlornly outside shops to buy air-conditioners for their sweltering apartments.

The new refrigerator arrived, and eventually everything else got repaired, but only after the heatwave had ended. My experience of Manhattan that July had strengthened me in my resolve to spend as much of August as possible in the country. Fashionable New Yorkers go for the summer to the seaside in Long Island, to the Hamptons, to continue their metropolitan socialising in fresher surroundings, but without change of pace or cast. But I had my eye instead on the Hudson Valley. Some time earlier I had met a nice man called John Dobkin at one of Jayne Wrightsman's dinner parties. He was president of Historic Hudson Valley, a trust for the conservation and maintenance of about half a dozen old country houses dotted along a 100-mile stretch of the Hudson River northwards from New York.

The showpiece of Historic Hudson Valley was Montgomery Place, a house at Allandale-on-Hudson, just north of Rhinebeck in upstate New York, which had just been restored for many millions of dollars. John Dobkin invited me up to Montgomery Place for a grand alfresco luncheon to celebrate the completion of the work; and when I arrived there, my heart leapt. The house itself was not the reason for my excitement, though it is an unusually charming Federal mansion containing its original early-to-mid-nineteenth-century furniture, wallpapers and even window panes. What excited me was the view.

The house sits on a terrace 160 feet above the Hudson River, and perhaps a mile back from it, surrounded by huge black locust trees. Through a steep stand of ancient forest just north of the house drops a rushing stream in a series of romantic waterfalls, spreading out at the bottom of the valley into a group of calm pools through which it eases its way into the great river. The prospect from the terrace of the house across these pools and the wild vegetation surrounding them, and then across the river itself to the Catskill Mountains beyond, is one of the most uplifting I have seen. The Catskills barely deserve to be called mountains, but are all the better for that. They are rolling green hills of exceptional loveliness which manage to suggest wilderness and mystery while being so gentle in their contours that they do not alarm or intimidate. When I saw them for the first time, they reminded me of the hills in Lanarkshire in the Lowlands of Scotland where I used to stay with my grandparents as a child.

Enthused by my visit to Montgomery Place, I asked John Dobkin if he knew of a cottage in the neighbourhood that I might be able to rent for the month of August, and he said he would look out for one. A week or two later, while I was on a visit to London, he called me there to say he had found me a cottage on the river, but that he needed to know immediately whether I would take it or not. The rent for August would be $1,000, he said, and he was sure that I would like it. The price seemed so low that I agreed. If the house turned out to be horrible, I would have wasted $1,000. This would be a pity, of course, but, thanks to Tina's generosity, it would be a sustainable loss.

In the event, the house could not have been more perfect for me. Situated a few miles from a little place called Germantown about twenty minutes' drive north of Montgomery Place, it was an isolated white weatherboarded cottage perched on the side of a steep hill beside the east bank of the Hudson. The main downstairs room was a good-sized kitchen containing a dining-room table and chairs and a bad but touching portrait of George Washington. Next to the kitchen was an outdoor wooden terrace—or 'deck', as the Americans say—from which one could sit in a wicker chair and gaze through a gap in a screen of tall trees at the mile-wide river and the beautiful Catskills beyond.

Rip Van Winkle had his long sleep in the Catskills, and Washington Irving's version of the famous legend opens with the following description:

> Every change of season, every change of weather, indeed, every hour of the day produces some change in the magical hues and shapes of these mountains. When the weather is fair and settled, they are clothed in blue and purple, and print their bold outlines on the evening sky; but, sometimes, when the rest of the landscape is cloudless, they will gather a hood of gray vapors about their summits, which, in the last rays of the setting sun, will glow and light up in a crown of glory.

I do not find that description exaggerated, nor do I argue with Karl Baedeker's opinion that the scenery of the Hudson is 'grander and more inspiring than that of the Rhine', nor even with the patriotic view of Thomas Cole, who emigrated from England, aged eighteen, in 1819, to become the leading figure of America's first home-grown school of artists, the Hudson River School, who said after a tour of Europe that 'the painter of American scenery has indeed

privileges superior to any other'. 'Although there is a peculiar softness and beauty in Italian skies,' Cole wrote, 'our
skies are far more gorgeous.'

But curiously, while I loved looking at the Catskills from
across the river, I never had the smallest desire to go into
them. I somehow acquired this fantasy that the Hudson
marked the limit of civilisation and that beyond it there
stretched an immense wilderness full of savages and wild
animals. And in fact I only once crossed to the other side
of the river during all of my time at the cottage—to the
town of Kingston, burned to the ground in 1777 by the
British under Major General John Vaughan, who later justified his action by writing that the town was a 'nursery for
almost every villain in the country'. It gave me rather the
same feeling.

Known as the River House, my cottage stood in the park
of a grand mansion called Midwood which was out of sight
to the north of it. Midwood and its estate belonged to the
energetic philanthropist Joan Davidson who had recently
been appointed Commissioner for Parks. Her duties included the vital task of protecting the Catskills. Joan Davidson was a country neighbour and good friend of John
Dobkin, who had his own tiny weekend cottage at Montgomery Place, and it was he who proposed me to her as a
tenant. I am deeply grateful to him for this.

After one trip up there in July to meet my landlady and
discuss the arrangements, I moved into the River House at
the beginning of August and found a note from Joan Davidson waiting for me on the kitchen table. 'Alexander, welcome!' it began. 'Please swim, canoe, explore and otherwise
enjoy your first Midwood weekend.' For my modest rental,
I had got not only a furnished cottage but also the use of a
handsome grey stone swimming pool concealed among trees
about halfway between my cottage and the manor house.
In addition, I had the use of a canoe. Having never been in
a canoe before, I was a little nervous about taking to the

water in it, especially as the river was so vast. But when I eventually found the courage, I enjoyed it. From the canoe one commanded views up and down the river and could admire Midwood and my own cottage from the unfamiliar perspective of the river boats.

The railroad hugs the east side of the Hudson for much of its distance, and one had to cross it by bridge to go from my cottage to the canoe in its boathouse, which stood on a little spit of land jutting picturesquely out into the river. Under the bridge, beside the railway line, there was a sign showing that New York City was exactly one hundred miles away. At the end of the spit there was a little group of trees providing shade for the barbecue lunches that I would occasionally give there, preceded or followed by a swim in the river. Once I had a weekend party consisting of Rick Hertzberg and his then girlfriend, the delightful Sara Mosle, a New York schoolteacher and journalist, Michael Kinsley, then still of the *New Republic* and CNN's *Crossfire*, and Henry Porter, a well-known British journalist who was then in New York doing a stint as an editor on *Vanity Fair*.

I had decided on a barbecue one lunchtime and, while I was getting the food together in the kitchen, responded to an offer of help from Rick by suggesting that he go in advance down to the river's edge to light the charcoal. Off he went, but when I eventually got down there with the food, I noticed there was something peculiar about the barbecue. The charcoal was burning away on top of the gridiron, instead of beneath it. Cruelly seizing the moment, I said to Rick I realised that the barbecue was an American contraption of which I, as an Englishman, had almost no experience, and I realised too that he, like every American, had been barbecuing things from childhood both in his parents' backyard and at annual summer camp, yet I still felt compelled to enquire whether it was quite normal to put the charcoal on top of the gridiron. His mortification was most gratifying.

Joan Davidson's note of welcome had also urged me to 'check out our towns':

> Hudson, to the North, is curious. An architectural trea-
> sure house, but a sad and dying place. No work. Lotsa
> interesting 'antiques' stores. Red Hook—a gutsy little
> blue-collar town, getting smarter by the day. Tivoli—sud-
> denly chic, artists moving in etc . . . Rhinebeck—lively
> and delightful. Nice shops, some good food (American
> Spoon, Food For Thought, new chef at the Beekman
> Arms). More tourist info to come, should it be required!

Under shopping tips, she mentioned Lee's Central Market in Germantown, 'very limited but with good meat'.

Germantown was the nearest town, just a ten-minute drive to the north of Midwood, and it was there that I did my basic shopping at Lee's Central Market, got money out of a cash machine, and bought the newspapers at the gas station. It was a cosy little place, notable for having its own telephone company—the Germantown Telephone Company Inc.—housed in the centre of town in a handsome neo-Georgian building with a lovingly tended garden at the front, and for listing (in 1993) twenty-eight people named Rockefeller in its very slim telephone directory. These were working-class Rockefellers, with jobs as plumbers, electricians, and so on. But all of them must have been somehow related to the still extremely rich descendants of John D. Rockefeller Senior, the founder of Standard Oil and America's first—and for several decades, only—billionaire.

For the first Rockefellers came to New York in 1710 among three thousand refugees from the war-ravaged German Palatinate, enticed there by Queen Anne of England with promises of land and religious freedom. Some of these Germans were eventually to found the settlement of Germantown, but in the meantime they had promised to repay their sea passage to America by manufacturing tar for the Royal Navy. Unfortunately for them, they were hijacked by a ruthless immigrant merchant called Robert Livingston, the eighth son and fourteenth child of a Scottish Presbyterian minister, who had emigrated to New York in 1674 and, by a fortunate marriage to Alida Van Rennselaer of the Dutch colonial aristocracy and a royal grant from King Charles II, had acquired an enormous estate of 157,640 acres along the east side of the Hudson (at the heart of which was the land on which Midwood was to be built more than two hundred years later).

The little I know of the history of the Livingston family is due entirely to a book I bought in a second-hand bookshop in Germantown entitled *An American Aristocracy: The Livingstons* by Clare Brandt, published by Doubleday in 1986. Mrs Brandt describes how the Germans soon went hungry. Robert Livingston wouldn't feed them properly because he couldn't get the Governor to refund him the cost of their food. At the same time, the Queen broke her promises to them by retaining title to their farms and to the houses they had built on them. So, after their first winter on starvation rations, the wretched and disillusioned Germans broke into an open rebellion which was repressed by British troops. Then, in the autumn of 1712, the Governor announced that the British government had decided to stop subsidising them altogether, but that they still had an obligation to the Royal Navy to stay put and start manufacturing tar again in the spring. Mayhem followed. Many of the Germans fled across the river to the west bank to take up freeholding, while others moved south into the next county where they were allowed to operate as independent tenant farmers. A large group of them eventually settled in Pennsylvania. But a substantial number just stayed where they were and signed themselves into feudal dependence on Robert Livingston.

In the eighteenth century, the Livingstons were prominent in the American Revolution and in public life. Philip Livingston ('Philip the Signer') signed the Declaration of Independence in 1776; eight Livingstons fought in the battle of Saratoga in 1777; Robert Livingston ('Robert the Chancellor') administered the presidential oath of office to George Washington in 1789 and, as Thomas Jefferson's minister to France, conducted the negotiations which led to the Louisiana Purchase in 1803. Many other Livingstons were to serve as US senators, governors, Supreme Court justices, cabinet members and ambassadors. But, according to Mrs Brandt, they came to regard politics under the American democratic system as ungentlemanly, and from early in the nineteenth century faded from public view as they concentrated instead on trying to be grand, aristocratic and rich.

Having already married into the cream of former colonial society—Delanos, Beekmans, Schuylers and Van Rennselaers—the Livingstons added Vanderbilts, Astors and Roosevelts to their family circle. And they dedicated all of their attention to their great Hudson Valley estate, referring to themselves, as their go-getting forebears had never done, as 'Lords of the Manor'. The Livingston consciousness, says Mrs Brandt, became focused as never before on 'the semifeudal society of landlord and tenant, lord and vassal'. 'In the absence of political and intellectual accomplishment outside the Hudson Valley, the Livingston *amour propre* came to depend almost entirely on the tenants' immutable servitude,' she adds. The New York rent system, at least as practised by the Livingstons, was more oppressive than anything in England and rested on the landlord's loathing and contempt for his tenants.

There were many tenants' rebellions against the Livingstons, in which the rebels would usually disguise themselves as Red Indians, and these did nothing to increase good will on either side. During one rebellion in 1753, the Robert Livingston of the day (most male Livingstons were called Robert) described his entire German tenantry as 'hoggish and brutish', while the rebels responded by posting a reward for his capture 'Dad or Alife'. And one of them, as he evaded capture by a Livingston loyalist, shouted over his shoulder, 'Robert Livingston: Kiss his ass!' (Which shows that this popular vulgarism is at least two and a half centuries old.) The land-ownership system of New York State, by which tenants had to remain tenants in perpetuity, without ever acquiring the right to purchase their land, was only abolished in 1852, to the great distress of the Livingstons.

The decline of the Livingstons coincided with the rise of the Rockefellers, their former serfs, who returned in due course to the Hudson Valley, acquiring 5,000 acres in Westchester County just north of New York City and a long way south of Livingston territory where their ancestors had endured their miserable initiation into American life. There at Tarrytown, in 1908, John D. Rockefeller Senior finished building a house called Kykuit—pronounced 'Kye-cut'—which was made over to the public in 1979 on the initiative of his grandson, Nelson D. Rockefeller, former Governor of New York and Vice-President under Gerald Ford.

The same John Jr. in 1851 founded Sleepy Hollow Restorations, the precursor of Historic Hudson Valley, which is based in Tarrytown and still supported by the Rockefeller family. ('The Legend of Sleepy Hollow' is another much-loved story by Washington Irving, who, until his death in 1859, lived on the river at Tarrytown in a little house called Sunnyside, now a charming museum.) David Rockefeller Jr. was one of the guests at the lunch I attended at Montgomery Place, and Joan Davidson told me she had once arranged for him to meet some of his humble Germantown cousins. According to Clare Brandt, there had been another rather more difficult Germantown reunion in 1978 when the then self-styled Lord of the Manor, Henry Livingston of Oak Hill, received a group of descendants of the Palatine Germans who had ended up in Pennsylvania. His opening remarks, she writes, began with the words: 'We may have parted badly in 1712, but welcome back; all is forgiven.' After a moment of stunned silence, he was rewarded with a hearty Germanic laugh.

I became so attached to the River House that, as August approached its end, I asked Joan Davidson if I could keep it on until I went home to England at Christmas, and she kindly agreed. For most of the five months that it was mine, I used it only for weekends, even though, from the end of September onwards, I stopped editing 'The Talk of the Town' and didn't have much to do at the *New Yorker* except to collect my cheque once a week and take it to the bank. At a breakfast with Tina Brown at the Royalton on the 24th of May, I had confirmed that I would not be seeking a renewal of my contract when it expired at the end of October but wondered if I might be permitted to stay on at the *New Yorker* until Christmas. When Tina readily agreed to this, I had suggested that a successor be chosen soon, both to facilitate a smooth handover and to allow me more time to write pieces for the section myself—something which Tina had constantly urged me to do.

An experienced editor from *Harper's* magazine, Gerry Marzorati, was appointed to take over from me in the autumn; and although he was always very friendly towards me, it quickly became clear not only that he wanted to make a clean break with the past, but also that he had no wish to use me as a contributor to his section. I was disappointed by this, but it was compensation that I still had the cottage on the Hudson to go to. Having become effectively redundant, I could really have stayed at my cottage for long periods. But as I was still being handsomely paid by the *New Yorker*, a nagging guilt prevented me from doing this, and I continued to put in daily appearances at the magazine.

I would generally go back and forth to New York by train, having rented a car in Rhinebeck which I would leave at the railway station when I was away. In the country I explored the towns Joan Davidson had mentioned in her welcome note and found that each of them had its uses. Rhinebeck, a pretty but rather genteel place, had a large and excellent tobacconist standing without any hint of shame at the town's central crossroads. Opposite this was the Beekman Arms which—having been established in 1766—claimed to be the oldest inn in continual operation in the United States. It suffered, like most such establishments in America, from having a bar that was far too dark. George Washington had been one of its guests.

Hudson, about twenty miles to the north, was utterly different in atmosphere to Rhinebeck. It was a strange, almost sinister place. Founded after the American Revolution by Atlantic whalers who, feeling exposed on the sea coast to harassment by the British, retreated more than one hundred miles up the river from New York to create a new whaling headquarters there. Hudson became so prosperous and important that it was nearly made the capital of New York State instead of Albany. It even had an opera house older than the Royal Opera House in London. When the whaling industry disappeared, Hudson found a new role for itself as a centre of gambling and prostitution. Since it was easily reached by train from both New York City and Albany, it was popular with men from both cities as somewhere to spend a dissipated weekend. It was full of brothels and gambling dens when suddenly, in 1950, the police arrived from Albany and closed them all down.

Apart from an enterprising local politician who once appeared on my doorstep to ask for my vote, nobody ever turned up unexpectedly at my cottage. There was complete silence there and complete privacy. If it had been in England, there would have been trippers and ramblers all over the place. But in America private property is respected. The cottage didn't even have a key to its front door. There was no need for one. The door had never been locked, and no unwanted person had ever walked through it. The contrast with Manhattan could not have been greater.

Along the roads in summer there were fruit and vegetable stalls stacked with peaches, pears, apples, tomatoes, aubergines and all the other wonderful produce of the local orchards and farms. Often these stalls were left unattended all day long, with open boxes in which to put the money for one's purchases, but I never heard of anyone taking advantage of this situation. Once, when I stopped to buy some peaches at a stall in front of a farmhouse, I was approached by a distraught middle-aged man with an Italian accent. He had read a notice on the road inviting people to pick their own apples in the farmer's orchard and had been knocking for ages at the farmhouse door in the hope of arranging to do this. But there was nobody around.

I said that if he wanted apples so badly, why didn't he buy one of the boxes of ready-picked ones from the stall? But he was indignant at this suggestion. 'I've come all the way from Brooklyn,' he said. 'There's no fun in buying a *box* of apples. I want to pick my own.' So I left him there waiting to fulfil this modest ambition for which he had driven more than a hundred miles. I later read somewhere that in the United States fruit and vegetables have travelled on average a distance of 1,200 miles before being put on sale in shops. The information made me feel more understanding towards this man. I could see that he might find it satisfying to eat an apple which he had actually seen growing on a tree.

When I hadn't got people staying at the River House, and even when I had, my social life on the Hudson centred around John Dobkin, Joan Davidson, and Joan's brother Richard Kaplan, an architect, and his English wife, the painter Edwina Sandys (Winston Churchill's granddaughter), who lived a few miles to the north of Midwood in another riverside mansion near to the village of Linlithgo, a corruption of Linlithgow in West Lothian which gave its name to the Earls of Linlithgow from whom the Hudson Livingstons were descended.

A gay divorcee with grown-up children and several grandchildren, Joan brought boundless energy and enthusiasm to all her tasks. She was immensely hospitable and liked having weekend parties at Midwood for her New York City friends. The Independence Day and Thanksgiving holidays were occasions for great family gatherings for which the River House had to be briefly surrendered by its tenant for family occupation. Joan was a cultivated and widely travelled woman, with a model of Shakespeare's Globe Theatre in her front hall, but she was also a fierce and unashamed American patriot. She was always talking up the United States in her conversations with me, and the only offensive sight in the glorious view from her terrace at Midwood was a very tall pole flying the Stars and Stripes. But the flag was taken down for the winter, as if there was less to feel patriotic about when the trees were bare, the ground under snow, and the river frozen over.

One autumn evening Joan asked me to accompany her to dinner at Rokeby, the family seat of the Aldrich family near Rhinebeck. The Aldriches were direct descendants of Alida Livingston who built the house with her husband General John Armstrong in 1815, and also of William B. Astor, once the richest man in America, who enlarged and embellished it in the mid-nineteenth century, adding a fine octagonal Gothic Revival library. But the situation at Rokeby in the nineties was one more familiar in Britain than in the United States—that of an aristocratic family struggling in reduced circumstances to keep its ancestral home. Although the Aldriches were poorer than most of their country neighbours, invitations to Rokeby were nevertheless prized for the legitimacy they conferred on wealthy newcomers to Livingston territory. Joan, who was one of them, was excited about taking me there; it would be like entering a time warp, she said, an experience I would not forget.

The house was indeed delightful, full of family portraits and other heirlooms, but in rather a crumbling and peeling state. There were about twenty people at dinner, seated around one long dining-room table, and it turned out that three of them had some connection with me or my family. One was an American woman I hadn't seen since I had once kissed her more than thirty years ago in Scotland; another was an elderly American gentleman who as a boy had befriended my uncle Robin at an English prep school and tried to protect him from bullies; the third was an Englishman my father had employed at Reuters news agency after ousting *his* father as head of the company in 1939. Somehow their presence there made me think that perhaps the 'special relationship' wasn't a total myth after all.

Our principal host was Winthrop Aldrich, who owned Rokeby with his brother Richard and their mother and sister. I had read about him in my copy of *The Traveler's Guide to the Hudson River Valley* by Tim Mulligan:

> Winthrop Aldrich is much more than merely a descendant and a relative of a good part of the Valley's most ancient families. His mission in life is to preserve this and other places in the state as a national trust, maintaining them for a mixture of private, public and semi-public uses that would fix for all time what is a centuries-old and unique national heritage. It would be an understatement to say that Mr Aldrich goes about his task with a near-messianic zeal . . .

As we finished dinner, this admirable fantatic, obsessed with his own ancestry, addressed us on the subject of heritage conservation before inviting us into the library for coffee. I took this opportunity to ask where the bathroom was. Joan pointed to a door under the stairs across the hall and urged me to go through it. 'It will remind you of home,' she said. Through the door was a small room with a cracked and stained washbasin in it and a notice about defective plumbing and how to flush the lavatory despite it. When I returned, Joan asked me for my impressions. I feigned puzzlement. 'I could find nothing in there that reminded me particularly of England,' I said.

CHAPTER 16

Goodbye to It All

In October 1996, nearly three years after I left New York, I got an aggrieved letter from Tina complaining that whenever she received the press cuttings from London 'there is usually one from you making some genially shitty comment about the *New Yorker* or about me'. I was genuinely surprised by this. I had occasionally written about Tina and her magazine in British Press columns, but never, I thought, in a way that could have been considered 'shitty'.

Wondering if there was any particular thing that might have offended her, I could only think of a column I had written in the *Guardian* a couple of weeks earlier about a controversy that had broken around Harry and Tina and Dick Morris, the Clinton election strategist who had resigned from the White House after being caught sharing presidential confidences with a prostitute. When Harry offered the disgraced Mr Morris a multi-million-dollar advance on his memoirs, the American Press started squealing again about British subversion of its ethical standards. Harry was even accused by one newspaper of being a 'co-conspirator' in Mr Morris's adultery. Then Tina compounded the outrage by inviting Mr Morris down to the *New Yorker*'s offices to address members of her staff on 'ethics'. My column had once again stressed the gulf between British and American attitudes to journalism and concluded that, since Tina and Harry remained incurably British in theirs, it might be time for them to return home.

I was never to learn exactly why Tina thought I had betrayed her, but her letter got nastier as it went along. She said how unpopular my recruitment to the *New Yorker* had been with its writers and editors, and how 'The Talk of the Town', while I was its editor, had been the object of 'pretty much universal' derision. She had been constantly petitioned by 'the old guard' to get rid of me, she wrote; but despite this, and despite all the 'flak' she had received on my account, she had always remained loyal to me because she had seen how hard it had been for me to come from England without a knowledge of New York and hadn't wanted to embarrass me 'with a precipitous change'. Nor, 'despite all the provocations', had she ever denigrated my work. Yet her reward had been 'snide commentary' from me ever since.

The letter was signed 'affectionately, Tina', but with the word 'affectionately' printed in smaller type than the rest of the letter. When I asked her British secretary Brenda Phipps, to whom she had dictated it, why this was so, Brenda said Tina had asked her to add the 'affectionately' only after the letter had already been printed out from her computer; and that rather than go to the bother of changing the text on the computer screen and printing it out again, she had slipped the letter into a typewriter and added 'affectionately' on to the bottom of it there. It seemed that Tina had wanted to soften the impact of the letter with a friendly sign-off, but had balked at doing it in her own handwriting.

If this stunted little 'affectionately' was really intended to mollify me, it failed in its purpose; for I couldn't avoid the impression that her letter had set out to be hurtful. And I wasn't convinced that she was telling the whole truth when she claimed that 'the old guard' petitioned her constantly for my dismissal, or that the derision I attracted had been 'pretty much universal'. These, I felt, were exaggerations designed to sharpen the contrast between her loyalty and my ingratitude.

Invoking 'the old guard' and portraying it collectively as my enemy was at odds with my own experience, for it was among members of the old guard that most of my friendships at the *New Yorker* were made. I also felt more in tune with their attitudes than with those of some of the new guard, having been inculcated in the same belief—they by Ross and Shawn, I by my Reuters training—that journalism should not be practised for personal glory and self-aggrandisement.

My failure, as Tina put it, to make 'a towering success' of 'The Talk of the Town' was largely due to my inability to generate stories worthy of the blue-butterfly treatment. When Tina realised this, she attempted to remedy the situation by encouraging me to hire my own reporters and by instituting a weekly meeting in her office at which people from other editorial departments were asked to propose story ideas. If none of these measures completely worked, one reason was that there was no kind of consensus at the *New Yorker* about what the section ought to be like. Everyone had his prejudices. One of mine was against reverential accounts of trendy New York happenings, such as art shows, nightclub openings, film premières, and so on. Another was against adulatory interviews with artists, musicians, actors, writers, and even journalists, most of whom seemed to me to be quite self-satisfied already.

Tina's main prejudices were against anything 'old' and anything 'wet'. She wanted news stories—scoops, gossip, whatever would get people talking—and I could understand why. But given the practical impossibility of filling the section each week with items of this kind, there had to be, I thought, a greater emphasis on style and tone to make it enjoyable to read even when good newsy material was scarce. I had wanted to give the section an original and amusing voice, and it was my failure to do this that I most regret.

As time went on, I made the disconcerting discovery that stories that appealed to me seemed to appeal to practically nobody else. I will give two examples. One concerned Robert Maxwell, the owner of the *Daily Mirror*. One of his publishing acquisitions had been the *New York Daily News*, and now, in December 1992, the paper was up for sale again, and Mort Zuckerman, great friend and benefactor of Harry and Tina and godfather of one of their children, was negotiating with the trade unions for its purchase.

When I bumped into Zuckerman at a party, he told me the following story. During a recent negotiating bout at the newspaper's headquarters on East 42nd Street, talks had dragged on until so late in the evening that Mr Zuckerman had asked one of his aides to order up a supply of sandwiches from the Carnegie Deli (the most famous delicatessen in New York, at Seventh Avenue and 55th Street). The person at the end of the telephone line accepted the order, but said that the sandwiches would have to be paid for in cash on delivery—an insulting condition to impose on a man of Mr Zuckerman's standing. When asked the reason for it, the person replied that during similar negotiations at the *Daily News* when Robert Maxwell had been trying to buy it, 'the bouncing Czech', as he was pleasingly nicknamed in Britain, had accumulated a debt of $8,000 for food and drink, and had died without paying it.

That struck me as an amusing and instructive story, exemplifying not only the legendary greed of the obese Mr Maxwell, but also the range and variety of the financial mayhem he left behind him (his main crime having been, of course, to rob his *Daily Mirror* employees of their pensions to help him pay his own debts). But when I mentioned it to senior editors on the magazine, they felt—without explaining why—that it was somehow not 'right' for 'The Talk of the Town'.

I proceeded to have the story checked anyway, and found that the owner of the Carnegie Deli, Milt Parker, flatly denied it. He said Mr Maxwell had never placed any order with his restaurant and so could not have owed it any money. This denial strengthened the antagonism of the editors to the story, but I decided to go ahead and publish something anyway, because I thought it was still odd and interesting that Mr Zuckerman believed strongly in his anecdote while Mr Parker just as strongly denied it. In writing up the item, I concluded: 'Not only in the big matter of his death in the Atlantic but in all matters, even the smallest, Mr Maxwell managed to generate mysteries, and most of them seem to have survived him.'

The other example concerns a story which hung around in galley proofs for three months under the catchword 'cows', encountering every conceivable obstacle to its publication. It is a sad reflection on my stewardship of 'The Talk of the Town' that I still regard the publication of 'cows' in the last section I edited as the one triumph of my year in New York. The history of 'cows' was as follows. A young freelance journalist named William Green, an Englishman settled in the United States whose work I had sometimes published in London in the *Independent Magazine*, had come to see me at the *New Yorker* with various story ideas. Of all his proposals, 'cows' was the one which interested me the most.

It was while researching a story about insurance fraud in the horse industry that William Green met a private detective, a specialist in insurance fraud of fifteen years' standing, who told him that he really ought to be concentrating on a much more intriguing case involving not horses but cows. The detective, William Graham, a resident of South Carolina, had been sent by an insurance company in Florida to investigate the death of a prize black-and-white Holstein cow in Cortland County, New York. The cow had belonged to James T. Wright, a dairy farmer, who had insured it with the Florida company for $200,000. The insurers wanted to know why it had died and whether it had really been worth so much money.

The detective discovered that Mr Wright was a highly regarded figure in the world of show cows, having judged international Holstein competitions in countries as far apart as Colombia and Japan. He earned his living selling milk, dealing in Holsteins, and boarding other people's cows. His wife Margaret was a professional cow photographer. When the detective visited Mr Wright at his farm, he had found him completely relaxed. He could see no cause for suspicion except, possibly, the farmer's apparent indifference to his cow's death. 'I'd have been terribly distressed if it had been my cow,' the detective, oddly, told William Green.

The dead cow, it emerged, had recently been bought by Mr Wright from a Holstein breeder named Gregory Wilcom in Ijamsville, Maryland. Mr Wilcom's cows had won national competitions. But the detective became suspicious when he learned that Mr Wilcom had sold Mr Wright two other cows for many tens of thousands of dollars, and that both of these had also promptly died. His suspicions grew when he was told by one of Mr Wright's farmhands that one cow bought from Mr Wilcom for $85,000 had arrived at Mr Wright's farm wearing an udder halter. 'Now, an udder halter is like a bra,' the detective explained. 'It's for support of the udder. But a show cow doesn't supposedly need any kind of support. It's like Marilyn Monroe.'

The detective, Mr Graham, came to suspect that James Wright and Gregory Wilcom were buying dud cows cheaply, insuring them for much more than their real value, killing them—possibly by an injection of poison into their tail veins—and splitting the insurance money. But, having no evidence to support this theory, he decided that he would try to frighten his two suspects into a confession.

He started by telephoning Mr Wilcom in Maryland, telling him there were serious problems with his insurance claims and advising him to hire a lawyer. Next day, Mr Wilcom killed himself by swallowing strychnine. As he was dying, he asked his wife Pamela to bury him with a 'Premier Exhibitor Banner'—a top prize—he had won at a cow show. A few days after Gregory Wilcom's death came the news that Mr Wright too had committed suicide. He had left home, checked into the Comfort Inn hotel in Cortland, and shot himself in the chest with a pistol-grip gun.

When I first submitted this story for publication (written

much as above, but in greater detail), it was rejected on perfectly good legal grounds. The house lawyer at the *New Yorker* wanted formal police confirmation that the two farmers had committed suicide and confirmation by the detective of his reported version of events. In time, every legal objection was overcome, but still the story failed to find favour with Tina or Chip McGrath. I couldn't understand why.

It was a strange and tragic tale in which, it seemed to me, nobody could fail to be interested. Tina's lack of enthusiasm may have been partly the fault of an unidentified troublemaker in the fact-checking department, who had sent her a note saying that the story was not new. There had been something on the same subject in another magazine, the troublemaker said, knowing that this would be bound to put her off it. But this wasn't so. The article in the other magazine had been about horse-insurance fraud, and not about cow-insurance fraud or, indeed, about the suicides of two of the most eminent Holstein experts in America, possibly the world. Our story was a modest, but bona fide, scoop.

Week after week, I continued to include 'cows' in my menu of offerings for 'The Talk of the Town', and week after week it got rejected by Tina. I started to persuade myself that it was the most important story of the year, imagining it on the front page of a tabloid as REVENGE OF THE MURDERED COWS. One week in July, at Tina's suggestion, I filled the regular gap left by 'cows' by interviewing Martin Dunn, a British journalist whom Mr Zuckerman had just appointed Editor of the *New York Daily News*, and came into the office next morning to find a fax from Tina waiting for me: 'Alexander. Martin Dunn 1000% better than Cows. As it always is when you write it. It's improved the section no end. Thanks. T.'

I was grateful to Tina for her praise, but I didn't agree with her. 'Cows' seemed to me far better in every way than 'Martin Dunn'. The showdown over 'cows' came in the third week of September. It was press day for 'The Talk of the Town', and I had gone out to lunch at the Oyster Bar in Grand Central Station, believing that 'cows' had finally surmounted all obstacles and was about to make its way into the magazine. But when I got back to my office after lunch, there was a message on my telephone answering machine from Pam McCarthy, the managing editor, saying that 'cows' might have to be pulled because there were still some problems with it.

I may have drunk rather too much wine at lunch, for I had a rush of blood to the head and ran upstairs to the office of Martin Baron, head of the fact-checking department, demanding to know what these problems were. Because 'cows' had been submitted and re-submitted so often, it had been picked to pieces not only by the house lawyer, who had recently given it the all-clear, but also at different times by four different fact-checkers. At my request, Martin now called all four of them into his office to deliver their opinions once again. None of them seemed to like the story much—it wasn't fashionable, after all, to like it—but all of them agreed that it had passed the tests of accuracy required by the *New Yorker*'s fact-checking machine. So I went to Pam McCarthy and asked her to come and listen to what the fact-checkers had to say.

She went straight from doing that into a meeting in Tina's office which, a few minutes later, I was invited to join. The topic was 'cows'. There seemed still to be problems with 'cows', Tina said. I appealed to Pam McCarthy. There weren't any problems, were there? I said. A little grudgingly, I thought, she admitted that there weren't. So I put it to Tina and to the three or four other editors present that it would be hypocrisy for anybody to oppose 'cows' on the grounds that it was mired in factual or legal problems, because it was now clearly established that it wasn't.

The only honourable grounds for objecting to 'cows', I said, would be simple dislike of it as a story, so would peo-

ple please say what their position was. I can no longer remember how everyone reacted, but Chip McGrath quickly
raised his hand to show he was still unequivocally anti-
'cows', and I knew that his opinion carried more weight
than those of everyone else combined—apart from Tina's
opinion, of course. So I turned to Tina and said it was up
to her to decide whether 'cows' went into her magazine or
not. She didn't have to give her reasons, I said, and I would
unquestioningly accept whatever decision she made. But decide, I insisted, she must. She looked around the table and
then shrugged. 'OK,' she said. 'Put it in, then.' She was
smiling as she spoke. I think she may have been amused by
my absurd performance.

As I said earlier, Tina spent her first few months at the *New
Yorker* in fearful anticipation of the *New York Times*'s
judgement upon her editorship, which she knew could not
be long in coming. By the end of 1993, the *Times* had published two assessments of it, both of them essentially favourable. The first of these appeared on 12 April in the
main section of the paper under the byline of its media reporter, Deirdre Carmody. This was a typical exercise in
Times 'objectivity'—an on-the-one-hand, on-the-other-hand
kind of a piece, carefully balancing positive and negative
opinions without delivering any conclusion of its own. But
the piece was arranged and presented in such a manner that
the reader was left with the clear impression that Tina was
doing a very good job.

'Despite the lamentations of loyalists last summer that
Tina Brown would tart up the *New Yorker* and destroy its
very soul, six months into her tenure as Editor in Chief,
subscription renewals are strong, newsstand sales have dou-
bled, and advertising pages are up by a hefty 16 per cent
just since January 1,' the article began. This was a glaring
non sequitur, since nobody could regard rises in a magazine's circulation and advertising revenue as evidence that

it had a soul. Nevertheless, Ms Carmody appeared to imply that 'the lamentations of the loyalists' (loyal to whom, by the way?) had been proven unjustified.

The article allowed Tina's critics their say. Joseph Epstein, Editor of the *American Scholar*, who had bitterly attacked Tina's appointment before she took it up, was now writing, six months into her tenure: 'Read the magazine today, with its unbuttoned and often sloppy language, its edge of political meanness, the childish obviousness of its attempts to outrage, and one comes to yearn for the quiet good taste that could once be counted on in a magazine one has been reading for decades.' Lewis Lapham, the Editor of *Harper's*, said Tina was taking the *New Yorker* 'in the direction of a fashion magazine and presenting what's fashionable in culture and politics'.

'Ms Brown, tossing her blonde hair and speaking intently, dismissed much of the criticism,' Ms Carmody reported. ' "Rubbish!" she said. "It's that *New Yorker* fakery." ' This was a phrase Tina regularly used in interviews to suggest that the glorification of the magazine's recent past was largely phoney. She claimed that 'the pieces I'm publishing are exactly those kinds of pieces that were previously published, but are now being mixed up with other kinds of pieces'. By 'other kinds of pieces', she presumably meant the topical ones on 'hot' issues and 'hot' people which were now helping to fill the magazine each week.

To complaints about the use of obscene and vulgar language in the magazine, Tina replied, 'I think you cannot have street people talking like Connecticut WASPs, and we have done a number of pieces on street people . . . There is a lot of *faux* Puritanism out there,' she added. 'It's all part of the *New Yorker* fakery. Good taste in the prissy sense has never been of interest to me.' That was true. There had always been a raunchy side to Tina, and even on her pinnacle at the *New Yorker* she still enjoyed telling people to 'get a life' or to 'go out and kick ass'. Tina was never one to shy away from an American vulgarism.

A far more substantial and interesting assessment of Tina was a cover story in the *New York Times Magazine*, published in December 1993, just before I left New York. Written by Elizabeth Kolbert and given the cover title 'Soul of the Buzz Machine', it seemed to me to make most of the right points. Among Tina's many admirable qualities as an editor, it identified one quality as being unique to her and perhaps the one chiefly responsible for making her 'one of the most powerful editors in the country' and 'probably the most influential woman working in print journalism' in the United States. This was her Houdini-like 'ability to control appearances'. 'She has succeeded in no small part because she has been able to represent herself and her magazines as successful,' Ms Kolbert wrote. 'This is an especially impressive performance because what is least clear about Brown's magazines is whether they have, in a commercial sense, ever really succeeded.'

When Tina Brown left the *New Yorker* in 1998, the management let it be known that the magazine's losses throughout her time as its Editor had been running at millions of dollars a year. For a long time, this didn't appear to matter to Si Newhouse. Ms Kolbert had written:

For his money, Newhouse had clearly gotten something of value. Regardless of whether *Vanity Fair* and the new *New Yorker* are financially successful, Brown has fashioned them into splendid simulacra of success. For a billionaire like Newhouse, this glittering appearance may well be worth more than a genuine but unsung profit.

Tina, who claimed that *Vanity Fair* had been making a profit by the time she left it, always insisted that the *New Yorker* was destined to become profitable too. But when, after five years, there was still no sign of this happening, Mr Newhouse seemed to start losing patience. Without consulting Tina, his managers persuaded him to incorporate the formerly separate New Yorker Company into the Condé

Nast magazine empire and move it from its independent premises on West 43rd Street to a flashy new corporate sky-scraper under construction on Times Square, where the *New Yorker* would be subject to the same controls as New-house's other less exalted magazines.

Tina had been squeezed into a corner, so it is not surprising that she accepted an offer by Disney-owned Miramax Films to run a new 'multimedia' subsidiary which, among other things, would publish a monthly magazine called *Talk* to generate material for films and television shows. (Within days of her resignation from the *New Yorker*, in an ominous development, a twenty-storey workers' lift broke away from the side of the Condé Nast skyscraper and hurtled into the street, killing an eighty-five-year-old woman in a hotel room across the way.)

The New York Times recognised Tina's celebrity status by placing a large colour photograph of her right at the top of its front page, but in two editorials it first accused her of having shed the *New Yorker*'s 'other-worldly nature and steadfast elegance in favor of a tarty breathlessness' and then condemned her new magazine venture as inimical to the principles of good journalism. Having been so reluctant to criticise her in the past, it chose the moment of her departure from the *New Yorker* to heap opprobrium upon her, saying she had left 'a magazine regarded by old-guard intellectuals [of whom it implicitly approved] as having a multiple personality disorder and a slowly declining glide path'.

But Tina's success at the *New Yorker* had been more than a simulacrum. It was in many respects quite genuine. If advertising revenue had been disappointing, circulation had risen dramatically. Her redesign of the magazine, in which she reverted to its original 1925 typeface by Rea Irvin (the artist who created Eustace Tilley) and enlivened it with restrained colour illustrations and striking black-and-white photographs, was harmonious and self-assured. And, as Ms Kolbert pointed out in her article, Tina published many pieces of which Mr Shawn would have been proud. She had her blind spots—and maybe appointing me had been one of them—but at least she left the *New Yorker* a much livelier magazine than she had found it.

The contrast between Tina and Mr Shawn was enormous all the same. When Si Newhouse bought the magazine in 1985, Mr Shawn wrote in an editorial that his intention was to go on publishing 'in defiance of commercial pressures' and that the *New Yorker* had 'never published anything in order to sell magazines, to cause a sensation, to be popular or fashionable, to be "successful" '. Tina set out quite openly to do precisely the opposite. 'Few dispute that Brown is an exacting reader, an inventive editor, and a witty writer,' Ms Kolbert wrote. 'But some argue that, however substantial her literary talents, her real genius is for publicity.' That could be so. She tried to ensure that each issue of the *New Yorker* contained at least one controversial article, in which she often tried to pair a distinguished writer with a sensational subject. For example, she commissioned Gay Talese to tell the story of Lorena Bobbitt, the Virginia woman who cut off her husband's penis, though in the end he didn't do it.

As well as sending free advance issues of the magazine to everyone with real or imagined power or influence, Tina's publicity machine alerted individual newspaper reporters to pieces that might be considered newsworthy. A distasteful example of this was when, according to Ms Kolbert, 'reporters received frantic phone calls from the magazine's public relations office' to tell them that the next issue would contain an article by the *New Yorker*'s celebrated writer Harold Brodkey revealing that he had Aids. I had seen quite a lot of Brodkey at the office, and I was sad when eventually he died. He was a kindly, rather melancholy man who often lectured me about how lucky I was not to be, like him, a Jew from the Midwest.

Tina also went to great lengths to please and flatter the celebrities she wished to keep involved with her magazine.

One September day I received a hand-delivered letter at my apartment which I discovered, after opening it, had been intended not for me but for Professor Arthur Schlesinger. The *New Yorker* had just published a 'pictorial essay' by Richard Avedon on the key figures in President Kennedy's administration to mark the thirtieth anniversary of his death, and Arthur had been one of the subjects.

> An endeavor of this kind is obviously something of a milestone for the *New Yorker*, and Dick Avedon and I are enormously grateful for your contribution [Tina had written]. We think the pictures are extraordinary and memorable, and hope you are as pleased as we are with the portfolio. Dick is working on a special signed print of your portrait as a gift that we hope you have by the end of the year. On behalf of all of us at the *New Yorker*, please accept our thanks and appreciation.

Of all Tina's attempts to provoke controversy, the most notorious during my time in New York was a St Valentine's Day cover by Art Spiegelman of a black woman being kissed on the lips by a Hasidic Jew. Since this would clearly be found offensive by Hasidic Jews (not to mention black women), Tina took many soundings to establish what the reactions to its publication might be. A senior editor on the magazine, a non-Jew, told me he had noticed many animated staff meetings going on in Tina's office over a period of several days and, somewhat surprised at being excluded from all of them, had wondered what they were about. At a certain point, he noticed that everyone present at these meetings happened to be Jewish. Later still, he discovered that Tina had consulted not only every Jew employed on the magazine, but 'practically every Jew in New York'. He also noted that she didn't seem to have consulted any blacks at all.

The Jews in the office were sharply divided. Some found Spiegelman's drawing repellent, while others considered it a work of great social significance and campaigned excitedly for its publication. To me, it just seemed like one of those meretricious Benetton advertisements which imply that they are supporting the brotherhood of man but have no real purpose except to shock. The cover was published and was a huge success. It was scandalous enough to provoke some Hasidic protests and to be a big topic on the radio and television talk shows; and it was even parodied in the satirical magazine *Spy* with a drawing of Si Newhouse kissing Tina on the lips. But, at the same time, the adverse reactions were not strong enough to cause any real problems for the magazine. Questioned about the controversy by Deirdre Carmody, Tina said simply that it was her best-selling cover.

In my opinion, Tina's worst covers were those which seemed to be trying to make a political or social point. One by Spiegelman, entitled 'The Guns of September', of children returning to school with machine guns in their hands may have been quite well executed, but it was conceptually crass. Worse still was a St Patrick's Day cover by Sue Coe called 'Broomstick of the Lord'. Coloured in sludgy green, it showed a miserable-looking streetsweeper with an Aids loop on his lapel sweeping up an empty Guinness bottle in front of St Patrick's Cathedral.

I wished Charles Addams and Peter Arno had been alive in my day, but I was fortunate that two of the best *New Yorker* artists from the time of Harold Ross were still doing work for the magazine. The icily analytical Saul Steinberg, a Romanian who had emigrated to the United States from Italy during the Second World War, had been responsible many years earlier for a celebrated cover of America as seen from New York—a tiny little United States dwarfed by the Manhattan skyline. The romantic William Steig, who had started drawing for the *New Yorker* in 1930, when he was in his early twenties, was still producing covers from time to time, and I particularly loved one celebrating the arrival of summer which appeared in the issue of 24 May 1993. It showed a voluptuous young woman, with flowers in her hair and a joyful expression on her face, running naked across her drawing room, while an old lady, arranging flowers in a vase, looked quizzically on.

My last few weeks in New York were spent in a sort of haze. I had long weekends at the River House and spent much of my time in the city just wandering about in a peaceful sort of way. I ought to have started writing this book, which was due to be delivered to the publishers the following spring, but I didn't feel capable of it. I'd been advised to keep a diary. I started to do this, but could manage only a few days of it. My observations of New York were poignantly unoriginal. I noticed that the buildings were tall, that the taxis were yellow, and that steam gushed out of the streets from underground, but beyond that, very little. So I pushed the book out of my mind, even though I knew it would come back to haunt me soon unless I was prepared—which I wasn't—to repay the advances I had received.

I saw practically nothing of Tina during those last few weeks until suddenly she realised that I was about to leave New York for ever. A lunch was arranged at the Royalton for 8 December, and a few days beforehand I received a telephone call from Nina Train, who had succeeded Vanessa Friedman as my personal assistant and was now working in the same capacity for Gerry Marzorati. She said that Tina wanted to present me at lunch with an original *New Yorker* cover, and that she, Nina, had been asked to select one. Although this gift was intended as a surprise, Nina said she had decided to disobey orders and ask me which cover I would prefer. I was grateful to her for that, since it would have been sad if my memento of the *New Yorker* had been a drawing I didn't like. So in secrecy, I went through all the covers published during my time on the magazine and found myself irresistibly drawn to ones by Saul Steinberg and William Steig. My first choice was of a Steinberg, but this turned out to be unavailable. So what I got, to my great gratitude and happiness, was the original of the Steig cover I had so admired—that of the ecstatic young woman running naked across her drawing room.

At lunch, Tina could not have been sweeter or more kind. It was as if there had never been a problem of any kind between us. And at that point I felt nothing but gratitude to her for having allowed me to spend what had been, after all, a wonderful year in New York. The week after that was taken up almost entirely with farewells—a lavish dinner party generously given by Graydon and Cynthia Carter at their apartment in the Dakota Building, a drinks party at Julia Reed's, another at Peter and Eleanor Pringle's, and a party in Washington at Michael Kinsley's house.

There was also a drinks party given for me at 16 East 63rd Street in the apartment I had happily occupied for most of my time in New York. Its owners, Grisha and Beatrice von Rezzori, had reclaimed it for themselves a few weeks earlier, and I had been living since then in rooms kindly lent to me by Drue Heinz round the corner from her house on Sutton Place. My main memory of the Rezzoris' party is of the glamorous Isabella Rossellini sitting on the edge of 'my' bed, deep in conversation with Saul Steinberg.

I had melancholy, leave-taking meals with Chip McGrath, Arthur Schlesinger, Alison Rose, Lynn Wagenknecht, Christopher Hitchens, and Rick Hertzberg and Sara Mosle. At lunch in the Century club with Brendan Gill, I confided that I was worried about what to put in my book. 'What's the matter with you, Alexander?' he said. 'Make it up, for Christ's sake!' I was pleased to hear such irresponsible British advice from a celebrated American journalist.

I left New York on the evening of Friday, 17 December, the very day on which Tina had organised a farewell buffet lunch for me in the Royalton attended by about thirty members of the *New Yorker*'s staff. In a generous speech, she praised me for my courage in having quit a good job as a magazine editor in London for the hazardous, unfamiliar world of New York and claimed, with gentle mockery, that I would be deeply missed by countless rich widows. After that, I went home to pack. Just as I was about to catch a taxi to the airport, Sara Mosle turned up and presented me with a single red rose. I couldn't have asked for a more touching send-off.

When I returned to New York a year or two later, I paid an impromptu visit to West 43rd Street. There had been many staff changes since I had left—including the replacement of Marzorati as editor of 'The Talk of the Town'—and the offices appeared to be under continuous reconstruction as rooms were made larger or smaller to reflect each new change in the pecking order. I went to look for Tina, but her secretary, Brenda, said that she and all of the senior editors were away in Boston for a conference marking the *New Yorker*'s new 'black issue'. The magazine under Tina had increasingly gone in for 'themed' issues, but some mental dysfunction prevented me from understanding what a 'black issue' was. I asked Brenda if it meant that the magazine was going to be printed all in black, and she replied, 'No, no. Don't be silly. It's about black people, like me.'

I was reassured to find that one thing hadn't changed at the magazine. Stanley, the black receptionist, was still in position, guarding the entrance to the writers' floor. Even so, there was something strikingly different about him. He was wearing a jaunty hat and brightly coloured suspenders, and he was smoking a large cigar and drinking from a tumbler of red wine. When I expressed some surprise at this behaviour, Stanley replied, 'A man's got to have his pleasures, you know.' I said yes, but a man might also be in danger of getting fired if he had them where he shouldn't. 'I don't think so, Alexander,' he said. 'Not during black-issue week.' Isn't America wonderful?

Now, at the start of a new millennium, much has already changed. Si Newhouse has sold Random House to the Germans and incorporated the *New Yorker*—until recently a separate company—into Condé Nast. Tina Brown has cast her "last roll of the dice" and is editing yet another magazine, *Talk*. I work quietly at home in West London, writing columns mainly for the British press, but also for *Slate*—Microsoft's online magazine—which Mike Kinsley edits in Seattle. Although it seems to me unlikely I will ever live in the United States again, it seems equally unlikely that I will ever break my ties with it. The country means too much to me, and I have too many friends there. I will doubtless continue to come and go across the Atlantic, but I have reached the comforting conclusion that it is not essential to be in America to enjoy the American dream. One can do one's dreaming anywhere. But it wouldn't be as vivid without my time at the *New Yorker*, and I will always be grateful to Tina for letting me have it.

A NOTE ON THE AUTHOR

Alexander Chancellor is a freelance journalist who writes regularly for the *Guardian*, the *Daily Telegraph*, and the online magazine *Slate* which is published by the Microsoft Corporation in Seattle. He was formerly Editor of the *Spectator*, and the founding Editor of both the *Independent Magazine* and the *Sunday Telegraph Magazine*. He lives in London.